This vividly written book is the first comprehensive assessment of the origins of the present-day democratic regime in Portugal to be placed in a broad international historical context. It is written with the benefit of a long-term vision of Portuguese history, and it emphasizes the significance of Portugal's new European orientation after centuries of global and oceanic preoccupations.

After an account of the collapse of the old regime in 1974, the book studies the complex revolutionary period that followed, and the struggle in Europe and Africa to define the future role of Europe's then poorest country. These events also had international repercussions which transformed the balance of forces in southern Africa, following the collapse of Europe's last overseas empire. The consequent actions and reactions of the European powers and the United States are examined, and telling comparisons are also drawn with later developments in Eastern Europe and with the wider collapse of the communist movement.

THE MAKING OF PORTUGUESE
DEMOCRACY

THE MAKING OF
PORTUGUESE
DEMOCRACY

KENNETH MAXWELL

DP
681
.M39

CAMBRIDGE
UNIVERSITY PRESS

MAR 1 3 1996

490483

Published by the Press Syndicate of the University of Cambridge
The Pitt Building, Trumpington Street, Cambridge CB2 1RP
40 West 20th Street, New York, NY 10011–4211, USA
10 Stamford Road, Oakleigh, Melbourne 3166, Australia

© Cambridge University Press 1995

First published 1995

Printed in Great Britain by Redwood Books, Trowbridge, Wiltshire

A catalogue record for this book is available from the British Library

Library of Congress cataloguing in publication data

Maxwell, Kenneth, 1941–
The making of Portuguese democracy / Kenneth Maxwell.
p.   cm.
Includes bibliographical references and index.
ISBN 0 521 46077 8
1. Portugal–Politics and government–1974–   2. Portugal–Foreign
relations – 1974–   I. Title.
DP681.M39   1995
946.904'4 – dc20   94-36697 CIP

ISBN 0 521 46077 8 hardback

For Martha Muse

Contents

Acknowledgments

This book, like Portuguese democracy, has been a long time in the making and I have accumulated many debts, above all to the Portuguese from all walks of life and political persuasions who, over the years, have shared their thoughts and concerns and welcomed my inquisitive presence. I have also enjoyed spirited and worthwhile exchanges with my colleagues in the academic world who form the small coterie of Portugal watchers in the United States and elsewhere in Europe, as well as with many journalists and government officials who became involved in the dramatic events unfolding in Portugal after the coup of April 1974. I remain especially grateful, however, to Robert Silvers, the remarkable editor of the *New York Review*, who allowed me to follow a hunch and go to Portugal prior to the coup and to accompany and write about events as they occurred; and to Carl Kaysen, who also encouraged me to follow my nose and allowed me the great privilege of several years at the Institute for Advanced Study in Princeton. John Funt gave essential encouragement when the spirit lagged, and Martha Muse reminded me gently that this task, once begun, was worth completing. Allison C. de Cerreño helped prepare the final manuscript with her ineffable efficiency, and I am grateful again to William Davies for seeing it into print.

Glossary

AD	Democratic Alliance
AMI	an elite military intervention force
ASP	Portuguese Socialist Association
assimilados	Africans considered sufficiently "civilized" to participate in Portuguese civil society
CAP	Portuguese Confederation of Farmers
CCP	Coordinating Committee of the Program (of the MFA) Comissão Coordinatora do Programa
CDE	Democratic Election Committees
CDS	Democratic and Social Center Party
CIP	Portuguese Confederation of Industrialists
CONCP	Conference of the Nationalist Organizations of the Portuguese Colonies
COPCON	Operational Command for the Continent
cruzado	gold coin of the sixteenth century
CEUD	Electoral Committee for Democratic Unity
CUF	Companhia União Fabril
DGS	Directorate General of Security (formerly PIDE)
EFTA	European Free Trade Association
FBIS-WEU	Foreign Broadcast Information Service – Western Europe
FNLA	Frente Nacional de Libertação de Angola, National Front for the Liberation of Angola
FRELIMO	Frente de Libertação de Moçambique, Mozambique Liberation Front
GNR	Guarda Nacional Republicana, National Republican Guard
intentona	an attempted coup or *putsch*
Intersindical	the central union organization
inventona	a made-up coup or provocation

ITT	International Telephone and Telegraph Co.
latifundiários	owners of large rural landed estates
MDP	Portuguese Democratic Movement
MFA	Movimento das Forças Armadas; Armed Forces Movement
milicianos	civilian draftees of noncommissioned officer rank
Mocidade Portuguesa	Portuguese Youth Movement of the New State
MPLA	Movimento Popular de Libertação de Angola, People's movement for the Liberation of Angola
MRPP	Reorganizing movement of the Party of the Proletariat
MUD	Movement of Democratic Unity
musseques	slums surrounding Angolan cities
OAU	Organization of African Unity
OECD	Organization for Economic Cooperation and Development
PAIGC	Partido Africano de Indepêndencia de Guiné e Cabo Verde, African Party for the Independence of Guinea and Cape Verde
PCA	Angolan Communist Party
PCF	Parti Communiste Français
PCI	Partito Comunista Italiano
PCP	Portuguese Communist Party
PIDE	International Police for the Defense of the State (Portuguese secret police of the Salazar epoch)
PPD	Popular Democratic Party (later renamed PSD, Partido Social Democrata, Social Democratic Party)
PPM	Popular Monarchist Party
Praça do Comércio	waterfront square of Lisbon built by the marquis of Pombal after the great earthquake of 1755
Praça da Alegria	Lisbon square off Avenida da Liberdade
PS	Socialist Party
Rádio Renascença	Catholic radio station
SACLANT	Supreme Allied Command Atlantic
saneado	purged, literally cleaned out
saneamento	process of purging

SUV   Soldiers United Will Win
UNITA   National Union for the Total Independence of
               Angola

Introduction

This book is concerned with dictatorship and its legacy; with revolution and its history; and with the emergence and consolidation of democracy. It is an attempt to discuss and to explain the making of Portuguese democracy. The Portuguese revolution of 1974–76 is at the center of the transition to democracy in Portugal as it is in this book. It was an extraordinary period – unexpected, much misunderstood, dramatic in its effects on the international scene. The Portuguese upheaval was more like the European revolutions of the 1820s and 1848 than like the "great" revolutions of 1789 in France or 1917 in Russia. That is, it was startling in psychological power, yet limited in its ability to reorder society; significant enough in its impact to transform the context of social and political discourse and the institutional context within which political power is exercised but, once over, hard for many outsiders to take seriously.

In some peculiar ways, however, the extraordinary events of the mid 1970s are already ancient history, and the Portuguese constitution and economic system are both marked by a self-conscious escape from the legacy of this period. For reasons I hope to explain in this book, contemporary Portuguese democracy rests in part on the sublimation of this conflictive experience which tends to make for a highly fragmented view of these events, and risks making the history of those years the captive of selective memories. Much that has been written about Portuguese democracy has tended to reflect a self-imposed amnesia; the story often begins in 1976 with the establishment of constitutional government. The problem with this approach is that the constitution of 1976 emerged out of the conditions of the revolutionary period. It incorporated a rhetoric and imposed statutory limitations on economic activity that reflected a point of view then dominant, but which by the end of the decade no longer found resonance in the public or the political classes, not to mention Portugal's would-be partners within the European Community.

It is important to stress this point because there has been a tendency to homogenize the Portuguese case into a comparative framework, thus obscuring vital elements of its democratization. For those on the right, this homogenization stems from a desire to de-emphasize the history of the revolution and even to deny that it occurred. None of this is very surprising. The image of the revolution is, of course, very much part of a struggle for historical memory, a process which in itself can involve both affirmation and denial. The Portuguese Communist Party, for instance, appropriated to itself the defense of the "gains of the revolution" during the 1980s – principally the radical expropriation of the large monopolies and landholdings in 1975 and the socializing clauses in the 1976 constitution – and until 1982 they fought a rearguard action in the defense of these measures. The communists thus helped to disguise the fact (conveniently for many former radicals who had moved to the center and right) that the nationalizations and expropriations were very representative of the popular will at the time, and were prompted as much by the absence or collapse of state authority as by any preconceived or Machiavellian plot. And the communists contributed to a partial and limited view of what had occurred since they were always glad to accept credit for the very phenomena which others blamed for Portugal's problems, and some of which they had, in fact, opposed in the heat of the struggle with a popular movement often led by young firebrands to their left.

The sublimation of the revolution is also a product of the demilitarization of Portuguese politics. A key element in the political equation of 1975 was the radicalized military. Yet, over the course of the 1980s, the military radicals were marginalized both within the armed forces and in the political system. Even the "moderate" officers who had played a central role in stiffening the opposition to extremism on left and right, when increasing anarchy and institutional breakdown threatened to escalate into armed confrontation and civil war, proved too interventionist for the new European-style democracy that developed in Portugal. After the abolition of the Council of the Revolution in 1982, the coup makers of 1974, "captains of April" as they had been named in the euphoric spring of 1974, were reduced to little more than a coterie of aging veterans. As always, it is the victors who write history and, in the case of Portugal, the victors are the civilian politicians who, with much outside encouragement and financial help, joined forces to oppose the radicalization in Portugal in the summer of 1975.

This bowdlerization of the revolution, while understandable, does have the disadvantage of obscuring some of the dynamics vital to the new regime's formation. In particular, it obscures the fact that agonizing choices were faced by the Portuguese in 1975, and thereby hides the sources of the strength of Portuguese democracy. This strength flows from the fact that it was a democracy born of struggle.

II

It is also sometimes difficult to remember, twenty years later, the importance Portuguese affairs assumed on the world stage in the mid 1970s. But this oscillation between long periods of inattention followed by short bursts of international panic is hardly a new phenomenon for Portugal. In 1640 and 1820, as in 1974, Portuguese revolutions disturbed the international status quo. The panicked reactions to them by the Count-Duke of Olivares, Prince Metternich, and Henry Kissinger respectively were surprisingly similar. And, in many ways, the Portuguese upheavals, which for a time so preoccupied these statesmen, were in the long term dwarfed by their international consequences – the collapse of the attempt to regenerate Spanish imperial power in the 1640s, the independence of Brazil in the 1820s, and the beginning of the end of white rule in southern Africa in the 1970s. Perhaps because of this peculiar historical trajectory, historians have given more attention to outcomes than to initiations. The events themselves more often than not receive barely a line of historical narrative. The failed revolt of the Catalans in 1640 is the subject of a classic work by John H. Elliott, but the successful revolt of the Portuguese in 1640 awaits its historian. The importance Metternich attributed to Portugal's revolution of 1820 is usually passed over in two lines. The Portuguese revolution of 1974 is already dismissed by most as having been a figment of the imagination of wishful-thinking leftists, even if some participants have good reason to forget this period. Henry Kissinger's actions in the mid 1970s, for instance, did not display his finer qualities or reflect his soundest judgment and, not surprisingly, features nowhere in his lengthy book, *Diplomacy* (New York, 1994).

The contrast between short-term salience and long-term consequence is also, it should be noted, encouraged by the rhythm of Portuguese history; that is, by a certain alternation between short bursts of often precocious experimentation which are followed by long lulls. Both phases temporarily appear to exclude the possibility of the other. I distinctly remember sitting in a Lisbon café in early 1964 reading Edgar Prestage's account of Lisbon fifty years before, in which he writes of demonstrators marching in the streets and of political and military turmoil. Such a Lisbon appeared inconceivable to me at the time and I dismissed Professor Prestage's description as being that of an old man's exaggerated memories. But, only a decade later, most of the old cafés had been replaced by banks, whose employees were vociferous "antifascists" led by a communist cabinet minister, and the fastidious tidiness of 1964 was already inconceivable, just as the revolutionary upheaval of 1974–5 must seem inexplicable to students entering university twenty years later. All of this goes to show how quickly we all become antiquarians, and the closer the past is to us the further away it seems.

That does not mean, of course, that the events themselves (or even our perception of them at the time) are insignificant. The Portuguese experience was qualitatively different from many other contemporaneous regime changes, precisely because the transition in Portugal acquired many of the characteristics of a revolution. In some senses, what occurred thereafter was not only a process of establishing democracy, but a process of a revolution tamed. The Portuguese upheaval of 1974–5 did not "turn the world upside down" as the seventeenth-century English levellers put it, though for several months in 1975 Portugal recaptured much of the euphoria of revolutions past, if little of their bloodiness. In fact, it was because of this blood–free trajectory that the Portuguese revolution is not punctuated by indelible images such as the execution of Charles I, the storming of the Bastille, or the fall of the Winter Palace, which in other historical contexts have so dramatically marked a rupture with the past. It is true, of course, that in all these cases the past in one form or another returned to haunt the new regime, and old social inequalities resurfaced in new political structures. Yet the signal event remained forever in popular imagination and historical text to proclaim the intent of radical change if not its consummation. Even failed revolutions had such moments. They have faded from historical memory only because the consequences of the events were not those anticipated, or the old order outflanked the new, returning sometimes with new clothing to suppress the fact and even the memory of potential rupture. Portugal had such moments, and one objective of this book is to record them before they suffer the ministrations of the historical amnesiologists.

The dynamic of failure and success, played out in the coalescence and disintegration of alliances during the tumultuous period between the collapse of the old order and the crystallization of the new, is not slighted here. The brief interlude of euphoria, characteristic of all revolutionary moments, when anything and everything seems possible, is the most difficult to recapture retrospectively. It was the moment Wordsworth encapsulated by his famous phrase about the French Revolution, "Bliss was it in that dawn to be alive"; or Marx, writing of the 1848 revolution in France, called a moment of "sparkling brilliants." This moment is invariably lost by scholars of successful revolutions, who almost always see outcomes as inevitable. And it is a moment too often suppressed by scholars of failed revolutions since they see such moments as ephemeral, even phantasmagorical.

There are certainly structural constraints in any revolution – socio-economic and psychological, as well as those growing from the international context – that set powerful limits in any given case. But the views of the actors in the drama, and their interpretations of the balance of political and social forces, remain critical for political action, even if objectively their constructions and interpretations turn out afterwards to be incorrect. Hindsight has many advantages, but its disadvantage is to rob history of any feeling for the choices men and women confront in moments of turmoil. That is probably why, despite all the theories of revolution and the academic and ideological debates about their causes, every revolution is a shock and a surprise. Indeed, the Portuguese revolution was both a shock and a surprise.

CHAPTER I

Prisoners of history

A libertarian may properly disapprove of Dr. Salazar, but
I doubt whether Plato would.
                    Dean Acheson, US secretary of state (1950)

Dictatorships of this type are sometimes necessary in countries whose political institutions are not so far advanced as
ours.   President Dwight D. Eisenhower (1960)

I want this country poor but independent; and I do not
wish it colonized by American capital.   Salazar (1963)

I love Portugal because it is a country of political unreality.
                    André Malraux (1960)

I

During Portugal's golden age of exploration, in the late fifteenth
and early sixteenth centuries, its mariners – Vasco da Gama,
Bartolomeu Dias, Pedro Alvares Cabral, and Ferdinand Magellan – vastly expanded the world known to the Europeans. The
Portuguese established colonies in Africa, the Far East, and South
America. The places where they landed added scores of new
names to Europe's commercial lexicon – Luanda, Mombasa, the
Maldives, Ormuz, Diu, Goa, Macao, Malacca, Malindi, Timor,
Rio de Janeiro. The Portuguese named the waters off Salvador,
their first capital in Brazil, the Bay of All Saints (and nicknamed
it the Bay of All the Sins). They also exported such European
innovations as the movable-type printing press, which they introduced in the Middle East and possibly Japan. Portuguese words
entered the languages of the Japanese ("tempura"), the Indians

7

("Caste"), and other distant peoples. In sum, as Lisbon would
never forget, it was the Portuguese who first "linked up, for
better and for worse, the widely sundered branches of the great
human family," as historian Charles R. Boxer has noted. "It
was they who first made humanity conscious, however dimly, of
its essential unity."[1]

But why the Portuguese? During the fifteenth century, there
were scarcely more than one million Portuguese, most of them
illiterate peasants. Smaller than Scotland, just 130 miles wide at
its broadest point, Portugal is short of every natural resource
but shoreline. Between the mountainous north and the arid south,
only one-third of the country could be cultivated. And when
Portugal[2] came into being as an independent kingdom during
the twelfth century, other European mariners – the Basques, the
Catalans, the Genoese, and the Venetians – were already in the
business of seaborne commerce and navigation.

The Portuguese had a genius for survival by deftly exploiting
the rival ambitions of more powerful neighbors. Through most
of 700 years of turbulent European history this skill kept the tiny
country independent. The Portuguese were not conquistadors, like
the Spaniards who followed them, but maneuverers – "opportunists of action," as the twentieth-century dictator, António de
Oliveira Salazar, once described himself. Opportunity called
early. In the twelfth century Lisbon was on the sea route used
by both Venetian and Genoese traders sailing to northern Europe,
and by European crusaders bound for the Holy Land to fight
the Islamic legions they called "Moors." Afonso Henriques, the
founder of Portugal's first monarchy, the House of Burgundy,
received help from a group of passing English and French crusaders in taking Lisbon from the Moors in 1147. The last Moors
were expelled from Portugal in 1249, some 250 years before the
Spanish conquered their remaining Muslim fiefdom, Granada, in
1492.

Foreign help was again crucial to Portugal during the four-
teenth century. John of Aviz, the bastard son of Portugal's last
Burgundian monarch, defeated a larger force of Castilian invaders
at Aljubarrota in 1385 with the aid of archers provided by
England's John of Gaunt, who had dynastic ambitions in Castile.
Proclaimed King by the *Cortes*, John married John of Gaunt's
daughter, affirming what was to be a lasting link with the English.

The 1386 Anglo-Portuguese Treaty of Windsor – a classic treaty of alliance by a small country seeking maritime protection against a larger land-based neighbor – remains Europe's oldest mutual defense pact. It was to bring Portugal into World War I and serve as "neutral" Portugal's excuse to allow the Allies to establish antisubmarine bases in the Azores during World War II.

The Portuguese, however, learned the limits of their own power early. In 1415, King John led a force that seized the Moorish port of Ceuta, on the Moroccan side of the Strait of Gibraltar. The aim was to strike a blow at the infidels for Christendom but, in the process, the Portuguese learned that the Moroccans were enriched by a steady procession of camel caravans traveling north across the Sahara from Guinea, laden with gold and spices. The Portuguese had little military success in Morocco beyond seizing control of Ceuta and a series of coastal outposts. Portugal retained Ceuta until 1640 when it was permanently taken by Spain after Portugal's revolt against Habsburg domination. Thwarted on land in North Africa, Portugal turned to the sea. In 1419, King John's energetic third son, Prince Henry, better known to history as the Navigator, then twenty-five, took the lead in promoting maritime exploration. His efforts were to earn Portugal its niche in history. The timing was propitious. During the fifteenth century, Portugal was largely at peace while larger European powers were embroiled in various conflicts such as the Hundred Years War, the Wars of the Roses, and in fighting the advances of the Ottoman Turks in the Levant and the Balkans. Portugal's Spanish rivals, Castile and Aragon, were immobilized by a state of near anarchy that would last until their union in 1479 under the Catholic monarchs, Isabella I and Ferdinand V.

The great achievement of the Portuguese captains and cartographers was to determine the patterns of the prevailing ocean winds and currents in the Atlantic Ocean and to recognize that the sea could be used to link distant continents. That knowledge would give all of Europe access to a wider world, and the Portuguese had it first. The Portuguese mariners began sailing down the uncharted littoral of West Africa around 1420. The early returns were meager – the first Portuguese *feitoria* (trading post) was not set up until about 1445 – but the captains of the small but fast lateen-rigged caravels gradually took part of the traffic in Guinean gold away from the Arab caravans. Coins called "Portugaloisers" appeared in Antwerp and other northern European cities.

Soon, the Portuguese were bartering brassware and trinkets, as well as cloth, carpets, and silks from Granada and Tunis for gold, slaves, and "grains of paradise," or Guinean pepper. By 1457, the Lisbon mint was able to issue a gold coin, the cruzado, for the first time in seventy-four years. Slaves – perhaps 150,000 were imported during the last half of the fifteenth century alone – were in demand in Portugal, Spain, and other European markets. The Atlantic outposts of Madeira and the Azores – first colonized to supply the ships in the West African trade – produced sugar cane, another prized commodity. Plantations were started on the Cape Verde Islands and São Tomé and Príncipe using slave labor imported from the African mainland. By that time, some sixty years after Prince Henry began launching his expeditions, Lisbon had replaced the Algarve as Portugal's maritime center. The Portuguese capital city on the Tagus offered easy access to favorable winds and currents. Lisbon also had old trading ties with the Muslim world as well as a community of expatriate Genoese and other Italians skilled in the use of exchange and credit and able to finance long-distance trade.

Italian merchants such as Lomellini, Affaitati, Giraldi, and Marchione, were bankers to the Portuguese court and its envoys. They invested in sugar and the slave trade, and forged links with bankers from southern Germany. Through the bankers, they traded Portuguese oil, wine, fruit, and salt, as well as African spices and gold, for German silver and copper. As Bartolomeu Dias was rounding the southern tip of Africa in 1488 and Cabral was discovering Brazil in 1500, they did so against a background of a Portuguese Atlantic commercial system based on sugar, slaves, and gold that was already thriving. The Portuguese provided the commodities; the foreign bankers saw to the capital and the markets.

After the epic voyage of Vasco da Gama in 1498, Lisbon's interest turned to Asia. The landing at Calicut launched what Indian historian K. M. Panikkar has called Asia's "Vasco da Gama epoch,"[3] a period of European intervention and hegemony that would not ebb until after World War II. As in Africa, the Portuguese did not initially seek to settle territory. They built a thalassocracy, a lucrative empire of sea routes and coastal trading cities. Europeans paid well for the Indian and Indonesian pepper, nutmeg, and cloves, the Ceylonese cinnamon, and the Chinese silks and porcelain that the Portuguese could buy cheaply with German (and later South American) silver.

By the sixteenth century, Portugal's thalassocracy had made it one of Europe's richest nations, and the kingdom enjoyed a period of commercial and cultural flowering. But that would soon change. King Manuel had ambitions of acquiring Aragon and Castile. To that end, he married Ferdinand and Isabella's daughter and matched their Christian zeal. In 1492 Portugal accepted some 60,000 Jews who had been expelled from Spain, but in 1496 Manuel reversed his decision and compelled those Jews who would not leave the country to convert to Christianity. The so-called "New Christians" were treated harshly. In Lisbon alone, hundreds were slain in a 1506 pogrom.

Manuel's Spanish ambitions faded, but Iberia's religious zealotry did not. Lisbon took the Catholic Counter-Reformation to heart. As Spain had done nearly sixty years earlier, in 1536 the Portuguese church established a Holy Office of the Inquisition. With the king's brother as inquisitor-general, the Inquisition tightened book censorship and began an epoch of repression. Armed with royal statutes requiring "purity of blood" for holders of key posts, Inquisition officials hounded the New Christians (many of them leading merchants) and anyone else who might be accused of "heretical" ideas. The Inquisition turned over to the state people who would not renounce their alleged heresies and conducted the gruesome spectacle of the *auto da fé* ("act of faith") – the public burning of heretics at the stake which became synonymous with Iberian religious intolerance. The first *auto da fé* was held in Lisbon in 1541. By the 1760s, when capital sentences were abolished, some 1,500 individuals had been garroted or burned; 45,000 subjected to interrogation.

Portugal's overseas fortunes also darkened. Within a century of Portugal's voyages of exploration, the Spanish, British, and Dutch were building their own empires, often at the expense of Portugal's pioneering role. Moreover, Europe was flooded with the imported commodities on which Lisbon had prospered. The empire's golden era had already passed by 1580, when Portugal lost its political independence to Spain – the result of a disastrous failure of leadership. King Sebastian, an impetuous twenty-two-year-old who admired his ancestors' overseas exploits and fancied himself "a captain of Christ," led an army of 23,000 to defeat in Morocco. Sebastian was slain, but rumors that he was held captive somewhere refused to die. Ordinary folk cherished a persistent belief that he would return to fulfill a grand destiny for Portugal. But the reality was different. Sebastian left no heir, and his throne went to an uncle who was also childless. Seizing the opportunity, Spain's Habsburg king, Philip II, claimed Portugal by right of his Portuguese mother (Sebastian's aunt) and sent troops to occupy Lisbon. For six decades, Portugal languished under Spanish domination. Not until 1640 did a successful rebellion, profiting from Spain's preoccupation with a war against France and a revolt in Catalonia, install a new Portuguese dynasty, the House of Bragança. By then, the empire was a shadow of its former extension. The Dutch had seized Ceylon, Luanda (Portugal's chief West African slaving port), and part of Brazil which, by the seventeenth century, was the world's largest sugar producer.

In need of assistance against further Spanish incursions, the Portuguese sought new alliances and again found the British willing – for a price. Under a 1661 treaty, England's King Charles II received a bride, the Portuguese princess Catherine of Bragança, and received a dowry of two million cruzados. Charles also obtained control of Tangier and Bombay, Britain's first foothold in India. Portugal's fortunes were increasingly tied to Brazil, and for a time this meant economic revival. The Dutch threat faded, and during the 1690s the first great gold rush of modern times began after a strike in the Brazilian interior.

During the eighteenth century Portugal prospered, mainly on Brazilian sugar, tobacco, cacao, hides, cotton, and gold, as well as on silver smuggled from Spain's South American colonies via the River Plate and Rio de Janeiro. Port became a valuable export as "the Englishman's wine" when Britain banned French claret in 1678. But prosperity brought change. Foreigners – Germans, Italians, and, above all, the English – came to Portugal to deal in wine or Brazilian sugar and tobacco. Welcomed as sources of capital and marketing skills, the foreigners gained an extraterritorial legal status that gave them their own courts and commercial organizations. In Oporto, the port wine capital, English "shippers" built an opulent "Factory House" where they dined lavishly while managing a virtual monopoly on wine exports.

After returning to London in 1752 from a visit to Portugal, the former British ambassador Lord Tyrawly reported that "a great body of His Majesty's subjects reside in Lisbon, rich, opulent, and every day increasing their fortunes and enlarging their dealings."[4] Another British traveler, Arthur William Costigan, anticipating Noel Coward by a century and a half, noted in 1787 that: "It is an observation of the natives [of Lisbon] that, excepting the lowest conditions of life, you shall not meet anyone on foot some hours of the violent heat . . . but mad dogs and Englishmen."[5]

At the same time, while northern Europe was caught up in that surge of interest in science, human freedom, and social progress known as the Enlightenment, Portugal's rulers insisted on church orthodoxy and absolute monarchy. The Inquisition was still pursuing heretics and censoring books. With 200,000 clerics on church rolls at a time when the population was less than three million, Portugal was, as C. R. Boxer put it, "more priest-ridden than any other country in the world, with the possible exception of Tibet."[6]

As time went on, King John V, modeling himself on France's "Sun King," Louis XIV, emptied his country's ample treasury on extravagances. Some 45,000 workers built a monastery-palace at Mafra; a Swiss who visited the site in 1726 marveled that "three-quarters of the king's treasures and of the gold brought by the Brazil fleets were changed here into stones."[7] Voltaire said of King John: "When he wanted a festival, he built a convent. When he wanted a mistress, he took a nun."[8]

Portugal's isolation from the Enlightenment increasingly disturbed the nation's more cosmopolitan officials and diplomats, among them the marquis of Pombal,[9] who became Portugal's virtual dictator for twenty-seven years until the death in 1777 of his patron, Joseph I, John V's successor. Pombal's aim of bringing the Enlightenment to Portugal was furthered by a dramatic event – the 1755 Lisbon earthquake. On November 1, All Saints' Day, about one-third of the opulent city was destroyed. Voltaire described the earthquake in *Candide*: "The sea was lashed into a froth, burst into the port, and smashed all the vessels lying at anchor there. Whirlwinds of fire and ash swirled through the streets and public squares; houses crumbled, roofs came crashing down on foundations."[10] The Royal Opera House and King Joseph's palace were in ruins. Of Lisbon's forty parish churches, thirty-five collapsed. Only 3,000 of the 20,000 houses remained habitable. The death toll was at least 15,000.

Pombal acted swiftly. Amid Lisbon's ruins, engineers went to work on what stands today as a classic product of rational eighteenth-century urban planning. New buildings were constructed to a standard economical design, hills were leveled, streets were laid out in a grid, and a large new riverfront square called the Praça do Comércio (Plaza of Commerce) was built. Portugal, Pombal had decided, would be an up-to-date country where both businessmen and aristocrats would have pride of place. He set up both a school of commerce and a college of nobles where Portugal's future leaders were to be taught foreign languages, mathematics, and the sciences, free of the influence of the Jesuits, whom Pombal blamed for many of Portugal's ills. Pombal closed the Jesuit college at Evora, purged the ancient University of Coimbra of Jesuit influence, and turned over the Inquisition's censorship powers (as well as control of primary and secondary education) to a royal board. The entire Jesuit order was banished from Portugal and its empire in 1759.

Besides curbing church power, Pombal also strove to limit foreign economic influence while retaining foreign (especially British) political and military support against Spain. To strengthen Portuguese business, he moved to bring "all the commerce of the kingdom" into monopoly firms and did so first in Brazil and the port wine region of Portugal where the British traders were most powerful. The aim, as Pombal's representative to the wine district said, "was to hurt them [the British] in such a way they cannot scream."[11]

All opposition to Pombal's measures was crushed. After 5,000 people in Oporto rioted over high wine prices, which they blamed on the monopoly company Pombal had created to supervise the vineyards of the upper Douro valley, 478 were tried for treason and 13 were hanged. As was the case with the Enlightenment everywhere, Pombal's efforts had mixed results. He advanced industry and education, ended slavery in Portugal, and abolished the distinction between "old" and "new" Christians. Yet he was ruthless even by eighteenth-century standards. Police and spies were everywhere, and jails were full of people held without charge. A contemporary, António Ribeiro dos Santos, noted that Pombal "wanted to civilize the nation and at the same time to enslave it; he wanted to spread the light of the philosophical sciences and at the same time to elevate the royal power to despotism."[12]

The competing goals of modernity and firm rule would surface repeatedly in Portugal over the years as its income from the overseas colonies slowly declined. Authority, and much else, was shattered by the Napoleonic Wars. The 1807 invasion of Portugal by the French army began a century of turmoil that would further erode the empire. British troops, led by the future Duke of Wellington, finally expelled the French in 1814, but by then Portugal was ravaged. Factories and vineyards were destroyed and art treasures were ruined. The Portuguese court, which had fled to Brazil, showed no desire to return. Instead, Brazil was raised to the status of a kingdom, co-equal with Portugal.

This trans-Atlantic arrangement was short-lived. In Portugal, a liberal rebellion erupted that led to the convening of the first *Cortes* since 1698. King John VI was forced to return to Lisbon in 1821 and accept a constitution providing for representative government and an end to the Inquisition. As Brazil declared its independence, its motherland fell into a series of struggles between constitutionalists, "absolutists," and other monarchists. Eventually, the diminished Portuguese crown was further weakened by another foreign humiliation – this one from its ancient ally Britain. The Portuguese mounted a claim, with Belgian and German support, to a stretch of the African hinterland separating Angola and Mozambique. But Britain had its own plans for the territory (now Zimbabwe and Malawi) and in 1890 demanded that Portugal drop its plans. Lisbon was obliged to comply.

By the twentieth century, agitation from emerging trade unions and political paralysis in Lisbon set the stage for a rebellion by civilian republicans. When the republican revolts occurred in 1910, almost without a shot, Portugal's last king, Manuel II, sailed off on the royal yacht to exile in England.[13] The republican regime never enjoyed a popular consensus. Its legalization of the separation of church and state pleased urban Portuguese but angered rural northerners. Political feuding and government deficits mounted, government followed government with alarming frequency, and by 1926 Portugal's military leaders decided that the republican experiment should be replaced by a dictatorship. To that end, they turned in 1928 to an obscure economics professor named António de Oliveira Salazar.[14]

II

An austere thirty-nine-year-old bachelor from central Portugal, Salazar (b. 1889) took complete control after 1930, ruling first as finance minister and later as president of the Council of Ministers. The "New State" constitution that he drew up in 1932 created a "corporate" regime on the pattern of what Benito Mussolini had just established in Italy. But despite fascist trappings, such as a Mussolini-inspired labor law that banned strikes and a ruthless secret police, the New State was essentially a Catholic authoritarian regime. A century and a half after the reign of Portugal's last strong man, Pombal, Salazar maintained stability by deftly balancing competing interests – small farmers and merchants, large landowners and big (often family-controlled) businesses. Yet Salazar's was also a regime with formidable means of repression. The political police spread their insidious influence throughout the country, relying on a network of collaborators and spies. Little recourse existed against their harassment.[15] With danger lurking in every political conversation, people became furtive, distrustful, and silent. The Republican Guard and the paramilitary security police (PSP) provided uniformed security men for all theaters and other public gathering places. Both groups brutally quashed public protest. The Portuguese legion, a militia raised to fight for Francisco Franco during the Spanish Civil War, complete with Roman salutes and green shirts, was the other paramilitary arm of the regime. Avoiding public excess or skillfully hiding it from foreign view, Salazar created a "moderate" terror which was relentless, vigilant, and devastatingly effective.[16]

The Salazar regime, thus, had at the core a condominium of conservative and quasi-fascist intellectuals, a brutal political police, and a handful of large monopolistic family concerns. In the country at large the regime sought support from the church, the small rural peasantry of the north, the large landowners of the south, and the petty functionaries who dominated the bureaucracy and its numerous agencies. Salazar provided order, balanced the budget, discouraged industrialization, and skillfully played off the great powers against each other. His basic philosophy was disarmingly simple. He wrote in 1928:

I have always been in favor of an administrative policy so clear and simple that it could be the work of any good housewife: a policy so ordinary and humble that it merely consists in spending well what one has to spend and in not living beyond one's means.[17]

Salazar always expressed an extreme distaste for change. The confining of Portugal within traditional economic and social patterns was deliberate. Archaic, isolated and puritanical, rejecting industrialization as a harbinger of class and labor problems, glorifying a sanitized peasant and folkloric tradition, Salazar's Portugal was firmly set against the twentieth century. The majority of the population remained agricultural. The regime promoted the family as the primary source of social harmony. Parental authority was extensive. Only "heads of families" were permitted for years to vote for the rubber stamp National Assembly and the regime's only permitted political party, the National Union. Salazar himself had his myopic eye on the smallest expenses. Yet, the social cost of backwardness was high. Portugal's rates of infectious disease, infant mortality, and illiteracy matched Turkey's. While Lisbon sparkled, the working-class towns on the other side of the Tagus did not. In Barreiro, families on aptly named "Sulfuric Acid Street" often had to move across town to escape fumes from the nearby chemical works.

Once in office Salazar never traveled outside Portugal (save for periodic meetings with General Franco in Spain) and eschewed ceremony. His strength lay in a talent for political manipulation combined with peasant stubbornness. Despite strong pressures from both Britain and the Axis powers, and mindful of his country's fruitless sufferings as a belligerent in previous wars, he kept Portugal neutral in World War II. Salazar sympathized with Hitler and Mussolini, and for a time Portugal supplied both Germany and the Allies with the critical metal tungsten. But in 1943, after the tide had clearly turned against the Axis, he allowed the Treaty of Windsor to be invoked to allow the British and their US allies to use submarine and air bases in the Azores.

His reward was a western guarantee that the integrity of Portugal's colonial territories in Africa and Asia would be respected and, later, membership of NATO.

Salazar seemed to savor a romantic image of Portugal and its empire, a vision of a world lost in time, certain of verities long dismissed elsewhere, that appealed not just to tourists. Salazar, the US diplomat George Ball noted after a 1963 Lisbon visit, appeared to live "in more than one century, as though Prince Henry the Navigator, Vasco da Gama, and Ferdinand Magellan were still active agents in the shaping of Portuguese policy."[18]

Unlike Pombal, who had used the power of the state to ruthlessly force through a crash program of modernization, Salazar froze Portugal's economic and social patterns. "We are antiparliamentarians, antidemocrats, antiliberals," Salazar said in 1936. "We are opposed to all forms of internationalism, communism, socialism, syndicalism." To govern, he said without apology, "is to protect the people from themselves."[19] Debt, which brought obligations, was to be avoided. Portugal accepted only $64 million in US Marshall Plan aid between 1949 and 1957, just 6 percent of Greece's total and 12 percent of Spain's.

Yet Salazar enjoyed sizable support. He had rooted his regime sufficiently in Portuguese social realities to garner for it a small measure of popular approbation. The church and the small landholders of the heavily Catholic north backed him. So did the *latifundiários*, the owners of big farming estates in the central and southern regions who feared a loss of their holdings if the left took power. (The outlawed Portuguese Communist Party, formed in 1921, was especially strong in the south.) Other backing came from Portugal's interlocking financial and industrial conglomerates. The Melo family's Companhia União Fabril (CUF) dominated commerce in Guinea and controlled 70 percent of Portugal's tobacco market. The Champalimaud group had a near monopoly of cement production.

But Salazar could not freeze the world. In 1961, India seized Goa from a 3,500-man Portuguese garrison that had been ordered to "conquer or die." In Africa, as the French and British were freeing their colonies, African nationalist guerrillas rose up against the Portuguese in Angola (1961), Guinea (1962), and Mozambique (1964). Salazar refused to negotiate. Portuguese claims to Guinea-Bissau, Mozambique, and Angola extended back to the fifteenth century, but the geographical delineation of these territories and modern economic exploitation of their natural resources were more recent. Portugal's African empire, more than the Portuguese ever cared to admit, was an empire by default, consisting of regions that more powerful competitors, during the halcyon days of imperialism, could not agree to divide among themselves. Angola and Mozambique, no less than the Belgian Congo or the Rhodesias, were creations of the nineteenth-century scramble for Africa.[20]

Portugal was the last European power in Africa to cling tenaciously to the panoply of formal domination. This was no accident. For a long time Portugal very successfully disguised the nature of her presence behind a skillful amalgam of historical mythmaking, claims of multiracialism, and good public relations.[21] But as the late Amílcar Cabral, founder of the liberation movement in Guinea-Bissau, said, "Portugal could not afford neocolonialism."[22] Economic weakness at home made intransigence in Africa inevitable. It was precisely through the exercise of sovereignty that Portugal was able to obtain any advantages at all from its "civilizing mission." These advantages were very considerable: cheap raw materials, large earnings from the transfer of export earnings, gold and diamonds, and protected markets for her wines and cotton textiles.

The problem was that this sovereignty limited the options of decolonization. Portugal faced real losses if control of her African territories were to end, and these would be difficult to sustain without major social and economic changes at home, changes which the Salazar dictatorship was not prepared to contemplate. In consequence, Lisbon was denied the chance for a clean exit. There was precious little room, for example, to manufacture the sort of commonwealth-style departure that had enabled some other European powers to cushion the end of empire by leading their peoples to think that nothing was altered, while at the same time beguiling the former colonies into believing that everything was new.

Intransigence in the defense of empire, even if it had a certain logic from the Portuguese point of view, was sustained only at very great cost. During the decade and a half when the world's attention was focused on Southeast Asia, a bitter struggle was going on in Portuguese Africa. By 1974 over a million Portuguese had seen service overseas. One of every four adult males was in the armed forces. In Africa the Portuguese army had deployed almost 150,000 men, but was nevertheless facing defeat in Guinea-Bissau, finding itself severely pressed in Mozambique, and stalemated in Angola.[23]

The white settler population in the Portuguese African territories had grown rapidly in the 1960s, especially in Angola. By 1974 it numbered some 350,000, only 20 percent of whom had been born there. For the most part the new settlers were peasants with minimal education and few skills. Despite some expensive government attempts to establish white agricultural settlements, almost all the poor whites ended up in cities, where they dominated commerce and semiskilled jobs to the exclusion of Africans.[24]

Elsewhere on the continent, the 1960s had produced much disillusionment with the venal regimes and military cliques that dominated many of the newly independent states. With time and experience, therefore, the ideological content of the anticolonial struggle was refined, and it moved beyond nationalism to a more explicit Marxian critique of dependency and its mechanisms. In the Portuguese colonies in particular, these issues were paramount in the thinking of the liberation movements. This was partly because of the peculiarities of Portuguese colonialism, and partly because of the accelerating penetration of large-scale foreign capital into the region after 1965.

The liberation movements that emerged in the Portuguese colonies differed in many ways from the earlier nationalist movements in the other European colonies which had achieved independence during the late 1950s and 1960s. With the important exception of Holden Roberto's Frente Nacional de Libertação de Angola (FNLA), the major liberation movements in Portuguese Africa – the Partido Africano de Indêpendencia da Guiné e Cabo Verde (PAIGC) in Guinea, the Frente de Libertação de Moçambique (FRELIMO) in Mozambique, and the Movimento Popular de Libertação de Angola (MPLA) in Angola – all perceived the enemy to be neocolonialism as much as it was the Portuguese *per se*. Led by Amílcar Cabral and Aristides Pereira, the PAIGC attempted to combine European revolutionary theory and Asian revolutionary experience to create a party self-consciously fitted to the special geographical, social, and economic conditions of Guinea-Bissau. The PAIGC called for an emphasis on "the people," for the "re-Africanization" of cultural life, and for social action and economic reconstruction to take place through constant discussion. It wanted to modernize the tribal culture, but to do so within the history and conditions of Guinea-Bissau. In Angola, Agostinho Neto, president of the MPLA, spoke of "a dual revolution, against traditional structures which can no longer serve them and against colonial rule." In Cabral's view, the "petty bourgeoisie," who had already achieved some education and modern skills, but had no real part in colonial power, had become a "revolutionary vanguard."[25]

The intensification of ideological consciousness was perhaps inevitable. The issues in Portuguese Africa were, after all, real and not theoretical, and were fortified daily in an armed struggle which the rest of Africa, with the exception of Algeria, had not experienced. It was also inevitable that the liberation movements developed their own heterogeneous international contacts, arms suppliers, and diplomatic supporters in Algeria, Cuba, the Soviet Union, Eastern Europe, China, Scandinavia, among western church groups, and even, during the early 1960s, the United States. Since those movements most strongly influenced by Marxian analysis (PAIGC, FRELIMO, and MPLA) saw the struggle with Portugal as only part of the problem, and because they focused on what they believed to be the realities of economic power rather than its vectors, a latent hostility to the west, especially to Western Europe, was built into their philosophy. It was a distrust only encouraged by the surreptitious aid the western powers gave to Portugal in Africa, aid that increased as the end neared.

Portugal's imperial pretensions had always been compromised by the fact that, for most of its history, Portugal itself was little more than a dependency of others.[26] This situation received every encouragement from Portugal's commercial and administrative leaders, who were content to act as front men for enterprising foreigners, or to see Portugal's bloated and incompetent bureaucracy supported by the legal and extra-legal kickbacks paid for by the passage of goods through the nation's ports. The arrangement relieved both businessmen and government of the more strenuous

and potentially disturbing task of constructing a modern industrial society. But it also created severe, if disguised, internal
social and economic tensions.

III

In 1968 Salazar's deck chair collapsed, knocking him into a coma
from which he never recovered. It fell to the president, Admiral
Américo Tomás, to replace him. Tomás, a simple but tough-
minded follower of Salazar, reluctantly appointed one of Salazar's
former protégés, a sixty-four-year-old law professor, Marcello
Caetano, as prime minister. But there was a bizarre hiatus until
1970, for the moribund Salazar resolutely refused to die, and
Tomás seemed to live in constant agitation that the old man
would revive and wonder why he had been removed from office.

Caetano was a reformer of sorts. He wanted to promote the
economic modernization of Portugal, but in combination with
extreme political caution. This was not feasible in a country
where institutions had been created to resist capitalism as much
as liberalism. The crisis in the countryside came most quickly
where it was least expected, and where its full impact would be
largely ignored. The economic managers in Lisbon, tinkering
with the economy without any reliable statistics, dealing with an
economic and social system in which the real sources of wealth
and power were disguised, continued to believe that agriculture
would take care of itself. Although reports by the Organization for
Economic Cooperation and Development (OECD) on Portugal
warned consistently in this period that the economic base of
agricultural production was being destroyed, little response or
corrective action was taken in Lisbon. The neglect of agriculture
had important political consequences since it strained to breaking
point one of the principal sources of support for the old system.[27]
One of the results of the agrarian crises was that food became
scarce. In the early 1970s crop yields in Portugal were exceptionally low. Wheat yields were half of the European average; rye,
three times lower; barley, four times lower. Extreme labor shortages on the great estates led to lower production rather than
mechanization, despite the fact that the great proprietors received
agricultural credits and subsidies for cereal production. The emigrants tended to purchase property as an investment, especially

in the north and the Algarve, and this took more land out of production while raising its value on a speculative market. Where year-round cultivation of diversified crops was required, the fields lay barren because of a lack of laborers.[28]

The cause was simple. Emigration had become a hemorrhage, while the money sent home by the emigrants hid the social and economic consequences of the deserted villages. The remittances of the overseas Portuguese had a significant economic impact, of course, and reached, by the early 1970s, a sum equal to 70 percent of the country's merchandise exports. Little of the money was used for productive investment. Rather, it helped bloat the money supply and fuel inflation, or was invested in property or land, which also helped raise prices. Portugal had always been a country of emigration but, beginning in the late 1950s and accelerating to a peak in 1970, there had been a dramatic shift away from traditional recipients of Portuguese emigration like Brazil, toward the nations of the European Economic Community (EEC). The conditions of Portuguese workers in France were hardly ideal, but the minimum monthly wage paid in France during the 1970s was more than the wage earned by 92 percent of the Portuguese population at home. Nine hundred thousand Portuguese emigrated between 1960 and 1971, most of them between the ages of eighteen and thirty-five. This represented 180 people for every 1,000 in the north of Portugal, and 185 per 1,000 in the Algarve region. By 1975 some 1.5 million Portuguese nationals were resident abroad, at least 700,000 in France and 115,000 in West Germany. Moreover, two out of every three people who left the countryside went abroad. Their departure helped create the statistical illusion of development since the proportion of the workforce engaged in agriculture declined dramatically from nearly 50 percent to under 30 percent in the 1960s. Another important consequence of these developments was to link Portugal's fortunes closely to the industrialized core of Western Europe and make it peculiarly vulnerable to Europe's economic woes.

Those young men who remained in Portugal faced at least four and sometimes six years of military service. By 1973 there was a marked growth in the number of skilled workers leaving. In that year, they made up as much as 34 percent of the 120,000 people who emigrated. With the demands of the colonial wars requiring the government to hold conscripts for longer terms of military service, severe labor shortages resulted in the modern sectors of the economy. Portugal was reduced to importing workers from the Cape Verde Islands, giving Lisbon a sizable black minority – something which, despite its grandiose claim to be the capital of a multicontinental and multiracial nation, it had lacked since the sixteenth century. As early as 1960, in 44 percent of Portugal, the birth rate was not replacing the population, and the absence of young males had a catastrophic effect on the ratio of males to females. Only Lisbon and Oporto increased in size over the decade before 1974. In the same period, the population as a whole actually declined to about 8,200,000.[29]

IV

Where the Portuguese had fled, tourists flocked in. The Spaniards were the most numerous, followed by Americans, Britons, French, and Germans. Ten thousand Britons settled in the Algarve. For the most part they were harmless couples, flotsam of an imperial past unable to adjust to their own wet and disputatious land, seeking docile natives, cheap servants, and sun.

Tourism was a mixed blessing for Portugal, particularly for the quiet fishing villages transformed into backdrops for monstrous hotels. There was sometimes hatred in the eyes of those whose way of life was being transformed, and resentful acceptance of their jobs as chambermaids or waiters. The state lavished public funds on tourist hotels, mainly in the luxury class, many of them owned and operated by foreigners. For the most part, the tourists were protected and shut off in sunny bubbles that filled in summer with large pink northerners and contracted in winter to receive a few Portuguese.

Tourism had also set off a speculative boom in construction and real estate operations, but it had some dubious social consequences. In the Algarve many Portuguese found themselves virtually expropriated in a very short period. Holiday villas, sometimes whole complexes, were built on public lands corruptly transferred to private ownership by venal municipal authorities. Resentment was no less because it was concealed for fear of the ever-present secret police. To be sure, the building boom provided many construction jobs – 244,000 jobs in 1973 alone, or 11.7

percent of the nonagricultural labor force. The other major source
of construction finance had been the emigrants. During the 1960s
and early 1970s neat little houses had sprouted throughout the
country on the outskirts of villages and towns, where they stood
empty for years on end, ready for the return of the prodigals.
Most Portuguese, meanwhile, lived without the most basic
facilities.

The largely urban middle class turned its back on the countryside, rejecting the dominantly rural ethos of the corporate state
that had, by its pompous promotion of the brilliant folk culture,
music, and art of the Portuguese countryside, succeeded only in
suffocating it. Living in indistinguishable apartments stuffed with
imitation furniture and plastic chandeliers, their imported cars
clogging the short stretches of divided highway and turnpike,
the Portuguese middle class desired nothing more than to be
"Europeans."

Those with the right family and business connections or money
could always resort to petty corruption and nepotism to mitigate
the authoritarianism of the state. But industrialization, the colonial wars, and rising prices meant that the small strategies,
deals, and bribes that kept many middle-class people going were
transformed into an intolerable system of speculation and favoritism. The small entrepreneurs and family enterprises that had
thrived under and been protected by Salazar found themselves
under attack from Caetano's economics ministers who decreed
that they were "uneconomic." Highly capitalized and competitive
"modern" businessmen moved into retail and distribution trades.
Government policy in the Finance Acts of 1971 and 1972 encouraged the concentration and consolidation of enterprises. With
both the distribution and supply of goods becoming constricted,
the result was outrageous profiteering and hoarding that the
state would not even recognize, let alone act against. Many
commodities, including codfish, a staple food of the Portuguese,
disappeared from the shelves.

The 1960s had seen substantial foreign investment in Portugal.
The Export–Import Bank helped finance a new suspension bridge
built by US Steel over the Tagus River. The bridge opened up the
possibility of industrial development in the sandy pine-forested
peninsula between the Tagus and Setúbal, and eased access to
the heavily industrialized working-class towns that sprawl along

the south bank of the Tagus opposite Lisbon. Furthermore, the bridge provided a link to the site of the petrochemical port and refining complex planned for Sines, and to the tourist zones of the Algarve. Official West German investment went to a new airport at Faro and a very expensive irrigation scheme in the Alentejo. The Faro airport, in turn, encouraged the growth of a large expatriate community along Portugal's southern coastline. The World Bank invested in electrical power supply facilities. And private foreign investment, a mere 2 percent of total private sector investment in 1970, climbed to 20 percent five years later; three-quarters of private investment came from the United States, Great Britain, West Germany, and Belgium.

The industrial development of the 1960s was of a new type, however, and not always looked upon with favor by the older Anglo-Portuguese interests which had long been the dominant foreign presence in Portugal. Many of the famous port wine companies had, by the 1970s, become subsidiaries of much less distinguished parents, exhibiting little of the sense of social obligation that had been central to the ethos of locally established and paternalistic predecessors. With the fall of the old families, some of the standards fell too. The boom conditions of the early 1970s, for instance, tempted some of the less scrupulous to adulteration. Portuguese, at the time, were careful to point out that the wine they served you was not, as they said, *feito do martelo* – made with a hammer. But the scandals, when they broke in 1974, came at a time of glut and low prices and they aggravated the depressed state of the wine trade.

The type of industrial expansion favored by foreign investment during the 1960s was extremely vulnerable both to political change in Portugal and to changes in the world economic situation. The profitability of industries that had attracted the most foreign capital during the 1960s was closely tied to the character of the political system. The absence of free trade unions and collective bargaining guaranteed exceptionally high profits by assuring exceptionally low wages. This was, of course, precisely why these industries were established in the first place, and the Caetano government advertised these attractions in its search for foreign businessmen. In 1970 wages in Portugal were seven times lower than those in Sweden and five times lower than those in Britain. Even these figures are deceptive, for the majority of the employees in the factories were women, whose wages were often less than half those of men, and averaged about two dollars a day. The European Free Trade Association (EFTA) agreement made Portugal especially attractive to enterprises that imported most of their raw materials and exported their products.

Two major types of enterprises were attracted by these conditions: electrical appliances and components assembled in Portugal by such companies as Timex, ITT, and Plessey; and the garment industry, where fifteen of the twenty-five major companies were under Swedish ownership. The electronic and component assembly plants employed about 16,000 in 1974; the garment factories some 70,000 out of a total industrial workforce of about one million.[30]

The most dramatic of all developments during the 1960s, however, was a change in direction within the oligarchy itself. The Companhia União Fabril (CUF) had grown into a huge conglomerate of over 100 companies and was the largest enterprise in the Iberian peninsula, controlling one-tenth of the corporate capital of Portugal. The old monopolies ceased to be so important, and CUF, like the Champalimaud group, entered into joint enterprises with foreign corporations, shifting its colonial and metropolitan ventures to more profitable investments in Brazil, the United States, and Europe. For Caetano and his economic experts, the conglomerates were well-managed enterprises, and in consequence they received a large share of state aid for investment, preferential tax incentives, and subsidies.[31]

The internationalization of the great conglomerates, however, represented a disintegration of the old alliance between landowners and the financial and industrial interests. Government economists were beginning to criticize not only the small fragmented plots of peasant proprietors, but also the great estates that, with the exception of meat producers, stubbornly refused to improve production techniques. Industrialists were impatient with the inadequate banking and financial network in the country and the lack of reliable information on which to base economic decision making. They were eager to capture the very large Portuguese savings (some 20 percent of the gross national product in 1972) for investment. Although they did not say much about it in public, they were strongly critical of the war in Africa, which was causing serious labor shortages and driving away money needed for expansion and which, by poisoning Portuguese international relations, threatened the chances of Portugal entering the EEC.

During 1973, in fact, as much as 48 percent of Portuguese exports were sent to the EEC and 15 percent to the overseas territories. About 45 percent of Portugal's imports came from the EEC; 10 percent from the overseas territories. The industrialists knew that Portugal's isolation was more a state of mind than an economic reality. To a segment of the great economic interests, therefore, the corporate state of Salazar and Caetano had become a positive hindrance. And by 1974 a conflict had emerged among the large Portuguese monopolies that dominated key parts of the internal and African markets between those who favored internal development along European lines and those who wanted to develop Portugal's African wealth.

During the early 1970s the regime's more European-minded reformers wanted to remove the worst rigidities of the corporate state but also to continue to give the monopolists special protection in the interest of efficient large-scale production. But not all the monopolists were convinced that liberal capitalism was the answer, especially if it involved a compromise with the nationalists in Africa, or any relaxation of the institutional intervention of the Portuguese state that protected their interests. Salazar's long-time foreign minister, Franco Nogueira, and the Espírito Santo Bank's interests saw any compromise with liberal demands as suicide – especially demands for compromise in Africa. Nogueira, in fact, on more than one occasion, observed that if Portugal lost Africa, it would "immediately be absorbed by Spain." But, as Nogueira well knew, if Portugal for most of her history had been in danger of being absorbed by anyone, it was Great Britain. Like several other former Portuguese foreign ministers, between leaving his official position and joining the board of directors of the Espírito Santo Bank, he served as chairman of the board of the Benguela Railway, the main outlet from the Katanga and Zambian copper belts to Lobito Bay in Angola, and owned by the British-based Tanganyika Concessions. Curiously, Nogueira's position on decolonization was the mirror image of those on the left. In his words,

Decolonization is a doctrinaire concept that covers the substitution of direct sovereignty for politico-economic domination. It aims to change the holders of effective power. It does not give real independence to the people, and the well-being and progress of these count for nothing.[32]

The regional context of Portugal's colonies was also extremely important, since multiple interconnections tied both Mozambique and Angola to every aspect of the explosive situation in central and southern Africa.[33] In South Africa no one doubted that the Portuguese colonies represented a breakwater against the tide of majority rule. In 1974 Angola had the largest white population in the continent outside of South Africa, and the *de facto* alliance of South Africa, Rhodesia, and Portugal against insurgency in southern Africa merely confirmed the obvious. The burden the Portuguese bore on South Africa's behalf, however, was very considerable indeed: an army of 150,000 in Africa in 1974 (60,000 in Angola alone) and defense expenditures of $425 million in the early 1970s, while South Africa, with a gross national product three times that of Portugal, spent about the same amount ($448 million).

The Portuguese empire was thus supported by economic linkages that combined an almost mercantilist restrictiveness, with complex networks representing the interests of Western European, North American, and South African capital. Though it was not always apparent on the surface, the pressures to hold on to Portuguese Africa, and to protect European capital in Portugal and its colonies, were closely interconnected. As long, that is, as the Portuguese government showed no willingness whatsoever to negotiate a settlement with the African nationalists.

CHAPTER 2

The praetorian guards

The Army must be honored and revered as being the scaf-
folding indispensable to the building of the New State.

Salazar (1939)

Nationalism does not exist in either Angola or Mozambique.
You Americans have invented it.   Salazar (1961)

Nations prefer to live prosaically rather than disappear in
glory.   General António Spínola (1974)

It was the contact with the people [of Guinea-Bissau] and
with you [my company] during two years that aided me
immensely in opening my eyes to see the injustice of the
colonial war and the illegitimacy of the fascist government
in Portugal and the consequent necessity to overthrow it.

Captain Vasco Lourenço (1974)

I

Even in early 1974 the withering of the old social basis of
Salazar's regime and the fragmentation of the coalition of interests
which long sustained the dictatorship were largely hidden from
view. Many outside observers, in fact, were impressed by the
solidity of the regime and even saw it as a model of corporatism
triumphant.[1] But as the fighting with the African liberation movements entered a second decade, bitter differences reemerged at
the top of the military hierarchy and these disputes were more
difficult to hide. Several of the civilian governors and military
commanders in Africa were ambitious men who became important public figures in Lisbon. General Spínola, commander-in-chief

of Guinea, was one of them, but the least typical. In Portuguese Guinea, he had dealt mostly with black Africans and Portuguese business interests. The proconsuls further south in Mozambique and Angola, men like Luz Cunha, Silvino Silvério Marques, and Kaúlza de Arriaga, governed territories with white settler populations and maintained close diplomatic and military connections with South Africa and Rhodesia, and, in the case of Angola, the foreign multinational corporations that exploited its large economic resources. Unlike Angola, where, by early 1974, the Portuguese army was holding back three rival liberation movements, or Mozambique, where Portugal's military position was not hopeless, in Portuguese Guinea the possibility of outright defeat had become very real. Indeed, as early as 1968, Spínola had reported to the government that the war was lost. Portugal's best hope, he recommended then, was to regain sufficient ground to force an honorable settlement through negotiation with the guerrillas.[2]

Acting on the premise contained in his gloomy assessment of Portuguese prospects in Guinea, Spínola did much to restore military confidence, implemented an extensive program of civic action aimed at winning support from the local population, and incorporated Africans into the colonial administration and armed forces. In 1972 Spínola met secretly with Senegalese President Senghor, whose country served as an important sanctuary for the guerrillas. Senghor suggested a cease-fire and a face-to-face meeting with Amílcar Cabral, the able Cape Verdean leader of the insurgency. Spínola believed he had succeeded in creating just the sort of favorable circumstances for the negotiated settlement he had recommended. Caetano, however, told an incredulous Spínola that "it is preferable to leave Guinea with an honorable military defeat rather than to negotiate with the terrorists, opening the door to other negotiations." Spínola, scandalized, exclaimed, "but Your Excellency would prefer a military defeat in Guinea?" Caetano replied: "Armies are made to fight and must fight to win, but it is not power which wins. If the Portuguese army is beaten in Guinea after having fought to the limits of possibilities, their defeat would allow us to initiate legal – political steps to continue the defense of the rest of the overseas provinces."[3]

To any military man, honor and defeat were not words that could be joined together so carelessly, and for Spínola the idea held no attraction whatsoever. He returned to his African post a deeply shaken man and determined to take his case to the people themselves. Caetano's comments also served to revive a nightmare of the Portuguese officer corps. In 1961, Salazar had ordered a vastly outnumbered Portuguese garrison in Goa to die heroically opposing India's military takeover of that tiny colonial outpost on the subcontinent. The Portuguese garrison sensibly surrendered after a perfunctory resistance, but Salazar had the survivors court-marshalled and branded as cowards by the government-controlled Portuguese press. "The example of Goa is a precedent which haunts the future we fear," Spínola was to write in *Portugal and the Future,* a book which, when published in February 1974, shook the regime to its core.[4]

There was also an added urgency to Spínola's message on the ground in Africa. The situation in Portuguese Guinea had deteriorated rapidly during the course of 1973. Amílcar Cabral, with whom Portugal might have negotiated a reasonable settlement, was assassinated on January 20, 1973, in front of his home in Conakry, the capital of the neighboring Republic of Guinea. On September 24, 1973, the PAIGC proclaimed from guerrilla-held territory an independent Republic of Guinea-Bissau, and by October 10, 1973, fifty-four nations had recognized the new state. In 1973 the Soviet Union began providing the PAIGC with sophisticated ground-to-air missiles, neutralizing the last advantage the Portuguese retained – control of the air.

General Spínola's book was published in response to this impasse and with the approval of his immediate superior, General Costa Gomes. "Nations prefer to live prosaically," Spínola wrote, "rather than disappear in glory."[5] The intention of his bold challenge to the government was to bring some realism and some flexibility into Portugal's position. It was less curious than appeared at first that a general legendary for his bravery in action should call for an end to the age of heroics. Indeed, he regarded his action as a patriotic act. Spínola argued that "to expect an exclusively military victory in Africa is unrealistic. To attempt to win a war of subversion by military solution is to accept defeat in advance." These were startling words coming from such a source. General Spínola, frontally attacking the justification elaborated by the Lisbon regime, argued that it was paternalistic and hypocritical to believe that Portugal defended the west and western civilization in Africa, that it remained there by historical or vocational right, and that it possessed a divine mission to civilize backward mortals. *Portugal and the Future* received wide attention in the international press and rapidly became a best-seller in Portugal. Spínola, moreover, was just the sort of improbable character, with a monocle, elaborately coiffed hair carefully pulled over an egg-shaped dome, and an elaborate and unconscious theatricality of manner, that reporters and cartoonists love.

Widely read in the literature of insurgency warfare and the liberation movements, a warm admirer of President Senghor of Senegal, and acutely aware of African society and culture and how to exploit them, Spínola concluded that the key to the struggle was not on the shifting battlefield, but in the mind of the population. He argued for a clear recognition of the right to self-determination, the necessity of establishing democratic institutions, and of accepting majority rule in the colonies. He believed that when Africans assessed their choices they would decide to remain connected with Portugal in some loose federation of autonomous states. He outlined in some detail a possible structure for such a federation.

Spínola's plea for new policies was based on hardheaded economic calculations. The future of Portugal, he believed, lay unequivocally with Europe. The endless war was fatally compromising the chances of raising Portuguese living standards to the rest of Europe's. A backward, isolated nation of a little over eight million people which was struggling to industrialize could not go on committing 50 percent of national expenditure to military operations and supporting an army of 170,000, especially when those called upon to fight had no political voice and the population was increasingly estranged from the regime.

In retrospect, General Spínola's proposals and critique in *Portugal and the Future* look modest, but the very publication of Spínola's book was itself an indication of the seriousness of the crisis caused by the long wars in Portugal's African colonies. The book's tone seemed unduly esoteric to outsiders, but it is precisely this quality that explains its effectiveness in Portugal. The mythology of empire as much as its reality trapped the Portuguese. The ethos of the old dictatorship was so enveloped by a carefully manufactured historical romanticism that Portugal could not reject it without rejecting something that was essential to the regime's being. Nor could Portugal in the end sustain the burdens that might give substance to the imperial dream. This in essence was Spínola's message.[6]

The impact of these arguments was given added weight because, when his book appeared in the Lisbon bookshops, General Spínola held the second most important post in the Portuguese defense establishment, with overall responsibility for the wars in Africa. He was a hero of the regime, the ideal man to state the unstatable. Spínola's father had been a close associate of Salazar. He had fought as a volunteer with Franco's armies during the Spanish Civil War, been an observer with the German army outside Leningrad, and was a former commander of the regime's praetorian Republican National Guard (GNR). His book laid out a position that many army officers, technocrats, and economists both within and outside the government believed might allow Portugal to retake the initiative, withdraw from untenable positions, and end its diplomatic isolation.

Many on the far right, as ever intransigent on the possibility of any compromise in Africa, saw the whole affair as an orchestrated plot by Caetano himself. The far right, which distrusted Caetano anyway, saw at once that the roots of Salazar's system had been called into question by General Spínola's book. The old fascists, who had created the regime and who had spent their lives in its service, found the liberal and democratic tone of Spínola's book anathema, especially since it was precisely this element that made *Portugal and the Future* a best-seller. Inevitably, the public concluded that no government could welcome popular participation in Africa while denying it in Portugal. While Spínola's blunt language made him a hero, it undermined Caetano, whose oft-promised liberalizations and constant retreats from those promises had lost him all credence.

Spínola's book was more than enough to panic the right-wing interests who had always suspected that Salazar's successor was a liberal sheep in wolf's clothing. Scrambling to keep their power, the leaders of the far right brought the fascist state down on their heads. Caetano had called the Portuguese system a "presidency by the prime minister." Now he found the head of state, seventy-nine-year-old Américo Tomas, threatening to use his legal power to dismiss the government. On March 14, 1974, in a vain attempt to reestablish his authority, Caetano insisted on a ceremonial act of obsequiousness by the military hierarchy. He ordered General Spínola, General Costa Gomes and 120 general-rank officers to gather together to pledge their loyalty to the government's African policies. Spínola and General Costa Gomes refused this vassalage. So too did the undeclared heroes of the right, General Kaúlza de Arriaga and General Silvério Marques, who viewed the request as an insult to the military. "Only in Mussolini's and Hitler's systems did the politicians ask the generals for public endorsement of their policy," Costa Gomes told Dr. Silva Cunha, the defense minister, before he and General Spínola were dismissed.[7] General Kaúlza de Arriaga was an old antagonist of General Costa Gomes, and their insubordination towards Caetano reflected a mutual contempt for the prime minister more than any convergence of views about Portugal's predicament. And so the ceremony, when it occurred, far from strengthening the regime, merely served to point up the open crisis at its highest levels.

II

While the generals squabbled and plotted, an even more formidable threat to the regime was emerging among junior officers. Known initially as the "Captains' Movement," the Armed Forces Movement (Movimento das Forças Armadas or MFA), originated among the lower levels of the officer corps in response to professional grievances and concerns with status and privilege.[8] The few western observers who were aware of these discontents tended to see the movement as a basically conservative or corporatist movement and paid it little heed. But the problem was only partly that of a coterie of captains angry about promotions, pay, and low esteem. Dissension within the officer corps was a reflection of a much deeper malaise which grew out of the scale, composition, and organization of the Portuguese armed forces, all of which, in turn, was a consequence of the seemingly endless military commitment in Africa.

In 1974 one in four men of military age was in the armed forces. The armed forces represented (at a low estimate) a proportion per thousand of the population (30.83) exceeded only by Israel (40.09) and North and South Vietnam (31.66) (55.36); five times that of the UK, and three times that of the United States or Spain. The military budget represented at least 7 percent of the GNP, more than that of the United States. With a per capita income of just over 1,000 dollars, Portugal spent a minimum per capita on military expenditure of 63.27 dollars, and this despite abysmal pay for officers, including deductions for uniforms, food, and other services. It was an army with almost no totally professional units; many of its private soldiers were illiterate, badly trained, and at times tenuously disciplined. The officer corps was composed of an aged group of generals, "the geriatric brigade" as they were called unlovingly by soldiers in the field; a segregated elite of staff officers, recruited from the upper classes of Portuguese society, exclusively devoted to administration, and relieved of combat duty; and a diminished cohort of junior and middle-rank officers, men in their thirties and forties, who had spent most of their professional lives overseas. The generals were promoted by the Council of Ministers and chosen for political reliability. They shuttled themselves back and forth between lucrative positions on the boards of state and private enterprises. The staff officers, if they appeared at their desks at all, rarely did so until late in the afternoon; only in the twilight months of the Caetano regime did a civilian minister of defense insist that work begin at nine in the morning. The defense ministry was little more than a coordinating agency, resented by the services, and the authority of the joint chiefs was never recognized by the navy. Corruption was so rampant that the war in Angola became known as "the war of the highrises," after the fat kickbacks invested in the booming Lisbon real estate market.

The resentment of the combat officers was well summed up by Captain Sousa e Castro, one of the original MFA members. "For thirteen years the soldiers – I am speaking of the cadres – were belittled and exploited in the war," he complained. "Personally I can say that as a sub-lieutenant in the combat corps I earned 4,500 escudos, less than a porter at the Imperial Cinema in Luanda. As a captain commanding a company in Mozambique I earned less than a barber in Nampula, 10,000 escudos a month. And I went for months on end without seeing my family or my friends."[9]

Since the fighting began in Angola, there had been a rapid decline in the number of applicants to the Military Academy and, as a result, a chronic shortage of manpower in the middle ranks. This aggravated a problem which had begun in the 1950s when the government shifted its recruiting policies, providing free tuition at the Military Academy in 1958, and offering a monthly stipend to cadets in 1969. By the mid 1970s this had produced a marked social cleavage within the professional officer corps at the rank of lieutenant colonel, and an extraordinary tangle of jealousy and dissension. The social background of the cadets at the Naval Academy, traditionally a preserve for the sons of the upper classes, also changed dramatically during the 1950s. Only 7 percent of the classes enrolled between 1955 and 1958 were upper class background, compared with 91 percent of cadets in 1944. Standards for admission to the service academies also fell after 1958, except in the engineering courses. The number of applicants continued to decline nevertheless. By 1969 they were down 80 percent from 1961.

Those most affected by these shifts were the middle-rank combat officers, caught between an extraordinarily archaic and slow-moving system of promotions on the one hand and a cohort of less than reliable subordinates on the other. The government, in order to cope with the armed forces' expansion, had been forced to rely increasingly on conscripted officers at the company command levels. The *milicianos*, as they were called, dominated the lower levels of the officer corps by 1974, though in status they were clearly differentiated from the regulars. Many of the *milicianos* were former university students, some of whom had been active in left-wing politics since the 1960s. These civilian soldiers, their careers, marriages, and professional prospects severely compromised by lengthy military service, showed even less enthusiasm for combat than the draftees they commanded. Yet although they became unreliable in military action, with 150,000 men in the field in Africa, the army could hardly function without them. The burden of combat thus fell mainly on a relatively small and diminishing generation of regulars, some facing their fifth two-year tour of duty overseas. A program to allow *milicianos* to take up permanent commissions was a particular affront to these men.

The government's motivation was to entice *milicianos* "who had proved themselves in combat" to abandon their amateur status and turn professional. Very few *milicianos*, however, relished the idea of entering the Military Academy with a group of green freshmen, so Decree-Law 353–73 created an accelerated two-semester course for conscript captains. By placating the conscripts the government enraged the regulars. Because the archaic system of promotion within the Portuguese armed forces recognized only seniority and not merit, Military Academy graduates were listed by class rank and moved forward to higher positions in this order. What so upset the regulars was that newly converted *milicianos* were now allowed to count all their service toward seniority, thus jumping forward in a seniority line which moved much too slowly anyway in the minds of most regular officers. It was out of the protest movement organized in response to these government measures that the MFA emerged.

Initially, the Captains' movement was composed exclusively of regular captains and majors. Later some trusted senior officers were incorporated or, more often, kept informed of developments. It was a small compact group, with strong personal interrelationships, numbering less than 200 out of a middle-rank corps of some 1,600. Members were spread out in most units and the MFA was especially strong in Guinea and Mozambique. After December 1, 1973, the Captains' movement was held together at the center by a fifteen-man coordinating committee subdivided into a military committee charged with the detailed planning of the uprising and a political committee which formulated the program for the post-coup situation.

For a determined minority within the army, a protest that originated in professional concerns provided a cover for political objectives. Major Melo Antunes, an artillery officer with a long record of opposition to the regime and who had at first dismissed the captains' protest movement as being "a reactionary cooperative in defense of privilege," was to play a key role in drawing up the MFA program. Colonel Vasco Gonçalves, another member of the political committee, had been involved in a *putsch* attempt a decade previously, and his actions on that occasion had closely paralleled those of the Communist Party. The leader of the military planning group, Mozambique-born Major Otelo Saraiva de Carvalho was much influenced by the theories of guerrilla struggle in Guinea where he had worked on psychological warfare. The movement as a whole, however, consisted of men with divergent political views. Their coalescence was less the result of any uniform conspiratorial objective than of a convergence of resentments, loss of a sense of purpose, and emotional and intellectual estrangement from the long colonial wars. Despite conventional wisdom, the work of the young officers had to be liberalizing and liberating. The intransigence of the Portuguese regime and its commitment to the wars made that inevitable. "The Revolution had come from the Left," one officer commented in April 1974. "After fifty years of right-wing dictatorship, where else could it come from?"[10]

Subtle differences separated Costa Gomes from Spínola, although both men at the time were close and old friends. Spínola was the more flamboyant of the two, but he lacked the flexibility which was Costa Gomes' trademark. Costa Gomes had a canny gift for survival. His success in riding out the storms which surrounded his career led his friends to call him "the cork." His enemies were less charitable. They called him "a congenital traitor." But it was Costa Gomes who had been first sought out by the disgruntled captains to convey their grievances over the government decision to allow conscript officers to join the permanent list and Costa Gomes was consistently the first choice among members of the embryonic Armed Forces Movement to lead the country once Caetano and Tomás had been overthrown. The importance of the publication of *Portugal and the Future*, and the international attention and prominence General Spínola achieved as a result, was to upset this order of preference at the last moment, and assure General Spínola the role of figurehead for the coup which the Armed Forces Movement had already decided to make.

III

In the face of these disagreements at the top and dissension in the ranks, none of which was any secret, the government first vacillated and then misjudged whence the most serious threat was likely to come. Part of the government's problem was the prime minister himself. Caetano was an unconvincing dictator. He embodied to an astonishing degree both the limitations as well as some of the qualities which had sustained the Salazarist system in Portugal for almost half a century. Caetano was a fine scholar and historian, in addition to being a successful lawyer and administrator. In these attributes he was not unlike many of the professors, lawyers and right-wing intellectuals with which the old dictator, Salazar, had chosen to surround himself. Often Salazar's protégés were men of humble origins like Caetano, whose father was a modest clerk, and who had risen by merit or patronage within the universities or public administration. Franco Nogueira's father was a shepherd and Adriano Moreira's a policeman. The Portuguese dictatorship was preeminently civilian and legalistic, despite the retention of military figure-heads in the presidency, and despite the fact that Salazar's authoritarian and corporativist New State had origins in a military coup.[11]

It was the domination of civilians and their ignorance of the military mind which had infuriated the would-be coup makers in 1961, horrified Spínola and his cohorts in the early 1970s, and determined that almost all the plots against the dictatorship since the early 1930s had begun in or had involved the military. The longevity of the colonial wars, of course, aggravated these long-standing tensions. General Costa Gomes observed in 1974 that "only politicians without imagination would think that military methods would solve the problems of subversive wars. Every educated soldier knows enough military history to be in no doubt of the truth proclaimed by Sun-Tzu in 500 BC, which is that subversive wars are political phenomena in which the military element while necessary is not sufficient alone."[12]

Caetano's relationship with the military was difficult from the beginning of his prime ministership. After his downfall, he would bitterly complain that the most vocal opposition to his appointment had come from those within the military hierarchy who were aware of his suggestion in the early 1960s that Portugal pursue a policy in Africa which would lead to a federation of states not unlike that proposed by General Spínola. Admiral Tomás, who had resented Salazar's failure to consult him on military matters (which he regarded as part of his presidential prerogative as commander-in-chief), made it clear to Caetano in 1968 that it was a condition of Caetano's appointment that the defense of the overseas territories was non-negotiable. Without such assurance, the admiral claimed, "the armed forces will intervene." Caetano's sensitivity to the threat from the extreme right within the military hierarchy, and his lack of sensitivity to the threat from the left among the middle-rank officers in 1974, are partly explained by this history.

The prime minister's problems were compounded by his personality and background. Caetano was a follower, not a leader. His caution, legalism, and indecisiveness proved fatal to the regime he headed. He had stood too long in the shadow of a mentor who rewarded diligence but distrusted initiative. Caetano was also an urban-based ideologue, something Salazar with his profound roots in rural Portugal had never been. Although Caetano had been closely associated with Salazar for more than three decades, he began his career considerably to the right of the conservative Catholic well-springs of Salazar's philosophy. Caetano had been a leading mover behind the Portuguese youth movement, the *Mocidade*, during the 1930s, one of the more overtly fascist institutions of the Portuguese New State. Much of the corporativist ethos of the Salazar regime was his handiwork, and he became, through his definitive textbook on administrative law, the most authoritative voice in interpreting the regime's legislation.[13] From his chair at the faculty of law of the University of Lisbon, he taught many of the leading figures in the coalition, including both the future communist leader, Alvaro Cunhal, and the socialist leader, Mário Soares. His view of his role as prime minister was, however, circumscribed by a highly legalistic and mechanistic view of the system. In reality the system worked not so much because of its legal niceties, as because of Salazar's skillful manipulation of factions, personal control of key decisions, and draconian control of the purse strings.

Caetano saw his task as being that of perfecting rather than fundamentally altering the authoritarian and corporativist dictatorship he had inherited. Caetano's ideological commitment to the system was somewhat obscured during the early months of his rule when he moved to liberalize some aspects of the dictatorship's image. Two prominent exiles, the bishop of Oporto, Dom António Ferreira Gomes, who had been prevented from reentering Portugal after a visit to Rome in 1958, and Dr. Mário Soares, a Lisbon lawyer and oppositionist who had been deported to the island of São Tomé in 1967, were both allowed back into Portugal. The regime's political movement in 1969 was permitted to incorporate a handful of liberal-minded candidates such as José Pedro Pinto Leite (the leader of the group who was killed in an accident in Guinea in 1971), Francisco Sá Carneiro, Francisco Pinto Balsemão, and Miller Guerra in its list of candidates for the National Assembly elections in 1969.[14] The notorious secret police (PIDE) was renamed the DGS (Directorate General of Security). Censorship was renamed "previous examinations."

But the "Lisbon spring" of 1968, such as it was, did not last much longer than the spring in Prague. Caetano rapidly retreated from his experiment with what one Portuguese socialist called "fascism with a human face." In retrospect, it is clear that too many misjudged Caetano's intention to carry off a successful transition to a more open and flexible system of government. He lost the opportunity to form a solid base of support for himself, which the small band of liberals in the National Assembly had been willing to provide if only he had collaborated with them in a process of gradual democratization. Disillusioned, they soon resigned their seats in protest. And, as a result, Caetano was forced further to the right, and further into the power of those who least trusted him.

Caetano's failure to act decisively during the final months of his rule can be attributed to his belief that the regime was solidly entrenched. Few inside or outside the government thought that it could be overthrown as easily as it was. The government also believed that the problem within the middle ranks had been resolved and was preoccupied with the threat from the extreme right, by labor unrest, and by the economic situation. In June 1973 a large congress of 8,000 right-wing "former overseas combatants" gathered in Oporto to support such hardline slogans as "the fatherland should be defended not debated" and "our generation will not be the generation of betrayal."[15] The officers in the field in Africa were outraged, and protested to the congress that it was unrepresentative of the sentiments of the combatants actually fighting in Africa.

By December 1973 Caetano had reluctantly rescinded the decree which had caused so much uproar in the army. Pressure from the army hierarchy first led him to exempt career officers with the rank of major and above. Then, under intense pressure from General Costa Gomes, he agreed to reconsider the whole package, and eventually the government withdrew the decree totally. Each grudging retreat had the opposite result from that intended. The first retreat, which took place in August 1973, stimulated the formation of the captains' movement, and by the time the decree was withdrawn in December, the Armed Forces Movement had already committed itself to overthrowing the regime.

In order to placate the irate officer corps, the government had also raised salaries in December. This pay rise was long overdue, but the timing was regarded by the officers as being a bribe to buy them out of political action. Nevertheless, Caetano cannot be blamed for believing that he had defused a potential source of danger. It was public knowledge that an attempt in December by General Kaúlza de Arriaga to use the Captains' movement to seize power from Caetano had failed. The MFA had rebuffed the right-wing general's plans which had envisioned the removal of General Spínola and Costa Gomes as well as Caetano. General Spínola, on being informed of General Kaúlza de Arriaga's plans, commented: "Kaúlza is an intelligent man, but it is a pity he is overambitious. He wants to be president of the Republic, but even if he succeeds in this ambition he will be in for a great disappointment. Portugal is not a monarchy, and he cannot be King."[16]

Again, the government misread the consequences of these events which, in fact, served to strengthen the links between the MFA, Spínola, and Costa Gomes at a critical time. Yet, the government had reason to take comfort in these developments. Given past history, the machinations of General Kaúlza de Arriaga were not to be taken lightly, and the failure of the MFA to respond to his overtures was a positive sign from the government's point of view. Moreover, in March, an uprising by the Fifth Infantry Battalion at Caldas da Rainha was easily suppressed by loyalist army units, including General Spínola's old regiment, the Seventh Cavalry, and the Republican Guard. Two hundred men and officers had been arrested by the DGS.

The security services were preoccupied with widespread labor unrest. Following the oil price rises, inflation was running at over 30 percent by early 1974 – the highest rate in Europe – and labor unrest was spreading not only among industrial workers but also for the first time among office workers and civil servants. Caetano had been warned to expect major disruptions and possibly a strike by government employees in May, a traditional month of labor militancy and antiregime demonstrations. The traditional methods of breaking labor unrest – the riot police, preventative detention, and censorship – he was warned, might not work. It was better to anticipate trouble by granting substantial salary increases before the storm broke. Caetano's response to this advice was to reshuffle his economic ministers. As to salary increases, this was a decision the government had intended to take the day it was overthrown. The secret police on April 24, 1974 had taps on the telephone lines of Generals Costa Gomes and Spínola, Major Melo Antunes, Captain Vasco Lourenço, General Kaúlza de Arriaga and, curious as it may seem, President Américo Tomás and the prime minister Marcello Caetano.[17]

If Caetano fiddled, it was because this was his method. If he had failed to act decisively, it was because the whole nature of his experience and the system he headed precluded decisive action. If he underestimated the threats, it was because few saw the regime in mortal danger. He was trapped both by his own personality and by the very institutions he had so diligently helped to create.

With the clear shift of power within the regime away from Caetano to President Américo Tomás and his ultra-right-wing allies, the captains realized that they would soon have to act. The dangers of delay were unmistakable. A steady stream of well-known reactionaries paid court daily at President Tomás' rose-walled palace at Belém. His photographs grew larger in the newspapers as Caetano's shrank. The purge of opposition elements in the army that had been taking place for months became harsher. Several army officers had already been arrested or shifted to posts deep in the interior of Portugal or on the Atlantic islands, among them Colonel Almeida Bruno, a close associate of General Spínola. The head of the military academy had already been removed. On April 18 the minister of the interior went to Oporto and gave a hard-line speech which later replaced the evening television programs and which ended with an ominous quotation from that old master whose words since 1970 had been carefully avoided, Dr. Salazar. The public were appalled. The last thing they wanted was a return to Salazarism which threatened even those modest liberal gains of the Caetano years, and would make virtually impossible a peaceful transition to the more open system most Portuguese now regarded as desirable.

CHAPTER 3

Coup d'état

If you fire, it will be civil war. Is the Army going to fire
on the Army?
>Captain Salgueiro Maia to loyalist tank commanders, Lisbon
>(April 25, 1974)

You must maintain control. I am frightened by the idea of
power loose in the street.
>Marcello Caetano to General Spínola as he surrendered
>(April 25, 1974)

When the Revolution took place in Portugal the United
States had "gone out to lunch." We were completely
surprised.
>Cord Meyer, CIA station chief in London (April 1974)

The alliance of the people and the military is, in the specific
situation existing today, an essential condition for the progress of democratization of Portuguese society.
>Alvaro Cunhal (April 1974)

I

As the base of the old regime in Lisbon was being undermined
by changing social and economic conditions, and with widespread
plotting and dissatisfaction spreading throughout the armed forces
from the highest ranks to the junior officers corps, Portugal's
NATO partners were blissfully unaware that anything was amiss
with their old, docile, and occasionally useful ally.

A major policy review of US relations with southern Africa
took place in 1969, early in the administration of Richard Nixon.
That summer an interdepartmental group on Africa reported to
the National Security Council that "the outlook for the rebellion

45

[in Portuguese Africa] is one of continued stalemate: the rebels cannot oust the Portuguese and the Portuguese can contain but not eliminate the rebels."[1] Nixon had promised Franco Nogueira, the Portuguese foreign minister, that he intended to rectify the errors in past US dealings with Portugal. He was true to his word. In 1970 the United States began to move closer to both Portugal and South Africa. Export-Import Bank facilities were extended in Portuguese colonies and the covert aid initiated during the Kennedy administration that had previously gone to the FNLA in Angola was curtailed, while in Mozambique aid to elements within FRELIMO that were considered "prowestern" was stopped.

Direct US economic interests in Portugal were relatively small. At the beginning of 1974 investments totaled $193 million, the largest belonging to General Tire and ITT. In Africa the economic stake was more important, especially that of Gulf Oil in the Cabinda enclave, a small territory separated from the rest of Angola to the north of the mouth of the Congo River. The interdepartmental group's report to the National Security Council in 1969 summed up the US position as follows: "Our policy positions in southern African issues affect a range of US interests. None of the interests are vital to our security, but they have political and material importance."[2] Important European assets tied into the southern African mining complex were, however, a significant factor. Raw materials and bullion, as well as the strategic allies' important Cape route, used by the tankers that carried almost all of Europe's oil supplies from the Arabian Gulf during the closure of the Suez canal from 1967 until 1975, had a strong influence on Washington's policies toward southern Africa. The same concern conditioned the US response to the collapse of Portugal's African empire.

Portugal is a founding member of NATO, though Salazar was to state in 1949 that Portugal's participation did not signify acceptance of what he regarded as the vague and wordy invocations of liberal and democratic principles in its charter. Portugal had sought to enter the United Nations in 1946 but had been opposed by the Soviet Union until a deal in 1955 between Moscow and Washington led to the admission of Portugal as well as sixteen other countries from the east and west, including Spain. Salazar had anticipated the problems that article 73, chapter XI of the UN Charter might cause for Portugal: the article concerning non-self-governing territories. To preempt the applicability of the obligations this imposed (promoting the economic and political development of these territories) Portugal's constitution was revised in 1951 to designate the Portuguese colonies as "provinces," hence constitutionally part of a unitary state. But this narrowly legalistic position was unsustainable, as the composition of the United Nations changed radically with the admission of newly independent nations in Africa and Asia throughout the 1960s, and it brought down on Portugal's head the disapprobation of the international community. Lisbon found itself at the center of the anticolonial campaign, causing increasing embarrassment and discomfort to its major western allies. On African policy, however, the Salazar regime at the time was not seriously challenged by the old republican opposition.[3]

Ironically, NATO began to find the notion of "pluricontinental Portugal" – the idea that Portugal was an intercontinental country with European and African provinces – to be a very convenient fiction just at the time when the whole edifice was under mortal challenge. NATO's charter excluded it from the South Atlantic, but US and European navy circles, in response to the growth of Soviet naval power in the late 1960s, had been voicing criticism of this stipulation for a number of years. After 1970, the US navy made increasing use of Mozambican and Angolan ports, mainly to avoid any embarrassment by visits to South Africa when the apartheid regime was itself coming under increasing international opposition. Particular interest was shown in the port of Nacala in Mozambique which, it was believed, with the proper technical facilities, could contain the entire US Seventh Fleet. In mid 1973, the Supreme Allied Command Atlantic (SACLANT) began contingency planning for air and naval operations in defense of South Africa. SACLANT carried out surveys of the state of the communications, airfields, and ports of Portugal's Atlantic islands and African colonies.

Between the 1940s and 1970s there was, nevertheless, a succession of distinct turning points, at which the United States came close to exercising significant pressure on Lisbon to change its intransigent stance in Africa. But on each occasion they occurred, Portugal, rather than compromising in the face of the inevitable, instead took a more stubborn stance. On each occasion the Azores was an ingredient in the equation. The relationship between the United States and Portugal had always had a special element to it as a result of the Azores base. Its most peculiar aspect is that the Azores base not only contributed to the longevity of Portugal's African empire but, also, its use by the United States to resupply Israel in 1973 during the Yom Kippur War became an important immediate cause of the coup.[4]

Between 1945 and 1947 many opponents of Salazar had hoped that a process of democratization would follow the Allied victory at the end of the war, and within Portugal the victory of the Allies provoked considerable political mobilization. The Salazar regime was compromised. It was a regime with the trappings of National Socialism and Italian fascism. The regime, therefore, was far from comfortable in a democratic world. The Roosevelt administration in the mid 1940s, moreover, had espoused a very strong anticolonialist position. So strong, in fact, that the British colonial office took the American policy seriously enough to initiate planning for a transfer of power in their own African colonies. The Portuguese were undoubtedly aware of this as well. The Cold War had not yet begun, so that the anticommunist arguments exploited so effectively later on by Salazar did not yet have credibility.

The Azores archipelago had become critical to naval warfare in the Atlantic during the Second World War, and Allied intentions in obtaining military facilities there and denying them to the Germans created a situation Salazar used to Portugal's advantage. During the war, the British, invoking the ancient Anglo-Portuguese treaties, had sought military facilities in the archipelago in order to combat German naval activity in the Atlantic, and had been prepared to seize the Azores if Salazar had persisted in denying them a base there, and Churchill had gone so far as to issue an ultimatum to Salazar. The negotiations, largely conducted by Humberto Delgado on the Portuguese side, were eventually successful and Salazar acquiesced in August 1943.[5] The Americans obtained access to the Azores facility under the cover of the British–Portuguese alliance, but in the negotiations conducted with George Kennan, chargé d'affaires in Lisbon, Salazar obtained a critical quid pro quo from Washington which committed the United States to respect the territorial integrity of Portuguese colonies in return for access to the Azores facilities.

The concession was the first significant breach in the United States' anticolonial position – subsequently the starting point for many of the problems which were to bedevil US policy toward Portugal and Portuguese Africa thereafter. The growing US role in international affairs, however, was deeply distrusted by Salazar. George Kennan told the secretary of state in 1943 that, "Salazar ... has almost as much fear of associating with us as he does with the Russians."[6]

Sometimes the internal situation in Portugal precluded change in colonial policy over the decades; sometimes it was external factors. Ironically, they never coincided to a degree that was able to bring about any significant transformation, leaving Portugal ever more isolated and intransigent in its position over Africa. Once the territorial integrity of the Portuguese empire had been assured and linked to US access to the Azores bases, the opportunity for a planned decolonization passed. With the beginning of the Cold War and Portugal's entry into NATO and the United Nations, Salazar took full advantage of the fear of communism in the United States and Western Europe to consolidate his power. President Eisenhower, who did not object to the dictatorial character of the regime in Lisbon, did gently suggest that Portugal should follow the British commonwealth example, in conversation with the American ambassador in Lisbon, C. Burke Elbrick. Portugal, Eisenhower believed, "obviously did not possess sufficient force to retain these vast territories [in Africa]." But Marcello Mathias, then Portuguese foreign minister, when told by Elbrick that the British had exported more to India since independence than before, replied that "for us, business was never the essential question."[7] Salazar told his minister of foreign affairs, Franco Nogueira, in March 1963, "I wish this country poor but independent; and I do not wish it colonized by American capital."[8]

The second period when the possibility of change occurred was between 1958 and 1962. The election campaign of General Humberto Delgado in 1958 prompted large-scale popular mobilization. Delgado, who was the negotiator of the original Azores agreement and a former airforce general, had challenged the regime in presidential elections and may well have won the election had it not been for fraud. This period also witnessed favorable external conditions for change. It was the grand period of African independence during which British and French colonies stampeded towards nationhood and which saw the inauguration of the Kennedy administration in Washington.

John F. Kennedy had been outspoken in his campaign against the remnants of European colonialism in Africa and he placed Africa high on his policy agenda once in office. The consequences of the precipitous Belgian withdrawal from the Congo, and the subsequent chaos in central Africa, also brought African concerns to center stage in Washington. On the first day of the new presidency, moreover, Portugal and its affairs hit the headlines with the spectacular hijacking by Henrique Galvão of the Portuguese liner, Santa Maria, on the high seas. Galvão and his co-conspirator, General Humberto Delgado, who, subsequent to his near victory in 1958, had sought refuge in the Brazilian embassy in Lisbon and later, from exile, had taken over the anti-Salazar opposition's leadership, timed the seizure of the Santa Maria with an eye to the inaugurations of Kennedy in the United States and of Janio Quadros in Brazil, both leaders considered sympathetic to the anti-Salazar cause. Galvão, as a former high official in Angola, had broken with the regime in 1947 when he wrote a scathing report on forced labor conditions and corruption in Angola.

Kennedy's response to the Santa Maria affair angered the Lisbon government, but the whole question was transformed as rebellion broke out in Angola in early February 1961 when 200 Africans, armed with machetes and clubs, attacked a police barracks and military prison in Luanda. The funerals held for the white policemen killed in the assault exploded into a violent rampage which left 300 Africans dead. The Kennedy administration warned Salazar that "step-by-step action towards full self-determination with a realistic timetable" was essential if further violence was to be avoided. In March, Adlai Stevenson, then Washington's UN ambassador, voted alongside the Soviet Union and with the three sponsors (Liberia, Ceylon, and the United Arab Republic) for a resolution calling on Portugal to begin "advancement" towards self-determination. By this time the revolt in Angola had spread to the north where a violent uprising resulted in 1,000 European and 20,000 African casualties.[9]

In March the United States was also closely monitoring and

surreptitiously encouraging a plot against Salazar among leading military officers, including the minister of defense, General Júlio Botelho Moniz. American ambassador Elbrick, in his meetings with Moniz, told the general that "urgent and drastic liberalization" was needed. Moniz agreed that reforms aimed at preparing for autonomy in the colonies were essential and that domestic reforms must include the participation of all noncommunist opposition in the government. The plotters failed to take account of the Salazar diehards within the military hierarchy or the resilience of Salazar himself, and delays by Moniz and his colleagues allowed the regime to mobilize loyal troops, the Republican Guard, and the Portuguese legion, and cut off the defense minister's means of communication. No less ominous was Franco's response in Spain; he mobilized tanks and sent them towards the frontier city of Badajoz, and apparently was intending to intervene in Portugal if Salazar was overthrown by left-wing forces.[10] Salazar dismissed Moniz and took over the ministry himself. "The Americans may succeed in killing me or I might die," Salazar remarked angrily to Franco Nogueira, "but if not, they will have to fight for years to bring me down."[11] Exercising his authority as minister of defense, Salazar ordered the speedy mobilization of forces and the reinforcement of the Portuguese garrison in Angola. A young political science professor, Adriano Moreira, was appointed to the post of overseas minister and quickly took the offensive to reform outdated policies and retake the initiative.[12]

The Kennedy administration's activist policy went so far as to give clandestine help to Holden Roberto and Eduardo Mondlane, leading anti-Portuguese nationalists in Angola and Mozambique, respectively.[13] Salazar reacted with fury to this intervention. "The present American government is a case where the lunatics have taken over the asylum," he told Franco Nogueira. "American policy is even more revoltingly imperialist than that of the Soviet Union."[14] Nevertheless, a unilateral embargo was imposed by the United States in June 1961 on the sale of arms to Portugal that might be used in Africa. US ambassador Burke Elbrick reported to Washington that "there is no question that the US is now identified as public enemy number one."[15]

By 1962–3, however, the moment when the possibility of change had existed again passed. The various opposition pressures in

Portugal faltered. By 1962, the attack on the army barracks at Beja when forty officers revolted was identified in the minds of American policymakers as being communist-influenced, a concern which had not been preeminent even one or two years before. The chaos which had followed the independence of the Belgian Congo, the Bay of Pigs episode, and the Cuban missile crisis, had hardened attitudes in Washington. Soviet premier Khrushchev told Kennedy in June 1961 that the Angolan uprising was a "sacred" war and that the Soviet Union would actively support the anticolonial struggle.[16] Again, the opportunities had been lost.

"Salazar was absorbed by a time dimension quite different from ours," George Ball reported after the frustrating visit to Salazar in 1963.[17] Ball was curiously more of a friend than Salazar supposed since he represented the more European-oriented side of the internal American debate over Portugal's role in Africa. Other Americans were complimentary in their view of Salazar; but their good will was not reciprocated. Marcello Mathias, the Portuguese ambassador in Paris and a close associate of Salazar, could hardly contain his diatribes against American "immaturity" in his letters to Salazar, especially where the Kennedy administration and its advisors were concerned.[18] Nevertheless, Salazar played the Azores card with skill and, in effect, the US administration capitulated. Admiral Anderson, the US ambassador in Lisbon during the mid 1960s devised an ingenious scheme to "buy" Portugal out of Africa, but the plan was doomed to failure because the possibilities of change had closed up again and the old intransigence dominated Portugal's position. Salazar was contemptuous of these efforts and economic arguments for decolonization carried little weight with some of Salazar's closest associates.[19]

Washington's contacts with the democratic opposition to Salazar were extremely limited. Marvine Howe, a correspondent for the *New York Times* in Lisbon had attempted to encourage a dialogue between the opposition and Washington in a letter to Bill Moyers, President Johnson's press secretary. She pointed out that "there are qualified spokesmen here [for the opposition] and if you'd like a name or two I'd be glad to submit them. After all, Premier Salazar is 76 and cannot last forever, and so the US may have to deal with someone else."[20] Ambassador Tapley Bennett, who succeeded Admiral Anderson as the US ambassador in Lisbon, did seek to maintain some contact with the opposition; and directly asked Nogueira if the Portuguese government had any objection. Nogueira acquiesced and Bennett assured him such contacts would be "always orthodox."[21] Surreptitious meetings subsequently took place in parks or out of the way cafés with individual opposition figures, including Mário Soares.

Finally, there was another dramatic moment of open options between 1968 and 1971. With Salazar's incapacitation and the appointment of Marcello Caetano, a great deal of hope for change emerged in Portugal. More European-oriented and modern-minded people entered into the government and National Assembly. Caetano himself hoped for some liberalization of colonial policies. The irony is that in this case it was external factors that mitigated against change. At just the point when some pressure might have produced results in Portugal, the Nixon administration came to the conclusion that, as the National Security memorandum puts it, "the Portuguese are in Africa to stay." Caetano visited Washington to attend the funeral of President Eisenhower in March 1969 and met with Nixon who promised him American support; subsequently Nixon ordered all American contacts with the nationalists in Portuguese Africa terminated.

When Franco Nogueira met with the new American president, Richard M. Nixon, in Washington in April 1969, Nixon assured him that he "was not in agreement with the policy until then followed with respect to Portugal." That night, at a banquet at the White House, Nixon told Nogueira that "the American policy towards Portugal was unjust. It will not be repeated."[22] Mondlane was assassinated in February 1969 by a book bomb, the work of FRELIMO dissidents, possibly assisted by PIDE.[23] This period of potential change ended with the murder, in 1973, of Amílcar Cabral, the African nationalist leader most open to a settlement and with whom Spínola had tried to persuade Caetano to negotiate, foreclosing the opening for an orderly disengagement from Africa. The liberals in Portugal had already resigned from the National Assembly in Lisbon, wiping out the possibilities of liberal reform in Portugal. The intransigence was back; the possibilities for orderly change had disappeared again.

There was a pathology to Portugal's intransigence. António de Figueiredo has called it the "metaphysics" of empire, though it can also be explained by the psychology of a small power as it responds to unwelcome outside pressure. Portugal is a classic case of a country that survived the enveloping power of its dominant neighbors. Sharing the Iberian peninsula with a larger and more powerful Spain and the oceans with the British, it is no accident that the Portuguese diplomatic service became absolute masters at delay, obfuscation, and manipulation, and finding ways of protecting Portuguese national interests in situations where overt power alone would have overwhelmed the Portuguese. Thus, while Salazar's ability to manipulate the international situation to Portugal's favor was considerable, it was also a skill that emerged out of Portuguese history. In the end, however, this skill was harnessed to the defense of intransigence and indefensible positions. The result was that Portugal was backed into a situation in which there remained no options whatsoever. Even under the pressure of the most sympathetic allies, such as General Eisenhower and Admiral Anderson, Portugal failed to come to terms with the inevitabilities of a world it was a part of, whether it liked it or not.

The final straw came, curiously, from precisely the old nexus between Atlantic geostrategic realities and imperial mythos.

On October 6 1973, the day of Yom Kippur, the Egyptian and Syrian armed forces launched a successful surprise attack on the state of Israel. The Soviet Union, which had long courted and armed the Arab belligerents, established a huge air support supply operation. Washington, like Tel Aviv, was taken completely by surprise; and what was worse both Israel and the United States found themselves isolated – Israel almost entirely dependent on the United States for supplies and materiel, and the US severely limited in its ability to establish the massive airbridge it urgently needed to put into place to resupply Israel. In the face of Arab threats to disrupt Europe's oil lifelines, the Nixon administration found itself denied landing and passage rights by all its NATO allies, as well as Spain, and turned urgently to Lisbon for permission to use the Azores air base facilities. But when the US approached the Portuguese they were smarting under the tightening of the congressional embargo against them, and the foreign ministry saw the US request as an opportunity to obtain a quid pro quo; most especially to obtain American Red Eye missiles, now regarded as essential to the Portuguese forces in Guinea. The urgency for the Portuguese government of this demand was driven home by the fact that the Soviets had begun to provide ground missiles to the PAIGC, thus making the retention of the remaining air-supplied enclaves the Portuguese still held in PAIGC territory virtually impossible. But the demand only demonstrated how totally out of touch the Portuguese were with both the urgency of the request and the inappropriateness of their demands. The US administration could not have lifted the congressionally mandated embargo even if it had wished. This was not within the executive's power, certainly not in the few hours needed to respond to the life-and-death crisis in the Middle East. Kissinger was infuriated and, on October 13, 1973, President Nixon issued a harsh démarche to Caetano personally, warning the Portuguese prime minister that a refusal to accede to the American request would lead to American retaliation which Portugal in its isolated position could ill afford. Caetano capitulated.

The tide turned in Israel's favor on October 16. But the economic consequences for Portugal of its role in the resupply of Israel were severe.

After a period of growing prosperity, the recession which followed the 1973 Yom Kippur War and the Arab oil boycott hit consumers in Portugal with high inflation, something they had not experienced in living memory. The oil boycott affected Portugal especially badly, precisely because the United States had used the Lajes air base in the Azores to ferry supplies to Israel. The Arab states continued to boycott Portugal even after they ended the ban on oil exports to other western nations. While visiting Lisbon in December 1973, Henry Kissinger secretly promised sophisticated ground-to-air missiles, "red-eye missiles," and other equipment to Portugal for use in Africa, a commitment which violated the US embargo on such arms sales to Portugal and a decision to which the US embassy, or at least the chargé d'affaires, was not privy.[24]

II

The failure of the revolt by the Fifth Infantry on March 16, 1974 had taught the MFA important lessons. "They behaved like what we call *espontâneos*, the rash young men who cannot contain themselves at a boring bull fight and leap into the ring and get gored,"[25] is how one member of the MFA's coordinating committee summed up the whole affair. Major Otelo Saraiva de Carvalho, who had been appointed to take charge of the military organization, also watched the behavior of the government's forces carefully. The security police and the Republican Guard had reacted quickly, but the security police worked in small units, and the Republican Guard, while it had protected vehicles, did not have armored cars. Moreover, neither security force possessed modern, automatic weapons comparable to the army's G-3 rifles. The Fifth Infantry rebels had been stopped by other army units, and it became clear to Major Saraiva de Carvalho that the security forces, while adequately prepared to control civilian disturbances, were not equipped to face the regular army. On March 24, Saraiva de Carvalho told the coordinating committee meeting at Major Vítor Alves' house in Oeiras that he would need twenty days to organize military operations and suggested that the coup take place in the week beginning Monday, April 22.

In the meantime, the political committee under the direction of Major Melo Antunes was putting the finishing touches to the MFA's political program. In a crackdown on nonconformist members of the officer corps, Caetano had ordered several of the movement's members posted to the Azores – Melo Antunes among them – and he arrived at the meeting with the draft at two in the morning and left for the airport an hour later. The program began with a general statement of principle: "After thirteen years of struggle in the overseas territories, the prevailing system has been unable to formulate concisely and objectively an overseas policy which would lead to peace among Portuguese of all races and creeds. It recognizes that only by the cleansing (*saneamento*) of the current internal political life of the nation could such a formulation occur."[26] The measures proposed in the Melo Antunes draft were presented in two stages – the immediate and the short term.

The immediate measures included the formation of the Junta of National Salvation, the dismissal of existing civil governors at home and overseas, the dissolution of the secret police and the Portuguese legion, amnesty for political prisoners, abolition of censorship, and the reorganization and purging of the armed forces. The short-term measures betrayed a more overtly political intent. A provisional government was envisioned which would include "representative personalities from political groups and trends and independent personalities who identify themselves with this program." The provisional government was to prepare for elections "by universal, direct and secret suffrage" to a Constituent Assembly which in turn would draw up a new Portuguese constitution. The provisional government would also promote measures "to guarantee the future effective exercise of citizens' political freedom." This included freedom of assembly and association – including political parties and trade unions, freedom of expression, and abolition of special courts. With regard to the justice system, the political program stated that "crimes committed against the state under the new regime will be subject to examination by judicial authority and will be tried in ordinary courts of law, and all the rights of the accused guaranteed."[27]

On domestic policy, the new regime would pursue "a new economic policy geared to the interests of the Portuguese people, in particular to that stratum of the population less favored until now, having as its immediate aim the fight against inflation . . . which will, of necessity, imply an antimonopoly strategy." A new social policy "will essentially have as its objective the defense of the interests of the laboring classes." As to external affairs, the MFA program promised "respect for international commitments resulting from treaties which are in force."

The key issue, African policy, was left to last. "Bearing in mind that responsibility for its formulation rests with the nation, the overseas policy of the provisional government will comply with the following principles: (a) recognition that the solution of the overseas war is political, not military; (b) creation of conditions for a frank and open debate of the overseas problem at the national level; (c) clear recognition of the right of the people to self-determination and the speedy adoption of measures which lead toward administrative and political autonomy for the overseas territories, with real and widespread participation by the indigenous people; and (d) laying the foundations for an overseas policy leading to peace."

The ambiguities of the MFA program were deliberate. The political committee wished to gather the widest possible support for the movement. Nevertheless, General Spínola, upon reading the program, found much of its political tone offensive. The last section on African policy in particular upset him. At Spínola's instigation, Section (c) – the right to self-determination – was struck out. Spínola also objected to the definition of the old regime as being "fascist" and the objectives of the coup as being "democratic." These words were not used in the final document.[28]

Major Otelo Saraiva de Carvalho's military plan aimed to seal off Lisbon rapidly, take control of key airports, radio stations and government installations, and to force a quick capitulation by the regime. Military units throughout the country were discreetly canvassed, a process inadvertently aided by the government when several key MFA leaders were dispersed to barracks throughout the interior in an effort to break up the movement during the weeks immediately prior to April 25.

The code for the coup was given out over the Portuguese Catholic radio station, Radio Renascença, during a midnight broadcast called "Limite" by José Vasconcelos. The tip-off that his program was to contain the code had been printed in the Lisbon evening newspaper *República*, edited by the socialist Raul Rego. An anonymous note was placed in the review section: "The program 'Limite' has been improving for some weeks. The quality of its news items and its choice of music make 'Limite' obligatory listening."[29]

Twenty-five minutes into April 25, José Vasconcelos read aloud the lyrics of the record he had on the turntable. The tune was "Grandola, Vila Morena," a popular song by José (Zeca) Afonso, a dissident from the Alentejo, the bread-basket of Portugal and the land of the *latifúndios*.

> Grandola, dark town
> Land of fraternity
> It is the people
> Who command more
> Within you, O city.
> On each corner a friend
> On each face equality
> Grandola, dark town
> Land of fraternity.[30]

This was the poetic signal for the revolt.

Fifty miles northeast of Lisbon in Santarém, on a steep bluff overlooking the Tagus River, ten armored vehicles from the Portuguese cavalry school were prepared. At 3 a.m. they moved

south at 40 m.p.h. along the highway to Lisbon. By first light
the column was in downtown Lisbon and had encountered no
opposition. Meanwhile, armed forces units had risen throughout
the country. The bridge up river from Lisbon was taken, and
the Salazar Bridge over the Tagus joining Lisbon and southern
Portugal was secured.

At 8 a.m., eight tanks from the seventh Cavalry barracks
appeared in the Praça do Comércio. They surrendered to Captain
Maia, the 29 year old commander of the Santarém detachment.
More tanks appeared from the west, rumbling along the cobbled
streets along the river front. Their commander, Brigadier Reis,
ordered them to fire. But the crews refused. A standoff continued
until 11 a.m. when Captain Salgueiro Maia persuaded the brigadier to surrender. The crowds were now thick in the streets and
Captain Maia and his tanks made their way with difficulty up
Lisbon's narrow streets to the Carmo Barracks, the headquarters
of the National Republican Guard, where Marcello Caetano and
several of his ministers had fled.

It takes two, however, to make a bloodless revolution, and on
April 25, 1974 the will to resist a coup did not exist. Only the
secret police, holed up in their headquarters with submachine
guns, opposed the coup, and their brief shootout caused the only
casualties. Marcello Caetano, sitting forlornly in a small room
at the back of the Carmo Barracks had feared the end was close
since February when he had read Spínola's book. He agreed to
surrender, but only to General Spínola. General Spínola meanwhile agreed to assume power, but only if he was assured of the
MFA's total backing and only if he received this assurance from
an officer above the rank of lieutenant colonel. Ironically, the
only such officer on the MFA's coordinating committee was
Colonel Vasco Gonçalves, an officer close to the communists.

General Spínola, horsewhip in hand, monocle in place, arrived
at the Carmo Barracks at 5.45 p.m. Ten thousand people were
now crammed into the narrow square in front of the National
Republican Guard headquarters. Spínola was taken to the room
where Caetano awaited him and the prime minister surrendered.
Caetano was then whisked away with other members of his
deposed government in an armored car and held overnight at
the engineering barracks of Pontinha outside Lisbon from whence
Major Otelo Saraiva de Carvalho had directed the coup d'état.

At 8 a.m. the next morning Caetano and Tómas were sent into temporary exile on Madeira.

It was done. With extraordinary speed, and without serious resistance, a regime which had ruled Portugal since the late 1920s was effortlessly overthrown. By April 26, 1974, the streets were full of joyful crowds. The MFA program was posted on walls where its democratic promises were avidly read. *Avante!* the Communist Party's newspaper, which had been printed underground without interruption since its founding, began immediate open publication. There seemed to be roses and red carnations everywhere.

III

Soon after the coup, a graffito appeared at the Technical Institute of Lisbon. It read: "Revolution of roses: petals for the bourgeoisie, thorns for the people." Twenty months later, Portugal was on the brink of civil war and Angola had plunged into fratricidal strife. It is surprising, in retrospect, that anyone should have been so sanguine. There would be thorns enough for everyone, once the issues at stake in Portugal and Africa became clearer. Although the uprising on April 25 had few revolutionary connotations at the time, it was no ordinary coup d'état either. It brought down Europe's oldest dictatorship, foreshadowed the end of its oldest empire, and thrust to the forefront a very curious hybrid – a group of young European military officers, profoundly influenced by the theory and practice of national liberation struggles outside Europe, who came increasingly, as the months wore on, to see themselves as a revolutionary vanguard. Portugal's western allies were unprepared for what happened, and during twelve critical months their reactions to events in Portugal were panicked, makeshift, and defensive.

Over the euphoric summer and early autumn of 1974, however, there was an illusion of Portugal as a kaleidoscopic theater of politics, sprung up after fifty years without political expression. Diplomatic relations with Russia were reestablished for the first time since the Bolshevik revolution of 1917. The ideological experience of the twentieth century became crammed into nine months. Best-seller lists harbored Lenin's *April Theses* along with the poems of Angola's nationalist leader, Agostinho Neto. There were marches and demonstrations where, before, a meeting of any political group would have been subject to brutal police attack. For gilded youth, with their neatly laundered blue jeans, it was a chance to spend hours stoned on whatever or whoever was available. Revolutionary homosexuals joined the anarchists. Revolutionary groupies flocked to Lisbon while the going was good. Middle-class families parked their cars wherever they felt like it. Hustlers inundated the Rossio, Lisbon's elegant downtown square, displaying their wares by the metro stop opposite the Pastelaria Suíça. Eventually even *Hair* arrived, with the "original English cast." It replaced an "international sexy festival" at the Teatro Monumental, a revue of naked German blondes in black leather jackboots, denounced by the Portuguese Communist Party (PCP) as "another CIA plot." At its worst, Portugal after the coup was like an ancient boulder suddenly turned over to reveal a thousand bugs scurrying frenetically in the light. At its best, Portugal was a garden of fragile, brilliant, and tangled foliage.

The "forces of order" of the old regime, apart from the secret police and the legion, still existed. But both the Public Security Police and the National Republican Guard were severely shaken by the collapse of clear lines of authority. More important, their self-confidence had been undermined and they were worried about their future. The ranks of both forces were made up of men of rural backgrounds and rudimentary education. They had few employment opportunities in civilian life. But they were also too much associated with repression under the old regime to be an effective power in the new situation. Thus, they saluted the scruffy students and *milicianos*, now ensconced in the old secret police headquarters, with as much deference as they had once saluted the former occupants. A job was better than none, and subservience was better than being in prison, which is where over 1,500 former secret policemen found themselves after April 25, 1974.

The coup also broke the dam of pent-up labor militancy. Hundreds of labor conflicts erupted throughout the country. Owners, unused to worker militancy and accustomed to calling on the security forces to prevent it, refused concessions, which led to strikes. The scale of popular response to the coup, the mobilization of workers, and the chanting crowds in the streets took the military by surprise.[31]

Across large parts of the political spectrum, rhetoric was more evident than organization as spring moved toward summer. The highly theoretical character of the debate in the immediate aftermath of the coup was not accidental. The Salazar regime had in cultural and intellectual matters come perilously close to totalitarianism. By raising the stakes of loyalty and narrowing its definition, the old regime had made all intellectual activity political. Historical myths were part of the regime's ideological essence. To deflate them brought instant retribution. Eventually the men who fabricated the myths by acting out their fantasies were destroyed by them, but the singular heritage of Salazar was to give words the appearance of action and sometimes even the power to create events. Paradoxically, therefore, the country with the highest illiteracy rate in Western Europe (37 percent) had a large and avid public of book readers attuned to the smallest political nuance, something that helps explain the impact of General Spínola's book and of the subsequent best-selling books by MFA officers.

The blanket condemnation by the old regime of all opposition as communistic also inevitably created, in the confusion following the coup, a situation where the mirror image of this view proved virtually irresistible. Overnight the communists, as the most persecuted of the old regime's opponents, became the most readily identifiable as the new regime's heroes. The terms of political discourse following the coup were, therefore, almost entirely framed in the phraseology of the left and the communists moved very rapidly to center stage.

The April revolution had thrown the high schools into chaos, and students spent the rest of the academic year purging the faculties of "fascists" and forming short-lived administrative committees of students, teachers, and maintenance personnel. Faced with the impossibility of holding examinations, the government rashly accepted all high school students in their final year into the universities, creating in the fall of 1974 a freshman class of 28,000 that the universities, themselves in chaos, would have been totally incapable of absorbing even at the best of times. The government was then forced to cancel the entire freshman class, turning 28,000 mostly middle-class students on to the streets of the cities with nothing to do but demonstrate, attend endless meetings, and engage in increasingly violent and intolerant internecine disputes, many attaching themselves to Marxist-Leninist, anarchist, and Maoist parties to the left of the PCP.[32]

The extreme visibility and volubility of the left was thus very deceptive. The uncomfortable truth was that until the very end of the old regime most Portuguese either approved of or acquiesced in the system overthrown by the coup. Not for nothing had that system survived for half a century. After April a large part of the population, intensely traditionalist and conservative, found themselves without spokesmen. They formed a political prize of some importance. The principal new political organizations of 1974, therefore, were not those of the left, most of which existed before the coup and had long-standing relations with one another, but the fledgling parties of the center and the right.

For those with an eye to power, this was not necessarily disadvantageous. Spínola's political strategy, on becoming provisional president, was based on three assumptions: (1) that the left would trip over itself and self-destruct; (2) that the high visibility of the leftists would in time make them an ideal scapegoat; and (3) that the left's lack of real support in the country would allow him to consolidate a centrist and reforming coalition that would strengthen his own authority, legitimize that authority by popular acclaim and, through the political process, circumvent the residual power of the MFA.

Spínola, moreover, started with formidable assets. He enjoyed vast popularity during months when the feeling of good will was palpable in Lisbon. The seven-member political committee that had drawn up the MFA program, the CCP (Comissão Coordinadora do Programa), was incorporated, however, into the Council of State, providing in effect the first form of institutionalization in the MFA. Under the transitional constitution the Council was to assume power until the election of the National Assembly. But Spínola could feel that the seven MFA officers were more than balanced on the Council by a conservative majority in the Junta of National Salvation – seven senior officers representing all branches of the armed services – and by his own seven appointees to the Council. The latter included two colonels from his personal entourage and five persons of some consequence from the old regime, such as Dr. Azeredo Perdigão, president of the Calouste Gulbenkian Foundation and the old opposition such as Henrique de Barros. Spínola appointed a loyalist, Colonel

Firmino Miguel, as defense minister, and put a leading rightist general in command of the critical Lisbon garrison. He sent to Angola as governor one of the main proponents of integrating the colonies with Portugal, General Silvino Silvério Marques, whose brother Jaime Silvério Marques was a member of the junta.[33]

How little these circles understood the attitudes of the MFA was shown by Spínola's first choice for prime minister, Professor Veiga Simão, the former minister of education under Caetano. Veiga Simão was a competent technocrat of modest background who had recently introduced a major reform of the university system, but his association with Caetano made him *persona non grata* to the old opposition. Spínola had then wanted Francisco Sá Carneiro, leader of the new Popular Democratic Party and a well-known liberal opponent of Caetano's, but eventually settled for Professor Palma Carlos, a liberal "apolitical" law professor. In fact, five members of Spínola's provisional government had been former students of both Caetano and Palma Carlos – most without any sympathy or even understanding of the potentially radical ideas implicit in the MFA program. But the closeness of the politicians to one another and their intimate connections with figures of the old regime were scarcely surprising. The situation was a function of the smallness of the Portuguese elite.

Spínola's failure to see the importance of the MFA was caused in part by the ambiguity of the transition, which was itself a result of Spínola's crafty political footwork and the desire of Caetano to give to the coup some semblance of a "transfer of power" to known figures of authority and responsibility. Spínola's "legalist" position was such that he both knew and did not know, a device that allowed him to state quite seriously on April 25 that "he was not one of those who take up arms against their government."[34] Thus the deceptive and contrived appearance of continuity when he arrived dramatically at the Carmo Barracks to "receive" a transfer of authority from the encircled prime minister. This was a maneuver to prevent, in Caetano's words, "power falling into the streets." It also served to disguise for a time, from many Portuguese and most foreigners, the importance of the young captains and majors who had executed the coup.

General Spínola's role in the overthrow of Caetano was, thus, much overestimated at the time and, when the old regime collapsed, scant attention was paid to the Armed Forces Movement, the phrase itself often being taken to be a descriptive epithet rather than the title adopted by the compact group of junior officers who had made the coup. While foreign correspondents and diplomats waded laboriously through the baroque syntax of Spínola's *Portugal and the Future* to seek some clue as to what might happen next in Lisbon, the movement's own program was little discussed, despite the fact that it was soon promulgated into the transitional constitution of the Portuguese republic. This was a serious misjudgment particularly on the part of Portugal's NATO allies. *Portugal and the Future* was important in the sense that it propelled Spínola into a position of leadership and international notoriety. But the book was of much less value as an indicator of thinking among those who had actually made the coup.

CHAPTER 4

Conflicts and confusions

> The silent majority of the Portuguese people must wake up
> and actively defend itself from the totalitarian extremisms
> growing in the shadows.
>
> General Spínola, provisional president of Portugal
> (September 10, 1974)

> No one should be in any doubt, and much less the Armed
> Forces Movement, that the true and only enemy of demo-
> cracy and the spirit of the 25th of April is reaction and its
> agents.
>
> Communiqué of the Fifth Division of the general staff of the
> Armed Forces Movement (September 25, 1974)

> Under the false flag of liberty, there are being prepared new
> forms of slavery.
>
> General Spínola on his resignation (September 30, 1974)

> Popular vigilance and the vigilance of the Armed Forces
> Movement must always be present to unmask all those that
> do not wish to see democracy consolidated in Portugal.
>
> Colonel Vasco Gonçalves, prime minister (October 5, 1974)

I

As Cord Meyer, the CIA station chief in London at the time
put it: "When the revolution occurred in Portugal the US was
out to lunch; we were completely surprised." The US ambassador
in Lisbon was an elderly and amiable lawyer, Stuart Nash Scott,
from the east coast establishment without diplomatic experience.
He was in the Azores visiting the US base there when the coup
occurred. Since Lisbon airport was closed he decided to go on
to Boston to attend a class reunion at Harvard Law School. It
was an extraordinary gaffe for an ambassador accredited to a
country in the midst of an armed insurrection, and it was one

of several factors which undermined the credibility of the ambassador in Henry Kissinger's eyes.

The story of Mr. Post, the deputy chief of mission left in charge of the embassy is even more poignant. In an interview with Portuguese journalist José Freire Antunes he described how he first heard of the coup: "It was still dark: the telephone rang in my bedroom. The guard at our house in Restelo, a former member of the DGS [the Portuguese secret police] was calling from the garage: he said to me '*perigo, perigo!*' [danger, danger!]. I did not understand. My wife, half awake, said 'Oh, that's the guard's name.' I hung up and we went back to sleep. It was about six in the morning when one of the military attachés called. He said there were tanks in the street and military music on the radio."

Washington, however, was more than usually nervous about the overthrow of Caetano. Only six months before the coup, the US base in the Azores at Lajes, which some had been claiming had lost its significance in an age of intercontinental ballistic missiles, was suddenly revealed to be of vital importance, not so much for NATO purposes *per se*, but for what in NATO jargon was called "out of the area contingencies"; the Middle East, for example. During the war between Israel and the Arab states following the Egyptian attack at Yom Kippur, in 1973, Portugal alone among America's European allies had permitted use of the base facilities for US resupply missions to Israel, and even this had required a virtual ultimatum to Caetano from Nixon. Given Caetano's isolation, he had had little option but to accede to American demands.

During the early 1970s, in fact, Portugal had been the perfect ally for the United States. It was docile, dependent, and had nowhere else to go. The United States' embassy in Lisbon became a quiet pasture for conservatives who had fallen temporarily from grace in Washington, including William Tapley Bennett, Jr., a former US ambassador to the Dominican Republic, and Admiral George W. Anderson, Jr., a former chief of naval operations and organizer of the Cuban blockade of 1961. In Portugal they were surrounded by an exceptionally congenial expatriate community. Ensconced among the mimosa groves of Estoril and Cascais or the almond blossoms of the Algarve were fallen dictators (the late Fulgencio Batista), would-be or former monarchs (Don Juan of Spain, ex-King Umberto of Italy), arthritic British colonels, a handful of ex-Nazis, and Elliot Roosevelt who owned a stud farm and had a stake in the Portuguese real estate company Torralta. They all enjoyed Portugal: Admiral Anderson bought a villa in the south. Like so many others rehabilitated by Nixon's election, such men were not without influence. William Tapley Bennett, Jr. was appointed assistant United States ambassador to the United Nations. Admiral Anderson became chairman of President Nixon's foreign intelligence advisory board. They were sure sources of "unbiased" views on the scruffy soldiers and assorted "reds" who emerged from the woodwork of old Portugal to ruin "their" paradise in 1974.

There were precious few other sources of information when the Caetano regime was toppled. On March 15, 1974, in Room 2200, Rayburn Office Building, Washington, DC, the sub-committee on Africa chaired by congressman Charles Diggs of Michigan, had met for hearings on "the complex of United States–Portuguese Relations." The rationale for the meeting was the ongoing negotiation between Portugal and the United States for the renewal of the Azores base agreement; but the principal topic proved to be General Spínola's book. The sub-committee had two distinguished State Department witnesses, the director of the Office of Iberian Affairs, Mr. Ellwood M. Rabenhold, Jr., and the director of the Office of Southern African Affairs, Mr. W. Paul O'Neill. Mr. O'Neill observed in a prepared statement: "We are not able to comment at this stage on what impact Spínola's book will have on the direction of Portuguese society. We are, however, aware of changes that have taken place over the last decade that lead us to conclude the Portuguese are working at an increasing tempo to bring non-white majorities in those countries into the mainstream of political and economic life." Mr. Rabenhold said, "I would like to make this observation: that change in Portugal occurs very slowly, very slowly and I don't think one can assume that anything, even this book, can bring about drastic change rapidly."

Just forty-two days later the tanks of the cavalry school at Santarém had rumbled into the silent city of Lisbon. Within twenty-four months, Portugal's presence in Africa, first established half a millennium before, had ended. Yet Mr. Rabenhold's comments accurately represented Washington's view. The only "irritant" in American–Portuguese relations during the early 1970s had been caused by the US government's own equivocation and double standards in its dealings with southern Africa. So oblivious had Washington been during the Nixon years to the political forces in Portugal, so unwilling to have even informal connections with the democratic groups opposing the dictatorship, that it knew none of them. On the eve of the coup a United States military attaché had boasted at a party that he had never talked to anyone below the rank of a colonel. With very few exceptions, no one who mattered in the new Portugal had yet reached that rank. As a Western diplomat bemusedly surveying the scene in Lisbon observed: "We don't know why they are doing all this, and we don't even know who most of them are."

The Central Intelligence Agency's presence in Portugal was held to be of low importance and Lisbon was regarded as a "retirement post." In 1973, William Colby, director of the agency, went so far as to recommend that the station in Lisbon be closed down. Since the late 1950s, however, the CIA had worked closely with the Portuguese political police (PIDE/DGS). Many Portuguese agents came to the United States for four-month training courses. Allen Dulles, the long-time CIA director, found them "of high caliber, diligent and gracious visitors," as he wrote in a letter discovered after the April 1974 coup. Most of those sent to the US were from the bureau of investigation, responsible for interrogation and, in some documented cases, for the torture of political prisoners. The inevitable result of these arrangements was that within a dying system the CIA was linked to the one element least anxious for change and, as it proved in the event, the last to know that the real threat to the regime existed within the army.

In Portugal PIDE/DGS formed a grotesque state within a state, locked in a continuing struggle with real or phantom communists of the PCP. As always, it was a struggle of mutual advantage, the importance of the PCP and the PIDE each reflected in the survival of the other. But when the PIDE was dissolved following the April coup, the CIA lost its local "assets" overnight. The nature of the CIA connections in Portugal, far from adding to Washington's knowledge, helped to blind it. After the coup, a "commission" including former political prisoners was set up to root out the political police and its vast network of spies and informers. (The scale of the network amazed PIDE's most strident critics, for the documents discovered at the fortress prison of Caxias outside Lisbon revealed that perhaps as many as one in every four hundred Portuguese had at some time been paid for information by the secret police.) As the twenty-two member central committee of the PCP had collectively spent 308 years in Salazarist jails, the commission inevitably contained communist militants. The CIA connection and that of several other intelligence agencies was thus threatened with exposure.

Or so they thought. In fact, the communists could be counted on for the utmost discretion. The PIDE archives were more useful for blackmail, and their contents were of as much concern to the communist leader Alvaro Cunhal as to anyone else, for the PCP had some embarrassing skeletons of its own, not least the secret police informers within its own ranks.

Certainly PIDE's connections with western intelligence were no surprise to the Portuguese communists. PIDE agents often boasted of the CIA connection to their prisoners, including on one occasion to Mário Soares, leader of the Portuguese Socialist Party. In fact, Abílio Pires, the PIDE agent who accompanied Soares to the plane that deported him to São Tomé had, since the late 1950s, been on the CIA payroll. (He started at $500 a month.) Initially, most of the work of the commission was handled by young *miliciano* noncommissioned officers in their twenties, many of whom regarded the Portuguese communists as "social fascists." And the commission contained members of the other political parties who saw no reason for discretion and were subject to no party discipline. Information did leak despite the frantic effort to prevent it by General Galvão de Melo, the member of the junta of National Salvation responsible for the "dismantling" process. *Le Nouvel Observateur* published highly damaging information on the role of French intelligence in Portugal and a photostat of Dulles' letter. Later, Bruno Crimi in *Jeune Afrique* reported in detail on those responsible for the assassination of Amílcar Cabral, not only implicating some of Spínola's closest associates in Guinea but again revealing some highly incriminating activities of French and German intelligence officers. None of these developments endeared the new regime in Lisbon to those shadowy forces on which western governments relied, perhaps with more confidence than was deserved, for accurate information.

II

Portuguese civil society was also caught by surprise at the suddenness and rapidity of the young officers' success. During the weeks prior to the coup, the MFA had deliberately avoided the civilian opposition for reasons of security. The clandestine political parties were known to be infiltrated by the secret police. Nevertheless, opposition to the dictatorship had always existed and almost automatically provided a cadre of civilian collaborators for the military in the political vacuum which had emerged in April 1974. The old republicans had never accepted the corporate state and its fascist overtones, for instance, even if their countless platforms of dissent never came close to shaking the formidable apparatus of censorship, repression, and cultural uniformity that Salazar imposed. The Communist Party had been the most serious thorn, which had in consequence suffered the most severe repression.[1]

Although no one under seventy had ever voted in anything resembling a free election in Portugal, local political organizations called "Democratic Election Committees" (CDE) did exist throughout Portugal. They were used principally (most recently in 1973) as an opportunity for criticism and debate during the regime's periodic contests for seats in the National Assembly. The electoral system itself was stacked in the regime's favor. Nevertheless, the opportunity was used to articulate a forceful critique of the dictatorship's positions. The CDE was comprised of coalitions of "anti-fascist forces," mainly middle-class liberals, social democrats, catholic radicals, independent Marxists, and the communists.

The Portuguese Communist Party (PCP) was founded in 1921. Originally, the communists had little representation among the working class, which, until the 1930s, was strongly influenced by anarcho-syndicalism and by the socialists. But after 1943, under the leadership of Alvaro Cunhal, the party began to develop a political base. Forced underground since the first days of the Salazar dictatorship, the long decades of clandestine existence profoundly affected the Portuguese communists' psyche and behavior. Party organization adhered to strict Leninist lines – small cells, tight discipline, members kept unaware of each others' identities, and decisions handed down from above. Cunhal himself

spent thirteen years behind bars in Portugal and another fourteen
years in exile in Eastern Europe and Moscow. The party was a
particularly classic cadre party; deeply dependent on and subser-
vient to Moscow. After Fidel Castro, for example, Cunhal was
the first communist leader to approve the 1968 Soviet intervention
in Prague, strongly diverging thereafter from his Iberian counterpart, Santiago Carrillo, in Spain. Cunhal was a man of upper-
middle-class origins, who studied law in Lisbon. He joined the
party in 1931 at the age of seventeen. In 1934, he organized the
federation of young communists in the Lisbon area and in 1935
the sixth Congress of Communist Youth in Moscow. He went
underground on his return to Portugal and became a member
of the Central Committee of the party in 1936.[2]

In Portugal the PCP possessed a strong base in the Alentejo,
the grain-producing lands south of the Tagus River – a region
of great landed estates. Here the party was strongly implanted
among the anticlerical, landless rural laborers. The Alentejo is
a region with a long history of communist militancy, and Cunhal
knew it well. He was the author of one of the few detailed
analyses of the social and economic structures of the Portuguese
countryside, *A questão agrária em Portugal* ("The Agrarian Question
in Portugal") published in Brazil in 1968.

The PCP was also strong within the labor movement. After
the incapacitation of Salazar in 1968 and during the early years
of Marcello Caetano, liberalization of the rules governing election
to positions within the corporative syndicate structure allowed
communists to take a leading role in the trade union committees.
In 1970 the communist-influenced unions joined in a coordinating
organization called Intersindical. Prior to the coup, the communists were strongly entrenched in the metallurgical unions and
increasingly influential among lower-middle-class white-collar
workers, especially the bank workers' unions in Lisbon and
Oporto.

There was a tradition of opposition, however, that coexisted
uncomfortably with the communists and gave rise in the 1960s
to the Portuguese Socialist Association (ASP), and in 1973 to
the Portuguese Socialist Party (PS). This current of opinion was
inspired by the leading intellectual opponents of the Salazar
regime, such as the Lisbon evening daily *República*, the monthly
journal *Seara Nova*, and its prominent contributors, the historian

Jaime Cortesão and the philosopher António Sérgio. In the 1960s, a younger generation took up the mantle as the old guard of dissident intellectuals passed from the scene. Three men were especially prominent: Lisbon lawyers Mário Soares and Francisco Salgado Zenha, and *República*'s editor, Raul Rego. Soares and Salgado Zenha founded the Portuguese Socialist Action in Geneva in 1964, and the organization was subsequently renamed the Portuguese Socialist Party at a congress held in Bad Munstereif-fel, West Germany, in April 1973. The Portuguese socialists affiliated with the Socialist International and developed strong ties with social democrats in Western Europe, especially with Willy Brandt and the West German Social Democratic Party. Soares and his colleagues were also in contact with Swedish and British socialists.[3]

Soares was the son of a former priest and politician prominent during the democratic republic that was overthrown in 1926 by the military; and thus Soares had been involved in opposition politics since childhood. He had been a student of Alvaro Cunhal, who taught at the financially successful private school owned and directed by Soares' father. Soares at that time regarded Cunhal as one of his political mentors, and the latter in turn aided Soares' rapid rise in the communist youth movement, of which he became a leader in the 1940s. Soares' break with the communists came after bitter infighting within the PCP over the issue of Marshal Tito's expulsion from the international communist movement.

Soares had trained as a lawyer at the University of Lisbon, when, like Cunhal, he had been a student of Marcello Caetano. He gained international stature as legal representative for the family of General Humberto Delgado. After the Santa Maria affair, Delgado had gone into exile in Algeria, where he organized an opposition movement. Lured to a meeting near the Portuguese–Spanish border in 1965, he was murdered under mysterious circumstances.[4] Soares' activity in investigating this case led to his deportation to the island of São Tomé, and to his later exile. At the time of the April coup, he held a teaching post at the University of Paris, Vincennes.

The socialists, unlike the communists, had a very small organizational base in Portugal prior to 1974. But whereas the communist leadership in general consisted of men who had been members since the 1930s and 1940s and were mostly in their

sixties at the time of the Caetano regime's overthrow, the socialists were of a younger generation, much more closely attuned to
the more recent developments in Western Europe. Soares, in
particular, had seen the unrest of the late 1960s in France at
close quarters. The socialists had rarely suffered the privations
that many of the Communist Party leadership had endured. But
men like Raul Rego, Soares, and Salgado Zenha had nonetheless
taken considerable risks and suffered several imprisonments for
their beliefs. The strength of their dedication was something the
communists tended to disparage, and in consequence tended to
underestimate.

The umbrella organization from which most of the postwar
opposition political groups trace their origins was the Movement
of Democratic Unity (MUD), formed in the mid 1940s. Communists and others had participated in the tightly controlled electoral
campaigns that the Salazar regime had periodically permitted
until opposition candidate General Delgado came so close to
success in 1958, when the system was modified to protect against
such near upsets in the future. After 1958, the opposition forces
split, and the socialists and social democrats competed in the 1969
election under their own umbrella organization, the Electoral
Committee for Democratic Unity (CEUD), while the communists
established an electoral front (CDE) with independents and radical Catholics led by the well-known economist Francisco Pereira
de Moura. It had been for this later group that Major Melo
Antunes had sought to be a candidate. In 1973, however, the
socialists and communists came together again in the semi legal
Portuguese Democratic Movement (MDP/CDE) and were so
allied at the time of the coup.[5]

The personalities and views of the opposition were thus well
known in 1974 – especially to Major Melo Antunes, who had
been largely responsible for drafting the MFA's program. Hence
there was much less cause for clandestine or conspiratorial contacts
between the military plotters and the opposition civilians than
might appear at first sight. Once the coup succeeded, there was
a ready-made group of clearly identified individuals to whom the
military could turn if it wished to form a government composed
of men whose hands were clean of any involvement with the fallen
regime. Even General Spínola was aware of this and he had sent
a signed copy of *Portugal and the Future* to Mário Soares in Paris.

The program of the Armed Forces Movement provided a framework and timetable for the transition. It called for a two-year period in which a new political system was to be defined. Hence, a large space was opened up in which new political parties were expected to engage in pre-electoral struggles, and define their approaches to the task of constitution making. This open-ended situation gave considerable advantages to the communists because, apart from the communists, no party in 1974 possessed a strong organization. In the weeks immediately after the coup, the PCP took full advantage of this organizational advantage to take over key positions, especially in the trade unions and the municipalities. The communist-dominated union-coordinating organization, Intersindical, became the basis of Portugal's new trade union federation. In trade unions which had formerly been controlled by supporters of the old regime, communist leaders were quickly elected to replace the old leaders. Also, on the initiative of the communists, new unions were organized for groups whose unionization had been prohibited by the old regime – most particularly public employees and farm workers. In most of the country's municipalities, new councils were elected by public assemblies, with the communists often taking key positions or securing places for reliable allies.

After April 1974, however, a large part of the population, intensely traditionalist and conservative, found themselves without spokesmen. Temporarily muted by the speed with which state power had evaporated, the conservative rural peasantry and the Catholic community constituted a political constituency of some importance.[6] Consequently, two major parties emerged representing centrist and conservative forces, although each was constrained for many months to maintain a "left" orientation. These were the Popular Democratic Party (PPD) and the Democratic and Social Center Party (CDS). General Spínola, the provisional president, wanted to consolidate a civilian centrist and reformist coalition that would strengthen his own authority against the MFA. He hoped to achieve this in collaboration with the new Popular Democratic Party, founded in May 1974 by the leading reformers of the early Caetano period, Francisco Sá Carneiro, Francisco Pinto Balsemão, and Joaquim Jorge Magalhães Mota. The CDS sought to capture the ground occupied in other Catholic countries by the christian democrats and among these leaders was a young law professor, Diogo Freitas do Amaral, who had been Caetano's favorite student and protégé.[7] Yet, in a move that surprised even the MFA, General Spínola also invited the PCP into the provisional government. He hoped that by placing a communist in the ministry of labor and bringing Cunhal into the cabinet as a minister without portfolio, he could moderate and restrain labor militancy. As it turned out, however, Spínola badly miscalculated the consequences of his invitation to the communists. He offered what the PCP was only too willing to concede, and he gained very little from the respite in labor agitation that he had hoped would follow.

The PCP's strategy in the aftermath of the coup was to act with moderation, whatever its position in or outside the new government. The recent Chilean experience of 1973, when Salvador Allende, an elected Marxist president, had been overthrown in a bloody military coup, was very much on the mind of the left in 1974 and had made communists wary of the military and anxious to coopt the middle class which in Chile had provided essential civilian support for General Pinochet. The Chilean experience seemed to confirm the communists' long-standing intention to direct their main attack against what they saw as the two pillars of the old regime – the great landowners and the oligarchic cartels – and to do so by forming an alliance with the urban and rural middle classes. The PCP's most recent gains, in fact, had been among lower-middle-class workers, especially the bank clerks, a leader of whom, Avelino Gonçalves, became labor minister in the first provisional government. During the early months following the coup, the communists thus urged restraint in labor disputes, often acted to end strikes, and sought to cement an alliance with the urban middle class.[8]

This "centrist" position of the communists, of course, had a totally different content from that of General Spínola and the PPD. The groups they supported and sought to encourage were diametrically opposed. Spínola hoped, as did some of the leading industrialists, especially José Manuel de Melo, that the change of regime might promote a rapid modernization of Portugal's economy and increase investments in new plants and methods, thereby raising Portugal's living standards to a level closer to the European norm. The same day Cunhal had arrived back in Portugal from exile, in fact, Spínola met with Sr. Champalimaud, Sr. Manuel de Melo, Dr. Miguel Quina, and Sr. Manuel Espírito Santo, still the ruling economic powers in Portugal. Afterwards, Champalimaud said: "the excuse of prudence drastically limited the activity of those who had initiative. Any delay in simplifying the economic situation even before restructuring it would lead to a loss of valuable opportunities." But "rationalization" of the economy along the lines proposed by Spínola's allies required the support of the very groups the communists aimed to curtail – the banks, which formed the linchpin of the Melo, Champalimaud, and Espírito Santo empires, and the network of industries, insurance companies, and financial holdings the oligarchy controlled.

This contradiction would not be easily unraveled without the victory of one position over the other, for they were wholly incompatible. Moreover, it was a conflict which, rather than pitting a view of the past against one of the future, pitted two views of the future against one another. Spínola's view of a modernized country, developing the kind of large-scale corporate technology and trade that had made other West European countries prosper, was as revolutionary for Portugal as was the objective of the communists. But as dissension between Spínola and the PCP became more apparent, it produced one result that was to be crucial for subsequent events. It created the conditions for closer collaboration between the coordinating committee of the program (CCP), of the MFA and the PCP, because it coincided with deep divergences within the armed forces between the MFA and Spínola over decolonization. But the principal immediate negative impact of Spínola's invitation to the communists was in Washington, DC.

The shocked reactions of Portugal's NATO allies to the presence of the first communists in a western government since the beginning of the Cold War, especially the presence of a party leader who made no bones about his devotion to the Soviet Union, meant that Spínola's attempt to buy peace at home succeeded only in buying him hostility abroad from friends whose support he would need if he were to survive. The irony, perhaps even the tragedy, of General Spínola's brief and turbulent term as provisional president of Portugal was that although he represented all that Portugal's western allies desired – a moderate, modernizing, market-oriented and reformist administration at home, and a gradualist transfer of power in Africa – this was hidden from them while Spínola ruled by their fear of the communists in his administration. Unlike the PCP, Spínola had not considered the lessons of Chile. He totally misjudged the reactions of secretary of state Kissinger to a communist-influenced government in Lisbon.[9]

Kissinger's response to events in Lisbon was very similar to his reaction to the election of Salvador Allende in Chile. The type of relationship that existed before April 1974 between the United States and Portugal and the growing estrangement after the coup were both logical consequences of the foreign policy of the Nixon years. The particular irony of the situation was that although Chile was, as Kissinger is supposed to have said, "a missile aimed at the heart of Antarctica," the geo-political import-ance of Portugal and its African territories were of quite a different order. Kissinger's assumptions failed to coincide with Ambassador Stuart Nash Scott's dispatches from Portugal and the secretary of state had little time and less inclination to understand the situation. When it became known that commu-nists would actually participate in the government in Lisbon, Kissinger's actions were reflexive and automatic. Almost immedi-ately NATO "secrets" were no longer passed to the Portuguese. Stories were leaked about a "Mediterranean domino theory." The American base in the Azores became a "decisive" element in the defense of Israel. General George Brown, chairman of the joint chiefs of staff, who had recently gained notoriety for blaming the "Jewish lobby" for overstretching the US commitment in the Middle East, claimed that, had Portugal not agreed to the use of the Azores in 1973, the United States would "have been hard pressed to help Israel" during the Yom Kippur War.[10]

Those arguments were exaggerated at best. Portugal is an Atlantic, not a Mediterranean, power; its strategic importance and that of its Atlantic islands are linked to the central and south Atlantic and the Cape routes. The "domino" argument was almost entirely ideological, concerned with what Kissinger regarded as the potential threat of participation by communists in the governments of Spain, Italy, France, and Greece. The Azores base was decisive in large part because the NATO allies and even Franco's Spain had refused the United States refueling rights during the Yom Kippur War. The Pentagon's own analysis had shown that air refueling would have made it possible to by-pass the Azores in resupplying Israel. Kissinger himself had delayed supplies to Israel to induce a cease-fire with the Egyptians at a crucial moment during the war.

The sudden change of regime and the emergence of an apparently powerful communist movement in Portugal, moreover, were greeted in Washington with more than the usual embarrassment because they threatened to expose the Nixon administration's recent approximation to South Africa and the secret agreements to provide embargoed weapons to the Caetano regime for use in the African wars. The communist role in Lisbon also posed a challenge to Nixon and Kissinger's policy of détente with the Soviet Union, already under attack by members of Congress. Washington consequently adopted a policy of "wait and see." It was like leaving a small baby in a bath for a week and wondering afterwards why it drowned. Yet, to have welcomed and supported the new regime would, in Kissinger's view, have set a precedent for Spain, Italy, and France that he had been prepared to destroy Allende to avoid.

III

When the coup occurred, the major part of the Portuguese armed forces were in Africa; the colonial warriors were weary, and the middle-rank officers were sorely pressed.[11] As a result *de facto* local cease-fires were soon arranged. General Spínola had hoped to establish a Portuguese-speaking federation of states, but the MFA overruled him and proceeded to effect decolonization. The first major crisis occurred in June 1974 when Spínola and the prime minister, Professor Palma Carlos, attempted to reduce the MFA's influence and found themselves outmaneuvered. The crisis led to Palma Carlos' resignation and to the elevation of procommunist, Colonel Vasco Gonçalves, as prime minister. To foreclose the possibility of a military challenge from Spínola, the MFA also moved to consolidate its military authority by establishing a command structure, COPCON (the Operational Command for the Continent), on July 8 under the effective command of Otelo Saraiva de Carvalho, who also became commander of the Lisbon military garrison.[12] In late September 1974, the conflict between the MFA and Spínola reached a climax. Spínola attempted to circumvent the MFA's influence by calling for a show of support from the "silent majority." Worried members of the old financial and business oligarchy helped finance the propaganda for Spínola's appeal. But by now the banking unions were keeping a careful watch on any unusual cash transfers and promptly published the clandestine financing of the PPD and the parties of the right.[13] The MFA, the communists (under the cover of their front organization, the Portuguese Democratic Movement), and the socialists mobilized their adherents and barricaded Lisbon against Spínola's supporters, forcing Spínola to cancel the event. As a consequence, the general resigned from the presidency on September 30. He was replaced by General Costa Gomes who had been the MFA's original choice, and whose political flexibility was reflected in his nickname, "the cork."

The crises which moved Portugal decisively to the left also moved Portuguese Africa equally decisively toward independence. They appeared as a series of sometimes lengthy struggles in which political tensions in Portugal, developments in Africa, and external pressures combined to force major confrontations. During these crises most politically sophisticated Portuguese were well aware of their underlying causes. But almost never did these surface in the Portuguese press, and when they did it was mainly by insinuation. Only when the crises were over and the consequences were patent – the resignation of Premier Palma Carlos on July 9 and the appointment of Colonel Vasco Gonçalves in his place; the resignation of General Spínola from the presidency on September 30 and his replacement by General Costa Gomes – were any of these crises publicly discussed by outsiders. No one involved ever doubted, however, that the shape and content of the political future in Portugal and the achievement of independence in the African colonies were intimately linked. The outcome of the struggle in one sphere would help to consolidate victory or bring defeat in the other.

Each crisis in Lisbon was connected with critical moments in the negotiations in Africa, where the liberation movements combined military pressures with diplomatic inducements to allow them a free hand. In Mozambique especially, FRELIMO stepped up its fighting while arranging local cease-fires. The MFA in Africa was already acting with a large degree of autonomy, each colony having a different MFA organization linked only informally to the others and, through Captain Vasco Lourenço, to the CCP in Lisbon. These arrangements prefigured independence, and they allowed a great deal of flexibility in local arrangements with the guerrillas.

In Portuguese Guinea, local peace came long before its recognition in a formal settlement. In May 1974, Spínola's friend and Council of State member, Colonel Almeida Bruno, went to London with foreign minister Mário Soares to negotiate with the PAIGC. When they failed to make a deal in June, a decisive shift took place. The negotiations moved out of the European orbit and shifted to secret diplomacy carried out in Algiers by Major Melo Antunes of the MFA. A settlement was finally arranged at the end of July, following Portuguese recognition of the right to self-determination, and after Vasco Gonçalves had been installed as premier and the MFA consolidated its military power in Portugal by setting up the COPCON.[14]

This was a crucial blow to Spínola's power and perhaps the most important one. The MFA and its leftist allies in Lisbon could make an African settlement when he could not, sustaining a momentum toward African independence that he opposed. Similar crises erupted over Mozambique in August and September of 1974 and over Angola from January to March, 1975. Both were complex, but in each case the settlements shored up the power of the MFA and allowed it to drive from power the moderate and conservative forces in Lisbon that wanted to maintain Portuguese Africa or slow the pace of decolonization.

Developments in Guinea were central to events in Portugal over the summer of 1974. A tiny, poverty-stricken territory with little economic and only indirect strategic importance, it was central to the drama. No other colony could have been a more poignant symbol to mark the end of Europe's imperial adventure. More than 500 years ago it was discovered by Portuguese mariners in search of a sea passage to the Guinean coast in order to capture control of the commerce in gold and slaves that previously reached Europe from West Africa along Saharan caravan routes. Edging around the difficult African littoral of Guinea, they found the systems of winds and currents that opened the way to the New World, the Cape of Good Hope, and the Indian Ocean. In a sense, it all ended where it began.

For the Portuguese, the war in Guinea was a patent absurdity, but for reasons of precedent and prestige, it could not be abandoned. The conflict tied down a vast army in proportion to the population. Toward the end Portuguese troops were restricted to enclaves, coexisting in the same small territory with a state that had already declared its independence. It was about Guinea that Caetano told Spínola, then military commander there, that he preferred defeat to a negotiation that might provide a precedent for Mozambique and Angola. More than anything else this comment by Caetano drove Spínola into opposition. But the circumstances of the struggle in Guinea had already exercised a profound influence, both on him and on the army he commanded. Soon after his arrival in the late 1960s, Spínola abandoned the largely American-inspired strategy of his predecessor, Arnaldo Schultz, and borrowed from the techniques of his enemy, the PAIGC. He formed civic action teams, started literacy campaigns, and attempted to encourage local participation in decision making. He cajoled Jorge de Melo, whose CUF had virtually run Portuguese Guinea as a private business fiefdom, into demonstrating some small social responsibility – distributing land and giving financial aid for settling peasant farmers. Spínola's tenure in Guinea not only made him appear a successful military commander at a time of gloomy disaffection and defeat, but gave him a sense of the possibilities of the firm and understanding exercise of power.

But there was another side to Spínola. Responsive to his men, he could be brutal if they failed him. He surrounded himself with an entourage of handsome cavalry officers with perfect manners and slim silhouettes (fat officers were banished to the outback). And sometimes bluntness in others is not appreciated by those who are blunt themselves. Spínola tended to like courtiers, and his court was resented. Saraiva de Carvalho, head of the MFA's military committee, and a psychological warfare expert in Guinea, was not one of Spínola's inner circle and resented it. Captain Vasco Lourenço, who had edited and published a collection of essays by soldiers in his company in Guinea and had served two tours there, was coordinator between the MFA and military units throughout Portugal, but he had no great love for the flamboyant General Spínola. In September 1974, Major Saraiva de Carvalho and Captain Lourenço were the key figures in Spínola's downfall. Captain Lourenço said: "General Spínola was a soldier in whom I saw enormous virtues, but in whom I also saw enormous defects

. . . We always feared that General Spínola wanted to be the only and exclusive interpreter of the [MFA's] program and to follow an autocratic line. That which we feared came to pass, and in consequence, a schism was inevitable."[15]

Many of the leading characters in the struggles within the Portuguese army between April 1974 and March 1975 worked with Spínola when he was governor in Guinea, and they either worshipped him or distrusted him because of it. Colonel Almeida Bruno had been one of his leading field commanders. Colonel Firmino Miguel, defense minister in the first and second provisional governments, and Spínola's choice for prime minister following the resignation of Professor Palma Carlos in July 1974, had headed special operations in Guinea. Carlos Fabião, the last Portuguese governor of Guinea and later commander-in-chief of the Portuguese army, was Spínola's other leading field commander.

Carlos Fabião illustrated the subtle impact of Guinea in the formation of the MFA leadership. A tough, quiet, hardheaded officer, Fabião spent almost a decade in Guinea and headed one of the Portuguese army's locally recruited crack African forces. He directed the major activities of the Portuguese army in Guinea's social and economic reconstruction. Working in the villages, he came to believe that such a program required a fundamental transformation of military ethics. Perhaps this was a natural conclusion for an intelligent man fighting an unpopular war with a conscript army in an undefendable place. In the case of Fabião, this transformation of social views and its depth was not appreciated in Lisbon. He had outlined his philosophy in some detail in the socialist daily, *República*, in October 1974. Speaking of the army's new internal relationships, he observed that leadership did not rest on any imposed or preordained authority but was exercised by the mutual perception of objectives and the means to achieve them. Speaking of Guinea, he said, "man alone, self-sufficient, omnipotent, has become a relic of the past, a type of extinct dinosaur, because productive work today is only possible by teamwork with the aid and confidence of all. It is a lesson I will never forget."[16] To outsiders such comments seemed like platitudes. For a country where such concepts never existed, and within a military establishment that had barely emerged from the nineteenth century, they were revolutionary.

The transformation which men like Fabião had brought about

in Africa during the weeks following the coup began to spread to Portugal once Spínola resigned the presidency in September. Committees of soldiers, sergeants, and commissioned officers began to function in quasi-legislative bodies within the army. In almost all these activities, Guinea was the progenitor. The teams of soldiers Colonel Fabião sent into the African villages to encourage expression of local opinion and the formation of cooperatives prefigured the MFA groups that ranged over Portugal before the Constituent Assembly elections. Long before the MFA in Portugal admitted private soldiers and sergeants to its membership and assemblies, or provided for the participation of conscript *miliciano* sergeants and officers in its deliberations, the MFA in Guinea under Fabião had institutionalized all these reforms. Indeed, they had done so as early as June 1974, and this fact was of central importance to the pace of decolonizing Africa.

Important *de facto* alliances were also strengthening the hand of those in favor of a rapid transfer of power to the liberation movements. In the first months after the coup d'état, the Portuguese communists placed themselves firmly in the center of the political spectrum. As a member of the first provisional government, Alvaro Cunhal followed a line of studied moderation. The communists' minister of labor resisted workers' demands and ensured that the minimum wage was as low as possible. At the Communist Party's October 1974 congress the PCP went so far as to drop the phrase "dictatorship of the proletariat" from its manifesto, the first West European communist party to do so. And the communists remained as sensitive as ever to criticism (which was not slow in coming) from the groups to their left which they had called "pseudo-revolutionary leftists" and "petty bourgeois radicals."[17] Cunhal explained:

The dictatorship of the proletariat is a regime more democratic than the most democratic of bourgeois democracies. However, the expression dictatorship used now in Portugal after fifty years of a fascist dictatorship, in the very particular situation that we are going through, does not facilitate the comprehension of the policy of the Party, nor aid in the realization of its objectives.[18]

As the fundamental divergences between Spínola and the PCP over the direction of domestic and colonial policy became more apparent it brought into closer collaboration the PCP and those members of the MFA who were also opposed to Spínola's attitudes toward decolonization. For each it was a tactical alliance. The young officers were, after all, the epitome of the "petty bourgeois radicals" that Cunhal had spent so much of his time denouncing, and the communists were appreciated more for their apparent willingness to follow the MFA's leadership and for their discipline and reliability than for their long-term vision of the future of Portuguese society. What united them was the fact that they shared enemies, not that they agreed on the same objectives.[19] For Cunhal, the emergence of a radical element within the military offered the possibility of forging alliances that might neutralize the potential source of a reactionary comeback. The alliance with the MFA became a fundamental pillar of Cunhal's strength.

After the coup in Lisbon, the liberation movements had supporters in influential places who proved to be highly effective allies. Spínola's views of a Lusitanian commonwealth were totally inappropriate to the real situation in which Portugal found herself. The armies in Africa were simply unwilling to act in any way which prolonged their stay in the overseas territories. Brazil, a supposed partner in Spínola's concept, had decided to cut her losses and make her own approaches to the new Portuguese-speaking states emerging in Africa.[20] Brazil recognized Guinea-Bissau on July 18, one week before Spínola himself made his declaration of July 27 that Portugal would begin an immediate transfer of power in its African colonies. By then, eighty-four countries had already recognized Guinea-Bissau.

Amílcar Cabral, founder of the PAIGC, held an important place in third world mythology. Cabral was assassinated on January 10, 1973 in mysterious circumstances, thereby making him one of independent Africa's most important martyrs. Many suspected the PIDE, but it seems likely that his death was brought about by factions within his own movement. Cabral had been a serious internationalist who had gained the support of the independent African states, established close relations with Castro's Cuba, and was well known and respected among the nonaligned nations. These connections proved vital in 1974. It was insufficiently appreciated at the time that the decolonization of Guinea-Bissau and Mozambique was a quiet triumph for African and nonaligned diplomacy. While Kissinger muttered about the PCP and sought to stir up right-wing opposition in

Portugal, a strenuous secret diplomacy was laying the basis for settlements with both PAIGC and FRELIMO. The diplomacy emanated largely from Algiers and Zambia. The process of making the settlements helped to bring Spínola down.

The underlying reasons for this African success were that Washington and Western Europe could not distinguish the forces at play in the Portuguese situation. They initially blundered into associations with groups so intransigent that they were doomed to help destroy the very solution that the United States and its NATO partners dearly wished to arrange. No such misjudgment took place within the liberation movements. They, after all, knew the Portuguese, appreciated their strengths, and were aware of their weaknesses. They knew the leaders involved – some of them only too well – and above all they knew that real power in Portugal was held by the MFA leaders and that a tacit alliance with them could be made against Spínola. These connections were to have a decisive impact in Angola, recognized by all sides as the most difficult and most important test of Portugal's intentions.

I V

Despite appearances to the contrary, the preeminence of the left within the military was by no means secure, nor were the communists prepared to leave to chance the predominance within the MFA of their allies. General Spínola tried over the first six months of the revolution to bring about the dissolution of the coordinating committee of the program (CCP) and hence to end the political role of the MFA. In response, the movement had expanded membership in order to secure its position within the military as a whole. From a restricted base of 350 to 400 officers, of which a mere 100 or so were active participants, the MFA grew to encompass some 2,000 officers in all three services by the time of the September 1974 showdown. All were still officers from the regular cadre but such a quick growth inevitably brought into the movement both a diversity of opinion and numerous opportunists. By the end of 1974 five broad groupings existed within the MFA.

On the right was the personal entourage of General Spínola. Some of its members, like Major Sánches Osório, had been with the MFA from the beginning. Others, like Lieutenant Colonel

Firmino Miguel, stood on the fringes. After September 1974, the Spínolists lost much of their influence, though it was only after March 11, 1975, that they were excluded. The Spínolists merged into a large group composed of men who upheld a strict interpretation of the original MFA' program. Closer to the center of the political spectrum, these men were increasingly alienated from the CCP, which they saw as creating a parallel authority structure within the military. They were often mistaken for Spínolists at the time but, as one of them, Lieutenant Colonel Ramalho Eanes, observed: "being a friend of General Spínola and being a Spínolist are very different things." In general, men like Major Monge, Captain Casanova Ferreira, Major Hugo dos Santos, and Captain Salgueiro Maia, believed that the armed forces should not espouse a political role but should rather act as guarantors of a democratic system on a western model.

As early as August 1974, Hugo dos Santos had organized a petition protesting the role of the CCP and circulated it with the approval of General Costa Gomes, then chief of staff. His petition gathered substantial support, especially among the cavalry regiments. The strength of the sentiment against the political stance of the MFA leaders emerged in the elections within the various branches of the army in January–February 1975. In voting by all regular officers in Portugal and Africa, several of the leading leftists were defeated. In the artillery, both Major Melo Antunes and Major (by now acting Brigadier General) Otelo Saraiva de Carvalho were rejected. In the cavalry, Major Monge and Captain Salgueiro Maia were elected. By and large the group composed of Hugo dos Santos, Salgueiro Maia, and Ramalho Eanes, reflected the professional interests of the officer corps, a current of opinion that had been a powerful element in the original captains' movement.

Among the more "political" officers were three groups, and again there was a great deal of fluctuation among them. Some of the more overtly leftist officers could not be clearly placed. Captain Vasco Lourenço and Lieutenant Colonel Carlos Fabião, for example, avoided clear typing, though both men were committed to a revolutionary role for the armed forces and each had been profoundly influenced by his experience in Africa. Broadly speaking, the three tendencies were democratic socialist, populist, and Marxist–Leninist.

After March 1975, the last group, associated with the prime minister, Colonel (by now Brigadier General) Vasco Gonçalves, was the most powerful. Close to the PCP, the Gonçalvists established formidable power bases during the months following July 1974. Among the procommunist group was Captain Varela Gomes, a hero of the Beja revolt of 1961 who, after years of exile in Algiers, had been reintegrated into the armed forces with the rank of colonel. Varela Gomes was a dominant figure in the Fifth Division of the general staff, the coordinating agency for propaganda and indoctrination, which soon embarked on a "cultural dynamization" program both within the armed forces and in the country. The Fifth Division became an embryonic political commissariat, strongly influenced by the PCP under the command of Lieutenant Ramiro Correia. The ministry of social communication, like the labor ministry, also came under the control of military men close to the PCP. After the March affair, the Gonçalvists also dominated the commission that had been established to dismantle the secret police, forcing out many of the nonparty men who had been influential previously. Control of the commission was important because of the access it afforded to the voluminous secret police files. Under the command of Almada Contreiras, a new intelligence and counter-intelligence agency, the SCDI, was established, also under Gonçalvist control.

Surrounding Major Melo Antunes and Major Vítor Alves, however, was a second group on the left. This faction saw the armed forces as an essential instrument in the revolutionary process, but its members increasingly objected to the vanguard role usurped by the Gonçalvists. They believed that a broader base of social support than that provided by the PCP was essential if the MFA was not to be placed in opposition to the majority of the population. Collaboration with the political parties was necessary, in their view, if an orderly and peaceful transition to socialism was to be achieved. Melo Antunes, a Marxist of the Gramscian school, was the main political articulator of this group, and it became associated with his name; but it was a broad group that had important operational support in the central and southern military regions, where the two commanders, General Pezerant and General Charais, both early members of the MFA, were close to Antunes.

To the left of both Melo Antunes and the PCP-influenced

Gonçalvists stood a populist radical group with fuzzy ideological views but with strong military support. Associated with Otelo Saraiva de Carvalho, it dominated the command structure of COPCON and several of the key regiments in the Lisbon area, especially the light artillery and the military police. Increasingly opposed to all political parties, including the PCP, the military populists stood for a vaguely defined people's power.

The showdown that pushed Spínola out of the presidency highlighted the power that the PCP and the MFA could exercise when acting together. On September 28, 1974, when the crisis broke, the Communist Party had moved efficiently and effectively to organize a blockade of Lisbon, thus preventing the thousands expected for a demonstration in support of General Spínola from assembling. The civilian pickets and barricades had been established with the connivance and support of COPCON, which functioned as the MFA's own command structure under Saraiva de Carvalho and circumvented the traditional military hierarchy and the politically "unreliable" elements still ensconced within it. In March 1975, COPCON once again coordinated the defense of the revolution against a rebellion among the airborne regiment and airforce: two planes and four helicopters attacked the barracks of the Lisbon light artillery regiment (RAL1), then among one of the most leftist units. And again, civilian vigilantes were mobilized. Both occasions were used to weed out and incarcerate purported enemies, including major figures of the old regime and the financial and industrial oligarchy, but also (in March) several military officers who were leading members of the MFA: Major Hugo dos Santos, Major Manuel Monge, and Captain Casanova Ferreira among them. The groups of soldiers and armed civilians who conducted the roundups often carried blank arrest warrants issued by COPCON headquarters. As a result, by April 1975, one year after the coup had opened the doors of the dictatorship's jails, there were more political prisoners in Portugal than there had been on the eve of Caetano's downfall.[21]

In the face of the disparate but formidable coalition of interests in favor of rapid decolonization and radical change in Portugal, General Spínola's potential support was divided and increasingly demoralized. Although the informal power groups of oligarchical and financial interests which had underpinned the old regime remained intact throughout this whole period, they were divided among themselves. The general could never count on the whole-hearted support of the conservative forces in Portugal since he was distrusted by the leading arch-conservatives for his role in the coup, and many were so shaken by the speed of change that they lacked the capacity to mobilize effective opposition to the leftward movement of politics. The urban middle class, the civil servants, and white-collar employees who might have joined the oligarchy against the left were, in this period, among the most vociferous leftists. During the dictatorship the very rich had felt no need to placate the less wealthy and had, on the whole, treated those less fortunate than themselves with contempt, particularly those who aspired to a modest fortune and had won middle-class respectability. Moreover, employers and employees were locked in bitter wage disputes and white-collar workers were making common cause with blue-collar workers against the bosses. An embittered Marcello Caetano, from his exile in Brazil, acidly summed up the situation in which the Portuguese middle class found themselves during most of 1974. "The truth is," he wrote, "that the Portuguese bourgeoisie, used to enjoying a climate of peace during half a century, under the protection of so many police institutions, which acted as their shield, had no combative spirit and did not know how to act in defense of the principles they said they professed."[22]

The forces of the right also acted in ways which compromised Spínola. The long and hidden struggle between the ultras, such as General Kaúlza de Arriaga and his friends, the MFA, and Spínola in 1974 and 1975, were rooted in the conflicts between forces that were lining up against one another in the years before the dictatorship collapsed. But the predisposition of Portugal's western allies to link up with discredited cliques in Portugal and in Africa in the months after the fall of Caetano also served to shut out the possibility of forming new alliances with the individuals and political movements in Portugal and Africa who were essential to any settlement of the colonial issue. The United States, in particular, was plugged into the most intransigent faction in the Portuguese establishment – admittedly on an improvised and informal basis – but nonetheless through an extremely influential channel. General Vernon Walters, deputy director of the CIA, arrived in Portugal on a "private visit to a friend" during August 1974. Walters spoke fluent Portuguese as a result of his service as liaison officer between the Brazilian expeditionary force and the US Fifth Army in Europe during World War II. On his return to Washington from Lisbon, Walters reported that "Portugal was as good as lost to the communists."[23] Admiral Anderson, chairman of President Nixon's Foreign Intelligence Advisory Board, was close to many of those Portuguese who had never believed Portugal was ready for democracy.

The fact that during the Nixon presidency the United States had chosen to move closer to Portugal and to the white minority regimes in southern Africa just as the whole situation was about to be transformed by the coup in Lisbon, created a predisposition by the western allies afterwards to link up with discredited cliques, and hence shut out the possibility of forming new alliances with the individuals or political movements the Portuguese dictatorship had opposed. This predisposition had serious consequences in both Portugal and Africa. It had been a short-sighted policy to have allowed this to happen while the Portuguese empire remained intact. Once Portugal's authority had collapsed and the advantages the west enjoyed as a function of good relations with the colonial power were lost, to persist in such relationships was sheer folly. Accurate intelligence about, and good contacts with, the liberation movements in the Portuguese African territories were more essential than ever. Unfortunately for the west, the advantage of good contacts and good intelligence now rested with its geo-political rivals.

It need not have been so. Ironically, on the very day the Caetano regime fell, Agostinho Neto, leader of the MPLA was in Ottawa. The Canadian government had changed its policy regarding non-military aid to the liberation movements in Portugal's African colonies, and Neto had come to encourage this promising development in a leading western country. He next went to London, where he met with members of the government and Labour Party officials, then to Sweden, where the MPLA had long been supported by the Swedish International Development Agency and the Social Democratic Party. On May 2, 1974, through the good offices of Father Houtard of the University of Louvain, Neto met secretly in Brussels with Mário Soares, the Portuguese socialist leader, who only five days before had returned triumphantly to Lisbon from his exile in Paris.[24]

Ironically, the experience of the early 1960s was to have important ramifications for later US reactions to Portugal's decolonization. The choice made by the Kennedy administration in 1960
of Holden Roberto as a recipient of covert American aid was a
bold measure placing Washington's support behind an armed
insurrection against the government of one of its NATO allies.
At the time Roberto was supported by the two most radical
independent African governments – those of Kwame Nkrumah
in Ghana and of Sekou Touré in Guinea-Conakry. He was in
many respects a protégé of the American Committee on Africa.[25]
Despite the later withdrawal of Washington's support and the
Nixon-Kissinger decision in 1970 to move closer to Lisbon and the
white minority regimes in southern Africa, these early connections
remained. When Portugal's position in Africa disintegrated in
1974, the alliances forged in the early Kennedy years surfaced
almost unaltered as if nothing had happened during the interven-
ing fifteen years.

Washington, on the other hand, was suspicious of Agostinho
Neto, who had a long record of arrests for political activity. He
had been imprisoned while a medical student in Portugal, first
in 1951 and again between 1955 and 1957. He returned to Angola
in 1959 and was arrested a year later in his consulting room in
Luanda, flogged in front of his patients, and deported to the
Cape Verde Islands. International protests led to his transfer to
Lisbon, where he was incarcerated and later placed under house
arrest. In 1962 he escaped from Portugal and resurfaced in
Leopoldville (now Kinshasa). In December 1962 he became president of the MPLA.[26] If Neto's connections in the anti-Salazar
underground made him suspect to Washington (as indeed such
connections made Mário Soares until the April 1975 Portuguese
elections revealed him to be the main democratic bulwark against
communism), they were to stand him in good stead in Portugal
after the April 25 coup. Unlike Holden Roberto, leader of the
Zaire-based FNLA, who had spent less than two years of his
life in Angola, and almost no time in Portugal, Agostinho Neto
knew the Portuguese left from the inside.

The MPLA itself was never a monolith. Among the groups in
its genealogy were the Angolan Communist Party (PCA), and the
MPLA's union organization was affiliated with the Prague-based
World Federation of Trade Unions. In essence, however, the

MPLA was a broad coalition, and it was led by a strong but often divided cadre of radical and Marxist intellectuals. The centrifugal tendencies within it were so strong that they seriously weakened its effectiveness and on several occasions threatened to destroy it altogether. Toward the end of the 1960s, there was a movement within the MPLA to form a disciplined and ideologically pure party organization. The movement intended to mobilize the broadest possible support, while at the same time the party provided a politically reliable cadre for leadership positions after the end of the war. But this seems to have increased rather than diminished contention and, during the early 1970s, Neto's position was challenged by two major competing groups. The first was associated with Mário de Andrade, a founding member of the MPLA and former member of the PCA, but later seen to prefer a Chinese orientation. The second was led by one of the MPLA's most successful field commanders, Daniel Chipenda, a former professional soccer star then considered closer to Moscow.

In early 1974, President Julius Nyerere of Tanzania, concerned that the MPLA's internal struggles had so weakened its ability to fight the Portuguese that Lisbon had been able to shift 10,000 troops from Angola to face FRELIMO's 1973 offensive in Mozambique, had persuaded China to provide technical assistance to the FNLA. The Chinese had already had considerable success in Mozambique, where they had aided the reorganization of FRELIMO following the setbacks and internal splits that racked the movement after the 1969 assassination of Eduardo Mondlane, FRELIMO's president. The division between the factions became so severe that, by 1974, Neto's survival as president of the MPLA seemed problematical, and he was reinstated to the presidency of the MPLA in mid 1974 only at the insistence of Kenneth Kaunda of Zambia. The MPLA, however, enjoyed exclusive relations with the major liberation fronts in Portuguese Guinea and Mozambique. Neto's personal relations with the leaders of both PAIGC and FRELIMO went back to his student days in Lisbon, and they had been fortified by a formal structure of mutual consultation among the three movements since 1961 (CONCP). Amílcar Cabral, president of PAIGC, while working as an agronomist on a sugar estate in Angola, had in fact been a founding member of the MPLA. Neto himself, since the assassinations of Mondlane (1969) and Cabral (1973), had enjoyed the prestigious and dangerous distinction of being the last of the founding leaders of the liberation movements in Portuguese Africa. Because of this, there was never any doubt about who, in the event of a dispute, the other newly independent Portuguese colonies would recognize as the legitimate aspirant to the government in Luanda.[27]

All three movements also had long-standing formal relationships with leading members of the nonaligned Afro-Asian and Latin American Solidarity Organization, founded in Havana in 1966. Some of Cabral's most important statements of revolutionary theory were delivered at the Havana conference. Cabral observed then that the Cuban revolution "constitutes a particular lesson for the national liberation movements, especially for those who want their national revolution to be a true revolution." There was never any mystery about these views, or about the fact that ideological affinity had been translated into concrete aid.[28] The establishment of diplomatic ties between Zaire and China in late 1973, and the decision of the Chinese to train the FNLA in 1974, had galvanized Soviet concerns about Chinese objectives in Africa. The Soviets had consistently supported the national liberation movements – support for the MPLA began in 1958 and, despite a cooling of the Soviet relationship with Neto in the early 1970s, Soviet support always went to one or the other of the MPLA's factions. Soviet long-term strategy placed considerable emphasis on Angola, since its geo-political position promised to give a sympathetic regime there considerable influence in Zaire, as well as providing a vital link to Zambia, Namibia, and South Africa itself.

The lines of conflict and alliance in Portugal and Africa were thus clearer in fact than they appeared to be on the surface. When the MFA overthrew the dictatorship in Lisbon the repercussions of its actions were almost bound to be startling. Portugal was a NATO ally, anachronistic and at times embarrassingly stubborn, but nevertheless an ally that had no doubt whatsoever on which side it stood in a bipolar world. The United States, because of the intimacy of relationships with the dictatorship, was unsettled by change in Portugal and especially unprepared for the sometimes bewildering reversals and turmoil that were the immediate consequences of the coup. And the United States, unlike its geo-political rivals, had next to no relationships with the old clandestine opposition in either Portugal or the African territories.[29]

On October 18, 1994, over lunch at the state department in Washington, Henry Kissinger made his misgivings about developments in Portugal abundantly clear to visiting President Costa Gomes and foreign minister Mário Soares. For the first time since 1949 communists were participating in the government of a NATO country, he complained, and communist penetration of the institutions, media, and trade unions, was so extensive that Portugal was probably lost to the west. When Soares protested, Kissinger told him he would be the Portuguese Kerensky. Soares said: "But I don't want to be Kerensky." And Kissinger replied: "Neither did Kerensky". To back up his concerns, Kissinger sacked ambassador Nash Scott and sent to Lisbon a high-powered new embassy team recommended by General Walters; it included as ambassador Frank C. Carlucci III, Herbert Okun as his deputy, and Colonel Robert Schuler as defense attaché. All three spoke fluent Portuguese, and had worked with Walters in Brazil in the 1960s, at the time of the American-backed coup against President Goulart. They had a clear mission in Lisbon as far as Washington was concerned. It was to get the communists out of the government and keep them out.

CHAPTER 5

African dilemmas

Spínola wanted to make the FNLA's Holden Roberto leader of Angola with Chipenda and UNITA's Jonas Savimbi at his side.　　　　Admiral Rosa Coutinho (July 1975)

The same forces that oppressed the peoples of the former territories under Portuguese administration also oppressed the Portuguese people. It is with great modesty and humility that we must say, without ambiguities, that the struggle of the colonial peoples against Portuguese fascism also aided our liberation from the same fascism.
Colonel Vasco Gonçalves in Lourenço Marques (June 1975)

I

In the first months after the April 25 coup, the young officers of the Armed Forces Movement stayed very much in the background, preferring to remain as anonymous as possible. This did not mean they had any desire to see the fruits of their victory taken away from them. In a conversation with David Martin of the London *Observer*, Major Vítor Alves commented pointedly that the problem with the coup of 1926 was that "although the soldiers knew what they did not want they did not know what they did want. They had no program."[1] In 1974 Major Alves' CCP had already rectified the error of their predecessors. The problem was how the program that existed was to be interpreted and by whom.

The MFA's ambiguous phrases about colonial policy and the "need of a political not military solution" had been, if anything, gross understatements. The MFA program and General Spínola's book in fact set out positions so diametrically opposed that they

96

contained seeds of a conflict that could be resolved only by the victory of one over the other. The nature of the revolution disguised for a long time the seriousness of the divergences within the new regime and, in particular, the degree to which the young officers who had made the coup were intensely political men. But the conflict staked out at the beginning was at its heart a conflict between revolutionary and evolutionary change in Europe and between immediate decolonization and gradual disengagement in Africa. Major Vítor Alves, however, regarded Spínola's book as "his personal dream." Yet during his first months in office, Spínola spoke privately of a timetable for decolonization over "a generation or so," during which time the people "would be given democracy and equipped to choose."[2]

The stakes in Mozambique and especially in Angola, however, were significant. With Portugal's own chronic trade deficits and economic recession in Europe affecting the remittances from Portuguese abroad and from tourism, the large surplus from the African territories would be painful to lose. In 1973 such earnings represented as much as 5 percent of the gross national product, about $540 million. All the cotton from Mozambique was exported to Portugal and 99.7 percent of its sugar, both at well below world prices. At the same time, the wages of the Mozambique miners working in South Africa were converted into gold shipments to Lisbon – in effect a hidden subsidy to the Portuguese war effort, since the bullion was valued at the official rate of $42.20 an ounce instead of the world market price that rose to nearly $200 an ounce in 1974. During the three years before the coup, the official value of this gold amounted to at least $180 million.

But to retain Mozambique and Angola even in the short term meant to continue the war the MFA had made the coup to end. Many officers of the MFA, who had all fought in Africa, were totally opposed to a solution that merely changed the terms of the game. They did not believe that Portugal as a whole benefited from retaining the African territories. Nor did they think, even in the improved international climate following the coup, that the Portuguese army could sustain the holding operation necessary if Spínola's model was to work. "We have no desire to construct a neocolonial community," one of them told Jean Daniel of *Le Nouvel Observateur*, "we are interested more in the formation of a

Socialist interdependence, and that only to the extent that our brothers in Guiné, Mozambique, and Angola accept, desire, and demand."[3]

The MFA's political solution for Africa thus signified much more than the type of autonomy within a Lusitanian Federation which Spínola foresaw. As the bulletin put out by the MFA explained with some bluntness: "Those who benefited from the war were the same financial groups that exploited the people in the metropolis and, comfortably installed in Lisbon and Oporto or abroad, by means of a venal government obliged the Portuguese people to fight in Africa in defense of their immense profits."[4]

In Guinea, Mozambique, and Angola, the liberation movements always made a careful distinction between the Portuguese people, on whom they counted for support, and the dictatorial government that was trying to crush them. PAIGC, MPLA, and FRELIMO had all feared from the first that a political revolution in Portuguese Africa could still leave them in a condition of neocolonial dependence on Lisbon, and on the European economic interests to which Lisbon was tied and for which it sometimes acted as agent. The emergence of "third world" notions within the Portuguese military establishment, as well as the growing *de facto* alliance between the radical wing of the MFA and the communists was, therefore, watched by the Marxist movements in Africa with considerable interest. It provided them with a wedge to speed up the process of decolonization and guarantee that, where competing nationalist groups existed, those which enjoyed long-term connections with the old Portuguese clandestine opposition such as the MPLA would receive special consideration.

An intimate part of these shared understandings between the MFA and the African movements was a deep hostility to liberalism, both political and economic; for the conundrum that the Portuguese have never been able to resolve is that whenever economic and political liberalism are wedded, orthodoxy in one makes the other hollow. The advent of individual liberties during the nineteenth century also threatened to remove the few traditional protections the poorer classes had against economic exploitation. The adoption of free trade, a policy that favored the strong expanding industrial powers of northwestern Europe, threatened a country like Portugal with total subjection. Hence the old oligarchies could always reclaim the mantle of nationalism despite the fact that it had been their own subjection to foreign interests that had often caused their overthrow in the first place.

The point is not merely esoteric, for it is important to an understanding of the philosophy of the MFA during its apogee between July 1974 and November 1975. It explains the quiet influence of historians and activists such as Piteira Santos and José Tengarrinha, scholars of the period of the 1820s when Portugal, struggling simultaneously to fend off anticolonialism in Brazil and to maintain a liberal constitution at home, succumbed to decades of civil strife. The distrust of liberalism also helps to explain the importance of the combination of eclectic Marxism and nationalism in the MFA's philosophy. As a consequence, there existed the basis for convergence between the PAIGC, MPLA, and FRELIMO on the one hand, and the MFA on the other. This unique, if temporary, alliance between the colonialist officer corps and its opponents was made possible both by the timing and the special circumstances of the liberation movement struggles and by the backwardness of Portugal which the MFA officers so resented. The alliance was bound to be temporary because, whereas the liberation movements had clear objectives, the MFA did not. Moreover, the liberation movements were committed by necessity to a permanent condition – national independence – while the MFA's commitment, important as it was, remained a commitment to a process that would end once the colonies were free. Nevertheless, temporary though it might be, the momentum which the convergence of views among former enemies brought to the internal politics of Portugal, and to the timetable for decolonization in Portuguese Africa, proved to be irresistible.

II

In the circumstances which emerged after the Lisbon coup, several of the factors that contributed to the MPLA's weakness as a guerrilla organization proved to be sources of strength. The MPLA's urban intellectual and cosmopolitan leaders had always strongly opposed tribalism and racism, and had enjoyed long-term relationships with the old antifascist opposition in Portugal, especially the communists. *Assimilados*, mulattoes, and whites had from the beginning, found places in its higher echelons. The

MPLA enjoyed wide support from urbanized Africans, who tended, whatever their ethnic or linguistic backgrounds, to form a distinct group in relation to the rural majority. The MPLA always had difficulty appealing beyond this base, especially in the FNLA-dominated Bakongo backlands of the north. MPLA support was concentrated, however, in the strategically located central zone of the country, along the 263-mile railway from Luanda to Malange, among the 1.3 million Kmbundu-speaking peoples, one of Angola's four main ethno-linguistic groups. MPLA support was almost monolithic among the African population of Luanda and in its teaming slums (*musseques*). But, above all, the MPLA enjoyed exclusive relations with the major liberation fronts in Portuguese Guinea and Mozambique, both of which, by the autumn of 1974, had successfully negotiated settlements with the Portuguese.[5]

Angola was always close to the center of the struggle between General Spínola and the Armed Forces Movement during the first turbulent months following the Lisbon coup. Outmaneuvered in July 1974 in the agreement with PAIGC over Guinea-Bissau, and thwarted in early September over Mozambique, Spínola attempted to retain personal control of the Angola negotiations.

The Spínola plan for Angola depended heavily on the collaboration of President Mobutu of Zaire. On September 14, 1974, Spínola flew to the island of Sal in the Cape Verde archipelago and met secretly with President Mobutu. Spínola's formal proposals for an Angolan settlement, which were made public at this time, envisioned a transitional two-year period during which a provisional government would be formed of representatives from the three nationalist groups (FNLA, MPLA, and UNITA), together with representatives of the major ethnic groups and the white population. Spínola wanted to recognise the Chipenda faction (the eastern revolt) as the MPLA's representative and to isolate Neto. Elections would follow for a constituent assembly, with the franchise based on universal suffrage. The private understanding reached between Mobutu and Spínola at Sal remained secret but was based on their common desire to see the MPLA neutralized and, if possible, eliminated. Vice Admiral Rosa Coutinho, Portuguese high commissioner in Angola, who had not been informed of the meeting, described the objectives later as being "to install Holden in first place, with Chipenda and Savimbi at his side, and to eliminate Neto."[6] Spínola, when insisting that no negotiations take place with the MPLA, said of Neto, "He received his orders from Moscow."[7]

Like so many of Spínola's projects, his plans for Angola were not without shrewdness. In 1974, the Portuguese military was under less pressure in Angola than in either Guinea or Mozambique. At the time Spínola met with Mobutu there were still 60,000 Portuguese troops in the colony, and beyond that an extensive paramilitary network. The secret police (PIDE/DGS) continued to operate in Angola under the authority of the chief of staff, and was renamed the Police of Military Information (PIM). Like the MPLA, Holden Roberto's FNLA had not yet agreed to a cease-fire and, in terms of the military struggle, the FNLA was by far the most formidable opponent of the Portuguese army. Mobutu was the obvious person to deal with, since Roberto depended entirely on Zairian support and certainly could not function without it. Jonas Savimbi of UNITA had already agreed to a cease-fire in June and opened negotiations with a variety of white civilian and business groups. In mid 1974 UNITA consisted of less than 1,000 trained guerrillas (probably closer to 400) with ancient and inadequate weapons. Savimbi appears to have enjoyed covert "protection" from Portuguese military intelligence and PIDE for some years, the objective being to split nationalist groups along tribal lines in eastern and southern Angola following the early successes of MPLA penetration into these regions after 1966. Rosa Coutinho, however, believed the role of PIDE was exaggerated by UNITA's enemies, and that UNITA was a genuine movement, even if limited to a tribal base.

On August 8, 1974, 400 MPLA militants meeting in Lusaka had split three ways: 165 delegates supporting Neto; 165, Chipenda; and 70, Mário de Andrade. Chipenda's group represented the major fighting force of the MPLA within Angola proper, and Chipenda himself had been elected president of the MPLA at a rump session of the conference. Despite his temporary role as a Moscow protégé, he had also, at various times, been a protégé of almost all the outsiders who had fingers in the Angolan pie, including the Portuguese secret police. At any rate, both Spínola and Mobutu regarded Chipenda as persuadable, given the right inducements. The scenario laid out between them at Sal was thus not entirely implausible, and shortly after his meeting with Spínola, General Mobutu attempted to persuade both Julius

Nyerere and Kenneth Kaunda of the merits of the project.

The plan failed, however, and for reasons that lay in Lisbon as much as in Luanda. On September 30, 1974, Spínola resigned from the presidency, having failed in his attempt to by-pass the MFA and the communists by a popular appeal for support from "the silent majority." Between October 1974 and January 1975, effective power in Portugal was in the hands of the MFA. It strengthened its hand by forming a broader based group to oversee its affairs called the Council of Twenty, and by constituting an assembly, the so-called Assembly of Two Hundred, to act as a quasi-legislative body where major policy issues could be discussed. During these four critical months, the MFA remained united in its commitment to immediate decolonization, since all the diverse leftist elements within the movement agreed on the need for a rapid disengagement from Africa. The ascendancy within the movement of its leftist elements also brought the Portuguese authorities ideologically closer to the MPLA than to either of the MPLA's two competitors. The period was a critical one because it allowed the MPLA to recuperate from its mid 1974 nadir. Above all, it allowed Agostinho Neto a breathing space to reestablish leadership over his badly divided movement.

Not least of the elements working in the MPLA's favor during these months was the aid the movement received between July 1974 and January 1975 from the Portuguese high commissioner in Luanda, Vice Admiral Rosa Coutinho, dubbed by Spínola and the white settlers as the "Red Admiral." Rosa Coutinho had a pathological hatred of the FNLA and made no secret of the fact that he regarded President Mobutu as a "black fascist." The most important result of Rosa Coutinho's intervention was to thwart a key element in the Mobutu–Spínola plan – the substitution of Agostinho Neto. Although the Andrade faction was reintegrated into the MPLA during the latter part of 1974 (friction reemerged after the MPLA's victory in early 1976), Chipenda, despite a brief *rapprochement*, was expelled from the MPLA in November.

The role of the Portuguese at this particular moment was critical. "One of the difficulties ... was the fact that militarily the colonial war [in Angola] did not present the same conditions as in Mozambique or Guinea. Thus, in Angola, the Portuguese forces controlled practically the whole of the territory. The movements, to some extent, were being defeated," was how Rosa Coutinho explained the situation. "The MPLA was virtually defeated from a military viewpoint. Of course, this situation subsequently complicated the decolonization problem, because the movement with the greatest political support was at the time militarily the weakest."[8]

The temporary resolution of the MPLA's internal squabbles, however, which Rosa Coutinho helped bring about by financial assistance to the movement (he claimed to have provided equal assistance to the others as well though his favoritism towards the MPLA was obvious to all), provided a basis for settlement. Under the patronage of President Boumedienne, Agostinho Neto and Major Melo Antunes met in Algiers between November 19 and 21, 1974, and negotiated a cease-fire agreement. A week later, the FNLA and the Portuguese made a similar agreement in Kinshasa. The Organization of African Unity (OAU), which had at different times recognized both the FNLA and the MPLA as the sole legitimate nationalist spokesman for Angola, now extended last-minute recognition to Jonas Savimbi's UNITA. In early January 1975, the three nationalist leaders, Roberto, Neto, and Savimbi came together under the chairmanship of Jomo Kenyatta in Mombasa. They agreed to mutual recognition and the speedy opening of negotiations on Angolan independence with the Portuguese government.

On January 10 the negotiations were moved to the Algarve in Portugal. The leaders of the three movements and their delegations met with the Portuguese government at the heavily guarded Penina Hotel, and by January 15 had thrashed out a delicately balanced and highly precarious agreement. Leading the Portuguese side were General Costa Gomes, who had replaced General Spínola as provisional president of Portugal the previous September; Mário Soares, the foreign minister; Major Melo Antunes; and the high commissioner, Admiral Rosa Coutinho.

The settlement, which became known as the Alvor Agreement, set the date for Angolan independence at November 11, 1975. During the transitional period, the country would be administered by a coalition government composed of the three nationalist groups and the Portuguese. At the head of the transitional administration would be a presidential college of three, each "president" representing one of the three movements. Lisbon's high commissioner was to control defense and security and to "arbitrate differences." Each movement and the Portuguese would hold three posts in the cabinet. A national army was to be formed, the movements contributing 8,000 men each, while the Portuguese retained a 24,000-man force in the country until independence. The Portuguese troops would be withdrawn by February 1976. Elections for a constituent assembly were to be held prior to independence. Meanwhile, the three movements agreed to place a freeze on their January 1975 military positions.

The settlement was no mean achievement. It had been brought about preeminently by the MFA, then at the height of its power and prestige. Agostinho Neto paid the Armed Forces Movement a quiet tribute at the end of the Alvor meeting, which was little noted at the time but was extremely significant in its implications. He called the MFA "the Fourth Liberation Movement."

III

The suddenness of the Caetano regime's demise, and the absence of any widespread violence or destruction, created a very unusual phenomenon. For a brief while, the bureaucratic structure of a dictatorship remained intact despite the fact that the state itself was discredited and powerless. It made for fascinating and at times indecent exposure. The situation reminded me of an elaborate Victorian doll's house, one of the type where the whole facade can be swung back to reveal a complex household. In Portugal, makeshift partitions were soon set up to keep out the sunlight, though they were far from effective. For almost twelve months information and documentation were available which, in normal circumstances, would have taken decades to reach public view.

By coincidence, the height of the turmoil in Portugal – essentially mid-1974 through mid-1976 – was marked by a very similar accessibility to information in Washington. Washington is a leaky bucket at the best of times, but in the mid 1970s it resembled nothing so much as a sieve. The reasons for this are obvious and need only brief exposition. The Vietnam war ended. The Watergate conspiracy was exposed. President Richard M. Nixon was forced to resign under the threat of imminent impeachment. Three major congressional investigations were conducted into the activities of US intelligence agencies. The foreign policy establishment was unusually fragmented, much of it in opposition, some of its members bitterly alienated. Relations between the executive and the Congress were strained and mutually suspicious. There was hypersensitivity to any hint of a new Chile or, worse, a new Vietnam. The star of the secretary of state, Henry A. Kissinger, once so bright, was in decline. In such circumstances much slipped out which in less frantic times would undoubtedly have remained hidden. As Portugal became more volatile, Washington became increasingly concerned at the turn of events; but the west found itself unusually constrained during these critical months, not least by the fact that whatever it did to contain or oppose the leftward drift in Portugal and Africa – especially what it did clandestinely – very soon found its way into public view.

No revolution can fail to suggest parallels. Yet too much attention to theory and too little to specific circumstance can hinder understanding. In Portugal this particular malaise affected participants as well as observers. On a number of occasions the highly theoretical and ideological interpretations espoused by the leaders of the revolution proved wildly unrelated to Portuguese realities. In fact, it was one of the peculiarities of the situation in Portugal, after April 1974, that the leaders of the three major groups which sought to give form to the new regime all worked from experience gained outside Portugal and not within it, usually from models drawn from the countries in which they had spent long years of enforced exile. The socialists looked to the advanced industrial societies of Western Europe, especially France and West Germany; the communists to the experience of the imposed revolutions of Eastern Europe, especially Czechoslovakia, and the military looked to the national liberation movements. None of these groups understood or appreciated the depth of commitment of the others and all had difficulty relating to the social circumstances in Portugal.

Another remarkable fact was the degree to which the fears of those on the political right reflected with almost absolute authenticity the most extravagant hopes of the left. In consequence, it was often difficult to distinguish concrete fact from wishful thinking. At times statements were made that did have importance in themselves, and the revolution produced a plethora of texts. They deserve to be read in their own right, since précis would not do them justice or reflect their tone, but in Portugal, more than most places, what a document says is rarely all that it says;

an understanding of context is essential and reading between the lines advisable.

The Portuguese are also masters at telling eager outsiders exactly what they want to hear. There is a time-worn phrase for the process – *para inglês ver* – for the Englishman to see. Not surprisingly, therefore, those who arrived seeking the "truth" were sure to return with it. The Portuguese themselves, knowing the rules of the game, remained more quizzical and they rarely underestimated the difficulties involved in discovering verifiable facts. A remark by a leading political commentator in Lisbon is as good a description as any I know of the problems that confronted those involved in the process. He described a pair of French communist intellectuals sent to write on the situation in Portugal for *La Nouvelle Critique* as "two characters out of Beckett, looking for Godot in the mists of Portuguese non-information."[9]

The situation changed so rapidly, in fact, that history had barely happened before it was rewritten. Individuals might not wish to be reminded of stands they had fervently espoused only weeks before. Once the euphoria of the early months passed there was sometimes xenophobia in the air, though its targets were far from consistent. None of this was very surprising after fifty years of dictatorship. Many were anxious to prove their "democratic" and "socialist" credentials. Few were not tainted by some association with the fallen regime. Noses were hypersensitive to any change in the wind. Most were afraid of being left behind as the crowd moved on. Ironically, it was those who had consistently stood apart at great personal risk, discomforture, and even torture, who were most viciously attacked for their lack of "revolutionary" fervor – Raul Rego, Mário Soares, Alvaro Cunhal, Vitorino Magalhães Godinho, to name but a few of the most prominent. On more than one occasion their most vociferous tormentors were exposed as informers of the old dictatorship's secret police. The habits of half a century were hard to break.

The problem for anyone who wanted to make some sense of the situation came back to the question of evidence; of how to distinguish fact from fiction among the welter of lies, forgeries and self-interested revelations that swamped anyone interested in interpreting Portuguese affairs. The *New Yorker*'s Jane Kramer summed up the situation well: "there's no way to describe the crisis here in its own rhetoric," she wrote at the time. "Portugal today is a place where Socialists are called Fascists, Marxists are called Moderates, Marxist–Leninist has become a code word for anything noisy and disruptive, where conservatives label the entire left Communist, Communists label the rest of the left conservative, and the foreign press has a field day."[10] Yet, despite this theater, beneath the surface decisive changes were occurring in Portugal – changes that would be irreversible. The decolonization of the territories in Africa were, in one sense, the easy changes, since in effect the Portuguese had been forced to recognize the inevitable and events moved under the pressure of circumstances largely beyond their control. Lisbon could not have resisted even if it had wanted to. The conditions in Portugal were more problematical. Here, pressures for change could and would be resisted. It was thus a curious fact about the situation in Portugal towards the end of 1974 and the beginning of 1975 that, just at the moment when many believed the move to the left to be irresistible, the fortuitous combination of elements which had contributed to the left's success was beginning to unravel.

The west was also beginning to find its way through the Portuguese thicket. Under Ambassador Carlucci, the US embassy had quickly established a formidable reporting and intelligence-gathering capability. Carlucci used the question of NATO membership as a test to help identify communists within the military. He also soon came to doubt Kissinger's dire predictions. "The pressures and forces that have been unleashed must be tempered, they cannot be stuffed back into the tube," he told Washington. Herbert Okun developed an efficient polling operation in anticipation of the constituent assembly elections, accurately predicting the results. And Colonel Schuler cultivated the younger members of the officer corps, working with General Alexander Haig, the NATO commander, to incorporate selected Portuguese officers in NATO training programs, among them an obscure colonel called António Ramalho Eanes. "A boy scout for democracy" was how Okun described Eanes. But the task of combating the communists proved only less arduous for Carlucci than confronting the presuppositions of Henry Kissinger in Washington. When Carlucci argued that Mário Soares was "the only game in town" Kissinger shouted at his staff: "Whoever sold me Carlucci as a tough guy?"

CHAPTER 6

Revolution

There are only two alternatives: either to be with the Revolution or to be with the reaction.
Brigadier General Vasco Gonçalves, prime minister
(May 1975)

The MFA is the liberation movement of the Portuguese people; it stands above party and its essential aim is that of national independence. The MFA recognizes that this national independence involves a process of domestic decolonization which can only be achieved by means of the construction of a socialist society.
Plan of Political Action, Armed Forces Movement
(June 1975)

There is nothing else now going on in the world – not in South East Asia; not even in the Middle East that is half so important and ominous as the communist drive for power in Portugal.
Senator James Buckley (1975)

Portugal is beginning to look like the tilting member in a new domino theory that envisions the whole northern rim of the Mediterranean possibly turning red in the not too distant future.
Howard Wiarda (January 1975)

I

If alliances were being forged on one front during the winter of 1974–5, alliances were disintegrating on another. Communist actions were alienating powerful elements of the Portuguese left which had previously collaborated with the communists in the "anti fascist" struggle. Most especially and dramatically, the communists were alienating the rapidly expanding socialists under the leadership of Mário Soares.

In Lisbon, January 1975 was a trying month – cold, misty, with great enveloping sea fogs rolling over the capital and surging in thick white-gray billows up its narrow cobbled streets as if propelled by some ancient wind machine. It was also the month that shattered some of the myths of the Portuguese revolution. When Mário Soares returned from Paris and Alvaro Cunhal from Prague the previous April, they had posed together, smiling, holding between them a red carnation. But in January the communists took to the streets in massive demonstrations to support legislation that aimed to impose a single central union organization that would effectively perpetuate communist control over the organized working class.

The MFA's leadership, known since September as the Council of Twenty, publicly endorsed the communists' position. But the Catholic church, breaking a long political silence, condemned the proposal for a centralized union structure and called for pluralism. The socialists and popular democrats in the cabinet succeeded in amending the details of the legislation to guarantee free elections for local union officials and committees. The voting on the issue in the cabinet, however, confirmed alignments long rumored. General Vasco Gonçalves, the prime minister, and Captain Costa Martins, the labor minister, voted with Alvaro Cunhal, the communist leader, against the amendments. Majors Melo Antunes and Alves, then ministers without portfolio, together with Mário Soares and the PPD ministers, voted for them. The split pointed up fundamental differences of approach and reflected divergences on the left, long antedating the present events in Portugal. It was in effect the classic debate between those in favor of a broad-based participatory and democratic route to socialism on the one hand, and those who espoused the role of a revolutionary vanguard on the other.

As the dispute between the communists and socialists over union organization was at its height, Avelino Gonçalves, the communist minister of labor in the first provisional government, and a banking union official in Oporto, was voted out of office in local union elections. This communist setback was a clear indication of the major inroads the socialists were making among traditional communist supporters disenchanted with the party's ambivalent attitude toward wage increases and labor militancy during the first year of the revolution. The socialists feared that a centralized union structure and communist-dominated Intersindical at its apex would block further erosion of communist support in the socialists' favor at the grassroots level. Thus, underneath the sharpening ideological debate were several immediate and pressing issues. These concerned the control of vital bureaucratic machinery, the growing regional polarization, and the escalating class and personal antagonisms. Before the year was out, the struggle between the socialists and the communists and between the political parties and the MFA, would so divide the country and its leaders as to bring Portugal close to civil war. When it was over, many wondered whether there had been, or could have been, a revolution at all.

The public dispute between the communists and the socialists that broke out in January had been simmering for some time. It was a conflict that reached beyond mere party factionalism because it paralleled, and to some extent intersected with, major divergences within the military. Whatever the leaders of the MFA may have intended, the intrusion of political and party division into the military after March 1975 was unavoidable. With the right and center effectively neutralized, the struggle for power began in earnest within the left and inside the MFA. It was almost inevitable that this should happen.

The crisis occurred on March 11, 1975.[1] It was the result of months of complex subterranean maneuvering by both sides. General Spínola was tricked into believing that an anticommunist *putsch* might succeed. When he arrived at the Tancos air base in central Portugal, ostensibly to take command of the revolt, he found instead a shambles. He barely escaped arrest before boarding a helicopter and fleeing across the border to Spain. After this comic-opera-like confrontation (in popular usage at the time, it was called an *intentona* by the left and an *inventona* by the right), the MFA's radical elements removed (and sometimes jailed) their more moderate colleagues and leading members of the old oligarchy were rounded up and imprisoned, including members of the Espírito Santo and Melo families, and sent to the old PIDE stronghold at Caxias; elsewhere in the country many others found themselves imprisoned. The old army general officer corps, with the notable exception of the new provisional president General Costa Gomes, had been flushed away (*saneado*) and the old staff officers corps abolished. On March 12, the Council of Twenty was transformed into the Council of the Revolution and became the supreme authority in the state. The Council of the Revolution absorbed the functions of the Junta of National Salvation, the Council of State and the Council of Twenty. It was intended to institutionalize the power of the Armed Forces Movement and become the clear center of authority in the state. This move was justified, as General Costa Gomes explained on 20 March 1975, "among other reasons also by the fact that the Portuguese people are not sufficiently enlightened politically to reject the elitist parties or pseudo-democrats."[2]

The Council of the Revolution was joined by an MFA Assembly, a confused amalgam of executive and legislative functions which usurped much of the authority intended for the yet-to-be elected Constituent Assembly. The MFA Assembly comprised 240 men, representing the three services. Following the precedent set in Guinea, the assembly also, for the first time in Portugal proper, incorporated sergeants and enlisted men in addition to regular officers. The sergeants and enlisted men were very much in the minority, to be sure, but the principle of representation by noncommissioned ranks and enlisted men was extended to the three service assemblies and to the committees that emerged at unit level in barracks throughout the country.

The MFA called the failed *putsch* a serious counter-revolutionary act which "made it an imperative, urgent need to give the Armed Forces Movement an institutional framework."[3] In an ominous phrase, the MFA bulletin spoke of seeking the collaboration of the "authentically democratic political parties" and left no doubt that the central political role in Portugal from now on was to be played by the MFA: "The Armed Forces will be the guarantor and motor of the revolutionary process, leading to the building of a true political, economic and social democracy."[4] The fourth provisional government, sworn in during March, included representatives of various political parties (PS, PCP, MDP/CDE, PPD), but it had at its core a strong team of radical economists in charge of the economic ministries, including the Catholic radical Francisco Pereira de Moura, leader of the MDP/CDE, and João Cravinho, a member of MES (Movement of the Socialist Left). But now it was not the politicians who held the initiative; it was the soldiers.

The MFA Assembly on March 11 and 12, 1975 imposed a series of drastic measures which the previous provisional governments had shied away from. The most critical of these actions was the nationalization of the banks and insurance companies. Because of the close interlocking of the Portuguese oligarchy and its control of major sectors of the economy, the nationalization of the banks took into the hands of the state the major part of privately owned Portuguese industry.[5] Since the banks also directly owned or held mortgages on virtually every Portuguese newspaper, one additional result was that, in taking control of the banks, the state assumed financial control of much of the communications media – all the Lisbon morning daily newspapers and a group of weekly magazines and newspapers. A rare exception was the Lisbon evening daily, *República*, one of the few voices of criticism during the long years of the dictatorship, owned by 3,500 small shareholders and edited by Raul Rego, a leading socialist.

At the time of the bank nationalizations, the Council of the Revolution also indicated that it would soon promulgate a major land expropriation, probably of estates over 500 hectares, a measure that would destroy the power of the great *latifundiários* of the south. The nationalizations and the threatened land expropriation struck at the two principal bases of the old regime and placed Portugal immediately among the most radical of European states, few of which dared to touch the banks or engage in large-scale land expropriation without a clear commitment to compensation.

On April 11, 1975 the Council of the Revolution forced the political parties to sign a pact with the MFA that guaranteed military supremacy for at least three years, relegated the provisional government to a subordinate position in the new hierarchy of power, and gave to the MFA Assembly a co-equal voice with any future National Assembly in the election of a president. The political parties had no choice but to acquiesce. They did not wish to jeopardize the Constituent Assembly elections scheduled for April 25. The timetable for Constituent Assembly elections and national parliamentary elections had been an integral part of the original MFA program, and to abandon them would have been an affront to the Portuguese people who, after fifty years of manipulated electoral contests and a narrow franchise, were eager to participate. It was a concession that the military radicals afterward regretted making. They should have recognized that, whatever the result of the poll, it was bound to represent a potential challenge to military supremacy because one unavoidable result of the election would be that, for the first time since the April coup, there would exist an alternate source of legitimacy to their own.

Leading military radicals, however, did little to disguise their contempt for "bourgeois" electoral politics. Lieutenant Ramiro Correia, a naval officer who had become a leading figure in the general staff's Fifth Division, responsible for information and propaganda, likened the contest to a "lottery" or "football pool." Admiral Rosa Coutinho, former high commissioner in Angola, and now the executive officer of the Council of the Revolution, attempted to persuade people to cast blank ballots. Admiral Coutinho hoped that, should such appeals be successful, the result might be used as an argument for a political role for the MFA and would allow it to dispense with civilian political parties altogether. Opinion polls commissioned by the MFA showed that as many as 50 percent of the electorate were undecided in early April as to whom they would support. Ironically, much of the foreign press, by now obsessed with the power of the communists, also dismissed the elections as being of minor significance.

They were wrong. In reality, the elections were an event of enormous political importance, and this was well recognized once the results were in. On April 25, 1975, in one of the highest turnouts ever recorded in a national election (91.7 percent), it was the new democratic political parties that won. It was the Portuguese Socialist Party led by Marío Soares that took 37.9 percent of the vote; the popular democrats led by Sá Carneiro gained 26.4 percent; Alvaro Cunhal's communists took a mere 12.5 percent nationwide, and the PCP's sister party, the Portuguese Democratic Movement (MDP/CDE), received a mere 4.1 percent; the conservative CDE got 7.6 percent. The blank votes numbered no more than 7.0 percent of the total votes cast. The constituent election returns showed that a majority of the Portuguese people wanted change, but they wanted change to come about by democratic means.[6]

Equally significant, the election revealed a marked regional polarization. Communist support was concentrated in the south of the country, especially in the industrial towns along the south bank of the Tagus estuary and in the Alentejo. But in the north the popular democrats (PPD) and the Social Democratic Center (CDS) dominated the returns. The elections had the effect of pointing out the profound differences in social and economic organization between the north and the south of Portugal. In the north, the size of the average farm holding in 1975 was small – a little under 5 hectares – but land ownership was almost universal. Agriculture was intensive and diverse, with abundant rainfall and access to ancient irrigation systems. The influence of the Catholic church was strong and religiosity fervent. Attachment to tradition and family and a strong suspicion of innovation were generalized among the population. In the south, on the plains and low plateau of the Alentejo, agriculture was monocultural (cereals, olives), the climate was characterized by long, hot, dry summers, and land ownership was highly concentrated (the average size of a farm in the south in 1975 was almost 40 hectares). The labor force was composed of salaried farm workers, most in precarious seasonal employment. Here, the influence of the church was negligible, often nonexistent, during the Salazar period. Among the landless laborers class consciousness was strong. This was the region that provided the backbone of support for the clandestine PCP, and it was from the Alentejo that the PCP, as soon as it emerged as a legal party in 1974, chose its folk heroes and official martyrs. Unlike the north, where most of those who left the land did so to go abroad to the factories of France or Germany, in the south migration tended to be internal. Hence, strong Alentejan influences extended into the industrial towns of the Lisbon–Setúbal area. In the north, however, few nonagricultural workers did not also have some access to land, and the factories in the region north of Oporto, up toward Braga, were often small paternalistic enterprises.[7]

There were curious similarities between the regions of PPD and PCP strength. The districts of Bragança and Vila Real in the north, like those of Beja and Evora in the south, suffered the highest rates of infant mortality. All had the highest percentage of the work force engaged in agriculture (over 70 percent). Each district had a high illiteracy rate (over 40 percent). All were backward and in many respects isolated rural communities; each was in its own way a highly traditional society. But in two critical respects they diverged: in religion and land ownership. These two elements were to be the fundamental issues in the struggle that was about to begin. Despite the regional divide, the socialists (PS) emerged from the Constituent Assembly elections as a national party, with respectable percentages in both north and south. Although they tended to be the right alternative to communists in the south, and the left alternative to the PPD and CDS in the north, it was in the central regions of the country and the major urban centers that the socialists did best of all. In Lisbon they won 46.1 percent of the vote; in Oporto, 42.15 percent; in Coimbra, 43.3 percent; and in Santarém, 42.9 percent. This reflected an important social phenomenon. The socialists were the first choice in the more modern, open area of Portugal. In the coastal plain between the two major cities of Oporto and Lisbon, and up the river valleys to Coimbra and Santarém, their support was concentrated in regions with good communications that tended to be at least partly industrialized.

Three complex factors now came into play. First, the coincidence between the seizure of power by the radical military and their communist backers in March, and the victory of the moderate parties in the Constituent Assembly elections in April, created potent and potentially conflicting sources of power and legitimacy. Second, the election returns demonstrated that the revolution's power base was narrower than had appeared to be the case. Third, the election revealed that the Socialist Party, because of its national reach, would be a key player in arbitrating the explosive division between a conservative north and a radical south. Thus, the returns inadvertently provided a geography for counter-revolution, a geography which the communists' enemies inside and outside Portugal were soon to take advantage of. The recently arrived American ambassador in Portugal, Frank C. Carlucci, put the point bluntly one year later in a congressional hearing in Washington: "I think it was the election that turned the situation around."[8] The communist leader, Alvaro Cunhal agreed, though he described the situation in his own language:

In the Portuguese Revolution two processes have intervened, two dynamics, with completely different characteristics. On one side, the revolutionary dynamic, created by the intervention of material force – popular and military – directly transforming situations, conquering and exercising liberties, defeating and throwing out the fascists, opposing the counter-revolutionary attempts, bringing about profound social and economic transformations, attempting to create a state in the service of the Revolution, and the creation of organs of power (including military organs) which will guarantee the democratic process and correspond to the revolutionary transformation.

On the other side, the electoral process, understood as the choice by universal suffrage of the organs of power, tending to subordinate any social transformation to a previous constitutional legality, and not reorganizing the intervention of the military in political life, or the creative, predominant intervention of the masses in the revolutionary process.[9]

What both Carlucci and Cunhal might have added was that Portugal throughout the 1970s was still a traditional society, and this did much to contain the potential for violence. The suspicion of outsiders was often a wall of protection for the stronger bonds within: those of family, relatives, and in-laws, and the outer networks of close acquaintances who might frequent the same cafés, go fishing together, come from the same village. Away from the small cosmopolitan elite, which is obviously the exception to this rule, the barriers could be insurmountable for the stranger – foreign or domestic – unless a social presence was established at some point within these networks. At its best this characteristic of social interaction in Portugal made for a depth of acceptance and hospitality that has been long lost in more modernized western societies where relationships rapidly established are more rapid of passage.

The strength of these traditional bonds helps to explain the resilience of Portuguese society under strains and stresses which by any objective measurement seem at times intolerable. Such social elasticity may not last, it is true. As Portugal is "modernized" it probably will not. But for the critical years I am discussing in this book, Portuguese society managed to absorb the traumatic psychological, economic, and political shocks that the end of empire and fifty years of dictatorship brought. Thus, the people participated in the election with great dignity and civic pride, despite the turmoil that surrounded it. The second factor was the extent and openness of the debate about politics that engulfed each household after April 1974. Each mealtime could become a small constituent assembly since families were large and children could cover the political spectrum. Politics

might bring generational conflict. Yet generational conflict in
Portugal had been growing throughout the 1970s, and politics
can mitigate as easily as irritate tensions which before had been
sullen and repressed. It was such family groups that watched
unseen in the wings and with increasing dismay as on center
stage the games of musical chairs took place in Lisbon. The
endless succession of governments, prime ministers, and presi-
dents; the coups and counter-coups; the resignations and recon-
ciliations; the endless debates; the interminable political and
military crises. The exasperation in the country was real enough
and the desire to participate was a palpable fact. Indeed, in
some ways it was this will to take some part in determining
their own destinies which was more important than the political
coloring under which it emerged. No one who had spent even a
day in a Portuguese home would have been the least bit surprised
that over 90 percent of the electorate turned out for the first
fully free and inclusive elections in Portuguese history, and in
all the key elections which took place after April 1975.

II

Events, however, were meanwhile quickly moving out of the
hands of the politicians and the military. In the rural areas,
especially in the Alentejo, rural workers were taking the law into
their own hands. By March 1975 many of the landowners in
this region had already fled the country and some were in jail.
The landowners of the south had always lived in fear of social
revolution and, well before expropriation measures had been
enacted in Lisbon, landless rural workers had moved onto several
estates and claimed the land for themselves.[10] Workers' committees also moved into place in the nationalized industries, and
the exodus of the oligarchs was joined by many middle-
management personnel seeking a more secure future abroad,
especially in Brazil.

The popular movement on the left had three main sources of
strength: the industrial workplace, the poorer urban neighborhoods and shanty towns, and the large farms worked by day
laborers. Each of the popular movements in these sectors began
with immediate demands – more pay, job security, housing. With
the old political police dismantled or jailed and the traditional

forces of public order confused and fearful, as the political battles over control of the state apparatus intensified, and as the divisions within the military became more obvious, the initiative did indeed pass to the streets and the workplace, as Caetano had feared and predicted. The joy of liberation that followed the coup soon acquired hard edges. In the small- and medium-sized firms workers commissions ousted and purged managers. There had been some precedent to workers' organization at plant level, which helps explain the speed with which many of these organs of workers control emerged; in many cases they grew out of the strike committees which had been formed during the period of labor unrest and wildcat strikes that preceeded the April 1974 coup. The communists had taken over the old regime's union structure which had been organized with separate unions representing each occupation; the new workers commissions in contrast were elected by workers assemblies on a factory-wide basis, and when the communists urged restraint in wage demands, the workers found more sympathetic collaborators among the small, more militant parties on the extreme left. The workers were also able to achieve quick acquiescence to their demands, diminishing the differentials between manual and clerical workers, increasing wages, and cutting back work rules and the working day. The most militant workers were those in the heavy industrial sector around Lisbon and Setúbal, where large numbers of younger male workers were concentrated. The leveling of wage differentials, however, alienated many white-collar staff from the revolutionary cause. In foreign-owned factories the workers commissions soon found that markets, supplies, and credit were closed off to them. The commissions thus became increasingly concerned with "industrial sabotage" and assigned workers to oversee the accounting departments, to keep an eye on shipments and overseas contracting and credit operations. After March, the workers commissions collaborated actively in the nationalizations, forcing the pace in those sectors where the communists were dominant.

The organization of the poorer neighborhoods arose initially out of the demand for housing and improved living conditions in the shanty towns surrounding the three major cities of Lisbon, Oporto, and Setúbal. The first takeover of empty public housing had occurred in Lisbon. On the outskirts of the city at Monsanto, empty public housing had been seized and occupied largely at

the instigation of a small far-left Maoist party, the MRPP.
Seizures and occupations followed in Oporto and Setúbal. Shanty
town residents in Lisbon and elsewhere refused to pay rent,
demanded better services, and turned to the nearby barracks
and the MFA for help. The young officers of the MFA, especially
the officers in command of COPCON, found themselves increasingly mediating local grassroots demands and disputes with the
local neighborhood committees (*comissões de moradores*). It was an
experience that radicalized them. Again, as in the factories, the
communists who had quickly taken over the old municipal and
parish governments, found themselves outflanked to their left by
the small but militant Marxist–Leninist and Maoist parties, and
these parties in turn found themselves in day-to-day contact with
the officers of COPCON. After March, the occupation of
"vacant" houses and apartments with military support became
widespread. Property owners found themselves without protection
and with little recourse in law.

The rural movement was concentrated largely in the Alentejo.
Here, the largest numbers of landless laborers were to be found.
No rural unions existed prior to the coup, but the communists
had long dominated the opposition to the old regime in these
areas, and here, unlike in the factories and the urban neighborhoods, there was little competition from the far left. The rural
workers wanted collective contracts, reduced hours, paid
vacations, transportation to the fields, higher wages. In Beja
they were initially successful in these demands, but opposition
emerged among the landowners in Evora. The crisis on the
southern plains quickly escalated after March, where workers
occupied over 400 great estates, often with military support.
The communist-dominated rural union made sure that the large
landholdings were not split up but transformed into cooperatives.
The workers, however, were ill prepared for their new responsi-
bilities. Illiteracy rates were high and the management of the
new cooperatives were often left in the hands of communist-party
and union officials or the small entrepreneurs and tractor owners
who had in some cases led the takeovers in the first place. It
was precisely these assertions of workers' control in the factories,
of people's power in the neighborhoods, and of peasants' power
in the countryside, that gave the Portuguese upheaval its revolutionary character. Nothing had been seen like this in Europe

since Spain in the 1930s, Germany in 1918–19, and Russia in 1905 and 1917.

Despite its sound and fury, the popular movement was restricted in geographical extension. It was not a movement that could emerge with a national dimension since it was limited to the larger concentrations of workers, and such concentrations in both the urban and the rural areas were largely a Lisbon and southern phenomenon. The popular movement elsewhere would emerge under different colors and with different objectives. In the center and north, where workers were often landowners, and where property was divided not concentrated, the mobilizing slogans were not socialism and jobs but religion and property. The leftist popular movement was also increasingly linked and dependent on the state for military support, credits, and post facto legalization of seizures and takeovers. When the popular movement was able to influence the armed forces, and most especially COPCON, this gave it great apparent power. But it was a power that was vulnerable if its allies within the state apparatus were removed or neutralized. It was thus a considerable irony that the temporary alliance between the state and the far left served to stimulate and then consolidate a counter-alliance between the frightened small property owners, largely concentrated in the center and north of the country on the one hand, and the emergent nationally based political parties and organizations such as the CAP on the other. Little of this was obvious in the spring and early summer of 1975. The communists and the radicalized officers of the MFA believed at the time that the peasants of the north and center of Portugal were manipulated and led by "caciques", priests, and local bigwigs. To change this, the northerners needed to be "culturally dynamized," which they set out to achieve with visiting military units and would-be political commissars. In one sense they were right about the north. The church was to take an active part in mobilizing anti-communist crowds in 1975. The larger landowners were involved in stirring up the fears of the small peasant proprietors. Embryonic clandestine networks linked to the now-exiled General Spínola were indeed being concocted in the northern provinces. But all these activities would have come to nothing had they not struck a responsive cord with ordinary men and women who believed that the left-dominated government in Lisbon was about to deprive them of all that they possessed: land and faith. Thousands of poor Catholics in black suits and dresses crawled painfully and fervently across the great tarmac plaza before the basilica where the Virgin Mary was said to have appeared in 1917. This phenomenon of Fátima was, to the left, no more than a false consciousness that could be dispelled by the truth according to Karl Marx. The left failed to anticipate that religiosity, culture and ingrained behavior might propel these peasant masses when aroused politically to shatter the wildest dreams of radical change.

III

Until January 1975, the rapidly changing situation in the Portuguese territories in Africa contributed to the dramatic shift to the left in Portugal. Events in Europe and in Africa coincided in a manner that strengthened the radical forces in each region. After March 1975, these circumstances were dramatically reversed. One of the keys to the implementation of the Alvor Agreement on Angolan independence was the MFA's ability to control the situation until the transfer of power could take place. The intrinsic problems in Africa were formidable enough. But contributing to the breakdown was the MFA's inability to fulfill its side of the bargain. At the time this was not yet apparent since the MFA, even as late as January 1975, still remained a mystery to many both inside and outside of Portugal. Above all, it appeared much more united and formidable than in fact it was.

Agostinho Neto was, as always, especially sensitive to the political situation in Portugal. Unlike Holden Roberto and Jonas Savimbi, who left Portugal quickly once the Alvor Agreements had been signed in January, Neto remained in MFA-ruled Portugal, traveled extensively throughout the country, and had lengthy meetings with political and military leaders. It was a critical time in Portugal. The euphoria that followed the fall of the old regime was passing. January 1975 saw a fundamental change in the atmosphere, a beginning of the long struggle between the communists and socialists. Within the military itself, conflicts were developing – indeed, had already developed – which would later split the MFA into warring factions. As shrewd and well-informed a politician as Agostinho Neto must have seen the warnings; they were not hard to recognize. Thus, while the ink on the Alvor Agreement was barely dry, the forces that would undo it were already gathering.

The Portuguese, their soldiers unwilling to become involved in armed confrontation, had virtually abandoned the Angolan frontiers. Between November 1974 and January 1975, some ten thousand FNLA troops moved into northeast Angola from their sanctuaries in Zaire, occupying the northern Uíge and Zaire districts of Angola and forcing out all MPLA and UNITA rivals. Behind the FNLA regulars came thousands of refugees, returning to the lands they had abandoned in the aftermath of the bloody rural uprising in 1961. As a result, thousands of Ovimbundu workers on the coffee estates were expelled from the region, and some sixty thousand fled south to their tribal homelands on the central highlands.

On the crowded Benguela-Bié plateau in southern Angola there were serious social and racial tensions too. The Portuguese army's counter-insurgency measures had uprooted thousands of peasants, concentrated them in "secure" village compounds, and in many cases opened up their lands to white settlers. In the capital, Luanda, the tension that had remained after the serious racial clashes of the previous summer was aggravated by the arrival, in February 1975, of heavily armed contingents from the rival nationalist movements.[11]

As had happened at several critical moments in the Angolan conflict, the situation in Luanda was aggravated by the vigilante action of the white population who, led by taxi drivers, rampaged into the *musseques*. In face of the increasing inability or unwillingness of the Portuguese authorities to deal with the violence, the Angolans within the Portuguese military demanded that they patrol the streets, and from this beginning many of the Angolans within the Portuguese armed forces shifted their allegiance to the MPLA, thus forming the nucleus of the MPLA's own army.[12]

The uneasy standoff between these factions lasted only until March when, coincident with the *intentona* by Spínolista soldiers in Portugal, widespread fighting broke out between the MPLA and the FNLA in the Angolan capital. In Caxito, to the north of the capital, the FNLA rounded up MPLA sympathizers and shot and mutilated them. It was the old nightmare of massacre and reprisal that had been a constant theme in the long Angolan struggle. To the massive internal ebb and flow of people and refugees was now added a mass exodus abroad. First to leave were Cape Verdeans caught between the rival African movements and deprived of their role as intermediaries and small tradesmen. Then followed the exodus of whites. In Lisbon, the airport began to fill with large boxes, crates, and the heavy humid smell of Africa as the settlers returned. First the official jargon referred to them as the "dislocated," then, the "returned." But they were refugees, and several hundred thousand of them poured into Portugal from Africa throughout the spring and summer of 1975. Their arrival was a rude awakening for many of those army officers who, a few months before, had been speaking naively about a socialist "commonwealth." In consequence, the process of decolonization – which, as it interacted with the internal situation in Portugal, had done so much to propel the country to the left in the months following the coup – now faltered.

The decolonization process that, until March, had helped cement the MFA's internal solidarity became, after March 1975, a major irritant and divider as the situation in Angola proved increasingly intractable and as outsiders intervened there at will. There was also an unforeseen consequence of the March nationalizations in Portugal which subtly altered Portuguese attitudes toward Africa. The state, by taking over the banks and industries which had been the core of the oligarchy's power, also assumed responsibility for vast assets in the former overseas territories. Ironically, the revolutionary governments held a more important economic stake in Angola than had the governments of the old regime. After March it was obvious to all that the Portuguese could neither contain outside intervention nor control internal security in Angola – both obligations which Portugal had assumed under the Alvor accords – and any pretence at a bipartite transitional government collapsed. There was open fighting in Angola, and in Portugal, too, the military factions were beginning to eye each other ominously. The initiative that had rested in the hands of the revolution for almost twelve months was gone.

The rapidly deteriorating situation in Angola was especially dangerous because it opened up opportunities for interference by outsiders which had not existed to the same degree in either the case of Guinea-Bissau or Mozambique. In Angola, three nationalist groups, all battle hardened, each with strong ethnic roots, competed with each other as much as they did with the Portuguese. The movements in Angola had regional bases; the FNLA in the northeast of the country; the MPLA in the western center and Luanda; and UNITA in the central highlands. The zones of influence were not clearly demarcated, however, and clashes between the rival movements were frequent. Fragmentation and rivalry within each organization was also common.

The schisms among and within the national liberation movements in Angola were partly ethnic, partly regional, partly the result of Portuguese colonial policy. The Salazar regime had ruthlessly rooted out nationalists, the educational system in the territory was woefully inadequate, and years of underground activity, exile, and infiltration had left psychological scars. Each of Angola's main ethno-linguistic communities was represented by a political movement and a guerrilla army. The FNLA was rooted in the 700,000-strong Bakongo community of northern Angola. After a bloody rural uprising in 1961 and the subsequent brutal repression vented on the Bakongo by the Portuguese, over 400,000 Bakongo refugees had crossed into Zaire, where they lived among kinsmen. The FNLA was deeply embedded in the Zairian political system and enjoyed sanctuary and support from President Mobutu. In 1973 the FNLA received military assistance from the Chinese. The movement was militarily strong but politically weak, and its leadership personalistic. UNITA, rooted in the two million Ovimbundu of the central Benguela plateau, was led by a former Roberto aide, Jonas Savimbi, the charismatic, Swiss-educated son of a Benguela railroad worker. After the Lisbon coup, UNITA had made overtures to the Angolan whites, who provided it with important support until the white presence and power collapsed as settlers fled from Angola in increasing numbers during 1975.

The MPLA's roots were in the 1.3 million Mbundu (Kimbundu-speaking) people of Luanda and its hinterland. Denied bases in Zaire, the MPLA operated from headquarters in Congo-Brazzaville, conducting military incursions in Cabinda, the oil-rich enclave, and in the grasslands of eastern Angola. The MPLA's leadership was urban, leftist, and racially mixed, with strong popular support from the rural Mbundu and the city slum-dwellers. Agostinho Neto, like Roberto of the FNLA, but unlike Savimbi, owed his survival largely to outside support.

The MPLA had been the exclusive recipient of Soviet, Cuban, and East European aid, and the MPLA had long been close to the Portuguese left. After 1965, Cuban assistance to the MPLA followed a meeting between Agostinho Neto and Che Guevara in Brazzaville (Mondlane had turned down a similar offer of assistance from Guevara in Dar es Salaam in 1965). The 1,000 Cuban troops sent to Congo-Brazzaville also assisted the MPLA with arms and training programs. Guevara was, however, highly critical of the MPLA's exiled leadership and when Neto was in Havana, Castro used Neto's personal inexperience in handling arms to humiliate the MPLA leader. "How can you expect to be a military leader?" Castro asked him.[13] The Liberation Committee of the OAU, assessing the strengths of the three movements in early 1975, found that UNITA enjoyed the most support and the MPLA the least, with the FNLA falling somewhere between them. In early 1975 the OAU, like the Portuguese and the Soviets, supported the idea of a coalition government.

Partly as a consequence of the factionalism within and among the liberation movements in Angola, the Portuguese had been much more successful there from a military point of view than they had been in either Guinea-Bissau or Mozambique. With the exception of UNITA, which in 1974 was a very poorly armed and small organization, the other nationalist movements were as much coalitions of exiles as they were effective insurgency forces. This was, of course, in striking contrast to both PAIGC in Guinea-Bissau or FRELIMO in Mozambique – movements which had formidable offensive capacity, controlled large areas of territory, and had developed rudimentary administrative structures. In 1974 Angola had the largest white population in Africa outside South Africa, and whites almost totally dominated Angola's agricultural, transportation, and administrative infrastructures. It was partly as a result of these differences from the other territories that Angola took on the importance it did when Lisbon's inability to control the decolonization process became apparent.

The speed with which the transfers of power to PAIGC and FRELIMO took place during 1974, therefore, proved to be deceptive precedents when it came to the complexities of the Angolan situation. Kissinger claimed after the event that the United States did not oppose the accession to power by "radical movements" in Guinea-Bissau and Mozambique. This is only partly true. The United States, in fact, was extremely disturbed about the consequences of the independence of the Cape Verde Islands under the auspices of the PAIGC, and there is evidence that it did contemplate support for anti-FRELIMO movements in Mozambique. It was not the lack of desire but lack of capacity that prevented the United States or anyone else from interfering in the decolonization process. The recognition by the Portuguese Armed Forces Movement of the necessity to deal exclusively with PAIGC and FRELIMO, and the firm action of the Portuguese in suppressing diversionary attempts, meant that in each situation, because the liberation movements and the Portuguese army worked in close collaboration, the opportunity for any effective interference never arose. In Angola, no single movement had the capacity to act with the effectiveness of either PAIGC or FRELIMO, and by the time Angolan decolonization became the prime order of business, the Portuguese were so divided among themselves that they too were unable to provide any consistent or effective opposition to the rapid internationalization of Angola's crisis.

Angola, moreover, with a population of about five and a half million, was different in other important ways from all the other Portuguese territories. It was immeasurably rich in natural resources (oil, diamonds, iron) and agricultural production (cotton, coffee, sisal, maize, sugar, tobacco). Unlike all the other territories, Angola had a favorable trade balance with the rest of the world and a firm basis for real independence. Yet the whole structure of Angola was so dominated by and dependent upon whites that the rapid deterioration of the security situation, the burgeoning and at times bloody confrontations between the three nationalist movements, soon created panic among them. After March 1975, as the whites began to stream out of Angola, they took with them almost everything that made the system of government and the economy work, throwing an already confused situation into chaos. In fact, by the summer of 1975, Angola had the misfortune to recreate some of the worst characteristics of two previous African crises – the Congo and the Algerian war – combining militarized, battle-hardened nationalists with an environment where the mechanisms which made society function had almost totally collapsed.[14]

The importance of stressing this chaos in Angola is to point out the contrast it presents to the situations which had transpired in much of the rest of Africa in the period of decolonization. Almost everywhere – except, perhaps, for the Congo, Algeria, and Guinea Conakry – the transfer of power occurred with the acquiescence (albeit sometimes reluctant) of the colonial powers and, in consequence, administrative and economic disruption had been surprisingly minimal. The experiences of outside powers in their relationships with the new African states were not appropriate to the situation that had developed in Angola. There, new circumstances required new policies which would have to be formulated within an international environment that had itself changed dramatically since 1962.

The decolonization of Angola was of special concern to the South African government, even more than the rapid withdrawal of the Portuguese from Mozambique. In Portugal's east African colony there was very little South Africa could do to influence the outcome once it became clear in September of 1974 that the Portuguese military in the colony, under the leadership of Admiral Vítor Crespo, would tolerate no interference with the smooth transfer of authority to FRELIMO. An independent Mozambique, moreover, even if ruled by a Marxist government, would be extremely vulnerable to South Africa and economically dependent on the good will of Pretoria.

Mozambique and South Africa were bound together by a mutual dependency. Much of Mozambique's foreign earnings depended on the use of its port and rail facilities by South Africans and the earnings of Mozambique workers in the South African gold mines. In 1975 South Africa relied on Mozambique for more than 25 percent of its mining labor force and needed the energy that would come from the Cabora Bassa dam. South Africa's own ports were overcongested. The South African government also hoped that good relations with FRELIMO would discourage any aid to guerrillas in Zululand and the eastern Transvaal. In Angola, by contrast, South Africa could exert very little economic leverage over any nationalist government in Luanda and, because of Namibia, South Africa was vulnerable where its own position was weakest. The temptation to interfere militarily was thus very great, and on the surface seemed to be relatively risk-free, given the divisions between the nationalist movements in Angola and South Africa's own logistical advantages.

The South African response to developments in Angola had thus to rely more on military capabilities than economic suasion. The defense posture that South Africa's military strategists had adopted during the 1970s set important conditions to South African options in Angola. While Dr. Vorster, the South African prime minister, had been talking of *détente* with neighboring black nations, he had also been rapidly building up the South African defense forces. South African military strategists, meanwhile, increasingly evoked the Israeli precedent of swift preemptive action, a doctrine that in the South African context was called "hot pursuit." Ironically, "hot pursuit" was first used against Kenneth Kaunda of Zambia in 1971 as a result of clashes in the Caprivi strip, when Botha, the South African defense minister, threatened to "hit him so hard he will never forget." The doctrine of "hot pursuit" was used to justify the first armed South African incursions into Angola in the summer of 1975. The "defense" of the Cunene Dam complex on Namibia's border was used to justify the first permanent installation of South African regular forces inside Angola in early August 1975. The deteriorating situation in Angola was also of concern to Zaire and Zambia. The closure of the Benguela railway over the summer of 1975 as a result of hostilities in Angola could not have come at a worse time for both countries. Each was in deep political and economic trouble – mainly, though by no means exclusively, as a result of the dramatic drop in world copper prices. Zaire, with an external debt of some $600 million, faced a chronic debt service problem and began, in July 1975, to fall behind in obligations to its international bankers.[15] Its foreign exchange reserves were sufficient for only about three weeks' imports. For Zambia, the economic problems were no less acute. The decline in copper prices had made the industry totally unprofitable, since the cost of production surpassed the market return. The result was to reduce the country's foreign earnings to nil. The social impact was very serious indeed. Copper exports had sustained an exceptionally high level of trade. In addition, 40 percent of direct government revenues came from the mining sector, and a large part of the food supply was imported from outside the country. It was these complex interrelationships in the region that made the escalating conflicts in Angola so dangerous. But it was the Zaire connection which entrapped the United States in the Angolan crisis and revived the old plan that General Spínola and President Mobutu had concocted the previous September.

In Zaire the United States' special sensitivity to President Mobutu's desires and his effectiveness in promoting them had five causes. First, through late 1974 and 1975, a result of Zaire's economic crisis was to give the viewpoints of the international financial community, especially in the United States, France, and Belgium,[16] unusual weight where Zairian affairs were concerned. Second, Mobutu used his very influential private lines of communication with Washington to circumvent and neutralize the less partisan and self-interested assessments made by many experienced African specialists in the US government.[17] Third, by the end of the summer of 1974, Mobutu had already pre-empted the west's strategy by providing the FNLA with privileged access to sources of western support. This was an inevitable consequence of acting in Angola through Zaire. Over the years, the FNLA had become little more than an extension of Mobutu's own armed forces, and Holden Roberto was a man linked to Mobutu by marriage and obligated to him for many past favors.

Fourth, Zaire played a key role in the overall structures within which the Nixon administration sought to organize its inter-national relationships. Recognition of the limits to the United States' power and ability to engage herself worldwide was the original rationale underlying the Nixon Doctrine – in effect, a policy of selective involvement in building up friendly states in important regions.[18] The fifth reason for the success of Mobutu's schemes was that, despite the fact that Zaire had been accorded a prime place in US relationships with Africa during the 1970s, top policymakers in Washington remained largely ignorant about what was happening there.[19] The reason for this ignorance had much to do with the personal style of the most influential US policymaker of the period, Henry Kissinger. The problem in the summer of 1975 was not that Kissinger gave Zaire and Angola too much attention, but that he gave them too little. He held Africa, Africans, and African specialists in low esteem, and they had been frequent butts for his jokes and humiliations. Moreover, between 1974 and 1976, there were four different assistant secretaries of state for African affairs, and two of them were forced out within less than a year for warning Kissinger that he was creating a debacle in Africa. Portuguese Africa, moreover, had been something of a Nixon specialty. The Spínola-Mobutu decolonization plan, in fact, had its roots in the Nixon-Spínola summit held on June 19, 1974, in the Azores, when Spínola had painted an extraordinary picture for Nixon of communist subversion in Europe and Africa.[20] But Nixon was out of office within two months, and Spínola only survived in his until the end of September. It should have been obvious that there was a debilitating weakness in an enterprise that had inherited its rationale from a dead colonialism, that sought to exercise power through informal influence over tenuously controlled clients, and where European predecessors who had possessed the formidable advantages of long local experience and formal sovereignty had just failed.

One major result of these circumstances was that, when top US policymakers eventually began taking a serious direct interest in what was happening in Central Africa, it was largely as a result of the direct and serious measures the Soviet Union was taking to counteract the all too obvious attempts by Zaire to exclude the MPLA and Neto from the fruits of the victory which they, with Soviet encouragement, had fought for twenty years to achieve.[21] But, by then, the United States was already trapped in a framework of alliances, assumptions, and barely comprehended past failures from which it was difficult to escape. The salience given in Washington to the MPLA's communist support served to conceal the fact that the roots of escalation lay in actions in which the United States had been directly and indirectly involved through her Zairian client.[22] The African dimension became almost irrelevant in the process.

CHAPTER 7

Counter-revolution

I'm telling you the elections have nothing to do with the
dynamics of a revolution ... I promise you there will be
no parliament in Portugal.   Alvaro Cunhal (June 1975)

... it was the election that turned the situation around.
Frank C. Carlucci, US ambassador to Portugal (1975–77)
Congressional hearing (1976)

Words like *revolution, agrarian reform, popular power, nationalization,*
and *praetorian power,* etc., have of course a great mobilizing
power and a value and political implication which I do not
minimize; but alone, they are not enough to deal adequately
with real situations.   Mário Soares (June 1975)

Friend Boss: The people are with you. Out with the Union
Committee. Death to the communists.
Anticommunist demonstration invading the offices of Têxtil
Manuel Gonçalves, Famalicão (August 1975)

I

As the situation in Angola deteriorated and the superpowers
began to maneuver ominously but clandestinely in the interests
of their African clients, international attention remained fixed on
the struggles in Lisbon. Between March and November 1975 the
fate of the revolution was settled and despite the left's apparently
formidable assets in March 1975 – control of the administration,
unions, army, the media, and political initiative – by the end of
November the left was disunited, weakened, on the defensive,
with its power broken. Why?
The answer lies in four aspects of those turbulent months.

First, the all-important alliance between the revolutionary left and the military radicals failed. The MFA leadership itself split into various factions, all ostensibly "on the left," but each with a different view of tactics and objectives. Simultaneously, discipline within the military collapsed, and it did so more quickly among the leftist units than among the centrist or rightist units. Secondly, the economic situation in Portugal became increasingly precarious and this allowed outsiders leverage which they had lacked before. Over the summer of 1975 western governments made it very clear to Lisbon that economic assistance would be dependent on political good behavior. Third, the communists made several major blunders. They misread the balance of forces in Portugal and hence the power of their enemies. They misunderstood the psychological impact of some of their actions, throwing potential allies into the embrace of their opponents, and they grossly overestimated the support they could count on from the Soviet Union. Finally, and perhaps most significant of all, the would-be victims of the revolution, most especially the small-holding peasants of the north, rose up to oppose the whole drift of events in Lisbon.

The atmosphere in Portugal, however, was permeated with a dangerous sense of unreality that lasted well through the late summer of 1975. There was a widening divorce between the highly ideological debate at the center and the heightened tensions in society at large. And, as the linkages among the central authorities were undermined, a type of popular power emerged at the local level to replace them. This, in turn, accentuated regional polarization and hardened political positions. Since popular power and the rule of local vigilantes could as easily be of the right as of the left, the resulting volatile situation had a much more immediate impact on the development of Portugal than the protracted debates in the Constituent Assembly on the new constitution, or among the officers of the MFA as to which of the many roads to socialism should be followed. The far left and the far right were the first to realize this and their activities over the summer and fall of 1975 took on an importance out of all proportion to their numbers or their real support in the country. Both the political parties and the more traditional military officers sensed the threat to them from the increasingly agitated grassroots activities. This concern also spread to the

Communist Party which deeply distrusted spontaneity and which had based its strategy in classic Leninist style on the seizure or subversion of the existing institutional structures.

The struggle in Portugal had by now also become a major concern for both the right and the left throughout Europe and was a worry high on the agenda of policymakers in Washington. The issues that most caught foreign attention were freedom of the press and freedom of religious expression. The first case focused on the old opposition newspaper, *República*; the second on the Catholic radio station, Rádio Renascença. Both were seized in late spring 1975 by radical workers' committees strongly influenced by the far left and with the acquiescence of the communists. Each case served to point up sensitive concerns, especially in France, that lay very close to the surface of uneasy alliances between social democrats and communists. The Portuguese socialists were, of all the political groups, the one most keenly attuned to west European politics, especially those in France where Mário Soares had spent the late 1960s and early 1970s as a university teacher and knew how best to exploit these foreign concerns in his own interests.

The comparisons, in fact, were decidedly forced. In France and Italy, the communists and socialists were in opposition and functioning within long-established parliamentary regimes. In Portugal, at the time the disputes erupted, communists and socialists were members of a coalition government during a transitional period both described as "parademocratic." The Portuguese communists and the socialists were each emerging from long years of clandestine activity. Neither had experience of political discourse within an open society. And the two most divisive *causes célèbres* over *República* and Rádio Renascença, both involving questions of press freedom, occurred as a bitter power struggle was in progress between them, not only at local and national levels for the control of unions, municipalities, and the communications media, but within the military itself.[1]

Yet, even though the speed of events was now moving well beyond the Communist Party's desires, the behavior of the Portuguese communists undoubtedly alarmed their co-religionists in the rest of Western Europe, especially in France, Spain and Italy. Again, the example of the 1973 overthrow of the Popular Unity Government of Salvador Allende in Chile was relevant. In June

1972 the French Communist Party had joined with the socialists in a common program which resembled the strategy that had ended in disaster in Chile. The Italian communists had gone even further, having opted for "a parliamentary road to social-ism." Major nonruling communist movements in Europe were also in the process of reassessing their relationship with the Communist Party of the Soviet Union. Both the French and the Italian communists thus had much to lose from the Leninist tactics adopted by the PCP; their differing responses to develop-ments in Portugal in the summer of 1975 led to a public quarrel between them. The French refused to condemn the PCP. The Italians publicly criticized the Portuguese communists for what they saw as their tendency to analyze events from a third-world perspective and for allying themselves too closely to the MFA. Later on, the French allowed themselves a retrospective comment about the PCP's sense of perspective when Jacques Fremontier remarked that "the African or third-world illusion" had done much "to cause the Portuguese Revolution to go off the rails."[2] The Italian Communist Party had also been insistent from the beginning that collaboration between communists and socialists was essential in Portugal. Unlike Georges Marchais, general secretary of the PCF (Parti Communiste Français), who visited Portugal in November 1974, and reiterated his support for the PCP, the Italians sent Ugo Pecchioli of the PCI's (Partito Com-munista Italiano) secretariat, who went out of his way to meet representatives of the other parties, and the Portuguese Socialist Party in particular, as did Santiago Carrillo.[3]

Foreign perceptions about what was happening in Portugal were nevertheless important. Outside assistance and money were welcomed by all Portuguese groups. After half a century during which Portugal had seemed largely irrelevant to the outside world, suddenly the most convoluted dispute of that nation's smallest political faction became a weighty matter of absorbing interest to Paris, London, and New York. João Abel Manta who had become something of the MFA's official artist summed up the situation well when he drew a poster for the Fifth Division's "cultural dynamization" campaign which showed a crowd of eager observers from the past including Karl Marx and Bertrand Russell, pencils in hand, eagerly staring at a map of Portugal drawn on a blackboard. It did not matter that this interest had as much to do with the political and economic situation elsewhere in Europe as with developments in Portugal.[4]

Portugal's preeminence rested in the belief that it had become a mirror held up at a most embarrassing moment in which Europe could see itself. Ideologists of both the left and right saw what they wanted to see. Reality most of the time was obscure, not least to the political and military leaders in Lisbon, suddenly thrust into the international limelight. Few luminaries, even Jean-Paul Sartre, could resist the chance to go see for themselves. In the chaotic spring and summer of 1975, the leftist intellectuals who then almost totally dominated the Portuguese daily press, radio, and television were also carried away with their own enthusiasm for and wishful thinking about the revolutionary potential of Portugal's situation. A consequence of this media consensus was that the left misread the popular mood, compromising their own cause in the process by preventing a rational assessment of the left's strengths and weaknesses. As the foreign press corps that descended on Lisbon did not wander far from the Tivoli hotel, their telex machines located in the building above Maxim's night club in the Praça da Alegria, or the Pastelaria Suíça in the Rossio, all in the heart of the city, the journalists also believed revolution was in the offing.

Both the left and the right initially underestimated the radicalism of the MFA and then, paradoxically, placed too much hope on its staying power once the revolution had moved from euphoric celebration to acrimony and factionalism. It would have been particularly surprising, however, if Alvaro Cunhal had ignored the possibility of the MFA's renewed concern for hierarchy and discipline once its own position was threatened by incipient rebellion in the ranks. The communists, therefore, despite temporary tactical alliances, first with General Spínola and then with the MFA, also made sure that their militants or sympathizers were placed in key roles within the military. But this power grab only served to split the military left and forced many non-communist military radicals into alliances with moderate officers.

Cunhal made the mistake of thinking that power could be achieved by the seizure of institutional structures and that such structures, inherited from the corporative quasi-fascist dictatorship, were transferable in the fluid situation that followed the April 1974 coup. He, along with many of the political leaders returning from exile, seriously underestimated the degree to which the authority of institutions had collapsed in the immediate aftermath of the coup. The communists were uncomfortable in the face of spontaneous action by the workers, and acted more often than not to curb such action when it occurred. It turned out, in fact, that the communists, by being associated with institutional structures and by attempting in many cases to prop them up, were badly mauled in the process. Between March and November 1975 the PCP behaved and talked very much like the dictatorial regime overthrown in 1974, and to do so was a critical error with a people emerging from fifty years of dictatorship.

Since the PCP had positioned itself disadvantageously, the political initiative was often taken by the radical left, a complex and often bitterly divided collection of small groups that included several Marxist–Leninist parties, Maoist, revolutionary leftists in all but name, and advocates of popular power. These groups, marginal to the political process in most European situations, became highly significant in Portugal, often because they tended to reflect what was happening at local or neighborhood levels, especially in the larger urban centers, better than the more formal and traditional political parties.

The tactical problems facing the PCP leadership in the spring and summer of 1975 were considerable, to be sure. They did confront a new situation after March, one which to every appearance had "revolutionary potential." Their policies had until that moment been based on defeating the great landowners and the monopolists. But by mid 1975 both of these enemies had been put to flight. In the Alentejo some 1.2 million hectares had been expropriated, often on the initiative of the workers themselves, sometimes by default, as workers carried on in the place of absentee owners. In any event, land seizures occurred on a massive scale and with minimal resistance. The nationalizations of industry likewise took place with ease, and again the PCP followed as much as initiated these moves. Now, with the power of the monopolies and *latifundiários* destroyed, the editors of Cunhal's 1974 book *For a Democratic and National Revolution*, when revising the work in July 1975, suggested that "the present historical stage of the revolution seems to be more correctly defined as a superior stage [than the title of Cunhal's book implied], that of socialist revolution."[5]

The difficulty with this "new stage" was that it inevitably showed up the ambivalent attitude of the communists toward their would-be allies, the small and medium-sized farmers of the center and north of Portugal and the small shopkeepers and property owners in the towns. Indeed, Cunhal had already made it clear that "the allies of the proletariat for the socialist revolution are not the same as those for the democratic and national revolution. In the first, the proletariat carried out the fundamental attack on the monopolies and *latifundiários* allied with part of the bourgeoisie, the *petite bourgeoisie*, and parts of the middle class interested in the antimonopolistic fight." "The socialist revolution," he continued, "is directed against the bourgeoisie in its totality and, for this reason, some of the allies of the proletariat in the first stage, sectors of the urban middle class, sectors of the rural peasantry, and some elements of the *petite bourgeoisie*, cease to be allies during the socialist revolution."[6] Cunhal was nothing if not blunt.

II

Nevertheless, because of the lack of reality permeating the political leadership and newspapers in Lisbon, it came as a considerable surprise to most observers in Lisbon and overseas when the intensely traditionalist Catholic, small landowning majority in the north and center of Portugal rose up and chased the communists out of much of the northern rural areas and small towns, ultimately creating a situation which forced the radical military back into their barracks. The *petite bourgeoisie*, as Cunhal defined the small proprietors of the towns and countryside, proved more resilient than the great family cartels and the large landowners of the south. The inevitability of history was not something that impressed them once they saw the threat to their livelihoods which the government in Lisbon appeared to promote and encourage.

As the land seizures continued in the south, a strong reaction was developing in the north and center of Portugal where land ownership was widespread, and many industrial workers owned land or had access to small plots. The landless rural workers in the Alentejo had been quickly organized by the communists (and other leftist groups) into collective and cooperative farms throughout the region, thus preventing the breakup of old estates.

But in north and central Portugal the landowners, most of them proprietors of small and medium-sized farms, were also mobilizing into the newly established Portuguese Confederation of Farmers (CAP). Small businessmen were likewise joining the Portuguese Confederation of Industrialists (CIP) in droves. The Catholic church was becoming increasingly outspoken and priests in countless villages throughout the interior were ending their sermons with the prayer: "God save us from the communists," to which their anxious congregations responded with fervent "Amens." Much of the MFA's "cultural dynamization" activity had been directed at the regions the Fifth Division considered dominated by superstition and local bosses. The activities of the propaganda teams, however, were totally counter-productive. Far from winning over the devout peasants, the military dynamizers had irreversibly alienated them. "Their field officers," Jane Kramer wrote, "were extremely young, extremely undereducated, and often extremely stupid, and their crash conversions to a few dimly comprehended slogans had turned them into zealots. Once out of Lisbon, they went their own way, convinced that proper thoughts inevitably produce a better life, and writing off as counter-revolutionary propaganda any suggestion that a sack of fertilizer delivered to the right person might make more converts than a sack of pamphlets."[7]

The disenchantment with the MFA opened up avenues for outside involvement, both by the disappropriated factory owners who had initially fled the country or had been purged, by the immigrant communities overseas, where many were opposed to the rise of the left in Portugal and were nostalgic for the old regime, and, no less importantly, by the church. In New Jersey and Massachusetts, action groups within the Portuguese communities soon linked up with anticommunist elements at home and the representatives of the MFA who visited were met with increasing hostility. Violent clashes broke out between union organizers and workers, who feared losing their employment and wanted to see the old bosses return, at several northern textile mills where credit had been cut at the instigation of the former owners, most notably at the Manuel Gonçalves factory in Vila Nova de Famalicão.[8]

As the spring and summer of 1975 wore on and the struggle between the socialists and the communists intensified, the radical left began to gain adherents among the military, most notably the commander of the MFA's main security force, Otelo Saraiva de Carvalho. These groups were, of course, as opposed to the communists as to anyone else. The radical left saw the Portuguese Communist Party as a group of "social fascism," by which they meant that they were the instruments of fascism hiding behind a socialist façade.

The failure to perceive the split that was occurring between the attitude of the radical political and military leaders in Lisbon and the mood of the country was aggravated by the peculiar way in which the African situation and the collapse of the economy affected the chronology of the revolution. The pressures emanating from Africa were undoubtedly the most important in the short run, but economic issues dominated the revolution's second stage, which began as disengagement from Africa was completed. The fact that the economic crisis was postponed for so long resulted from Salazar's last gift to Portugal: the large gold and foreign-currency reserves he had so avidly accumulated. These reserves, which stood at $2.8 billion at the end of 1973 ($1.2 billion in gold), provided a cushion that helped the revolution postpone the consequences of its actions. At least they allowed a series of far-reaching and radical transformations to be promulgated without much apparent pain to the population at large. In the first year after the coup, in fact, workers' real purchasing power increased dramatically, stimulating a sharp rise in sales of consumer goods.[9]

The reserves helped to obscure the fact that the reforms and transformations would, in time, have to be paid for, and paid for not merely by the revolution's immediate victims – conservative military officers, expropriated landowners, great industrialists, and banking magnates. High degrees of sacrifice, austerity, and disciplined collective action were unavoidable if a socialist revolution was to be made to work. Whether the Portuguese people, or a sufficiently large number of them, would be prepared for that route was a question that had been avoided. By the spring of 1975 it was apparent that the reserves could no longer provide the luxury of a revolution without tears and that Portugal had a major economic crisis in the making. With huge and accumulating trade and balance-of-payments deficits, Portugal became vulnerable to foreign pressure and increasingly dependent on foreign aid, giving back to the western powers – West Germany and the United States in particular – the initiative they had lost in April 1974.

The speed with which the economic crisis grew had as much to do with the chronic problems and imbalances in the Portuguese economy as it did with the failures of revolutionary leadership, grave as they were. The failures aggravated the crisis, but they did not cause it.

It was no accident that the electrical and component assembly plants and garment factories were the sites of the most bitter labor disputes after the 1974 coup. Long and acrimonious strikes occurred at the Timex and ITT plants in particular. Nor was it surprising, given the working conditions, that grassroots workers' movements erupted in the garment industry, where the first workers' takeovers occurred in Swedish-owned plants late in 1974. This development had dangerous implications for the general employment situation, because once free collective bargaining became a possibility, much of the attraction of Portugal for these particular industries vanished. Profit margins were bound to deteriorate under a more democratic system that allowed workers' organizations. Since most of the factories concerned were dependent on imported materials and were part of a chain of assembly plants spread throughout several different countries, the temptation to strip assets was very great. Those who moved did so quickly. In the garment industry, which was more often under individual ownership, many entrepreneurs simply packed their bags and went home. They were in Portugal, after all, to make money, not to finance a social revolution. But they left behind a fledgling workers' movement, since those employed had nowhere else to go and sought as well as they could to carry on. And when the question of credit arose, this in turn led to pressure for the nationalization of the banks.[10]

But as if these problems were not enough, the great show projects of the Caetano regime, which had seemed so logical when initiated during the euphoric 1960s, were singularly inappropriate for the 1970s. Portugal had based her most modern sector almost exclusively on oil. The great Lisnave dry dock facilities built by the Portuguese monopoly CUF in association with two Swedish and two Dutch shipyards were predicated on an expanding and prosperous tanker business. But after the 1973

Yom Kippur War and the world recession that came in its wake, the world's tanker capacity increased by a quarter while world trade in oil decreased by over 10 percent. The complex at Sines was based on refining and petrochemicals and the expansion of motor vehicle assembly plants. The western economic crisis made none of these projects particularly viable; nor could revolutionary Portugal well afford them. But the groundwork had been laid, and it was too late to turn back.

Thus, there was a serious maladjustment in the Portuguese economy that the revolution could only exacerbate. And beneath the economic troubles lay much social tinder to be ignited when Caetano fell, and with him the whole apparatus of a highly repressive state. Individually the problems were serious enough; cumulatively they were disastrous. Uncertainty and violence led to the collapse of tourism. Tourists are fickle creatures, not encouraged by militants marching through city streets. Only 2.6 million tourists entered Portugal in 1975, representing declines of 25 percent and 50 percent respectively, from the 1974 and 1973 totals. The falloff in tourist expenditures was probably much greater. Portuguese tourism had been oriented toward the luxury trade, but the "tourists" the new Portugal attracted more often than not stayed at camps organized by the PCP and leftist factions for youthful revolutionary groupies. Thus, as the revolution was radicalized, the tourist boom deflated. And with it construction ended.

The collapse of the authority structure had another serious economic consequence. Since there was almost no public housing and most Portuguese lived without the most basic facilities, takeovers of empty houses had begun almost as soon as Caetano had been overthrown. A vicious circle resulted. The new Portugal needed the money and good will of its overseas workers, but the occupation of "vacant" properties, many of them owned by emigrants, soon alienated them from the regime since many emigrants lost both their savings and their hopes for the future. Very soon, emigrants became a major source of financing for the clandestine right-wing opposition.

The old textile industry, which employed some 120,000 people in 1974, was highly dependent on the African colonies, and with decolonization, lost its source of raw materials and its markets. Growing unemployment first hit women, whose earnings, small as they were, had been a vital element in increasing the small internal market. The contraction of purchasing power in turn helped to create more unemployment. Government measures that prohibited the dismissal of workers drove many firms into bankruptcy and led to escalating demands for credit from the nationalized banks. The demobilization of the armed forces added more men to the rolls of the jobless. Portugal entered the winter of 1975 with some 400,000 unemployed, only 19,000 of whom received any form of social security. And on top of these were some 500,000 Angolan returnees, destitute for the most part, their money worthless.

Portugal, it seemed, was doomed to face the worst of all possible worlds at the worst of all possible times. It was a sober background against which to implement a democratic revolution. Nonetheless, it was a background that over many months the squabbling political and military leaders in Lisbon studiously ignored. The desperate state of the economy as much as anything else provided the leverage to bring down the government of Vasco Gonçalves.

III

If international press attention was focused on revolutionary Portugal, the international intelligence agencies were already becoming preoccupied with Angola, though this crisis received virtually no public attention at the time. The crisis was driven by the timetable for independence which was set for November 11, 1975. All sides were aware of the importance of establishing their own favorites in Luanda prior to that date. US policy in Portugal was now driven by the incidence of Soviet and Cuban support for the MPLA. As Helmut Sonnenfeldt, counselor in the State Department and Kissinger's closest advisor on Soviet affairs, later explained, the United States "had no intrinsic interest in Angola as such." But, "once a locale, no matter how remote and unimportant for us, becomes a focal point for Soviet, and in this instance, Soviet-supported Cuban military action, the United States acquires a derivative interest which we simply cannot avoid."[11]

Preoccupation with Soviet intentions overwhelmed the recommendations that were pouring into Washington from, among others, the US consul in Luanda, an interagency task force, two assistant secretaries of state for African affairs, and from such respected African specialists as John Marcum and Gerald Bender, and from US Senator Dick Clark. All of them argued that unless the United States pursued a broad-based political strategy aimed at conciliating the factions in Angola, instead of attempting to favor one side at the expense of others, the United States was doomed to face escalating demands in Angola with no certainty of success – doomed, indeed, to help create a situation where the resolution of the conflict would come through military means, with the United States unprepared and incapable of acting to aid the very forces it had egged into conflict. At no time, until too late, did the United States give any serious thought to what a purely military solution to the Angolan crisis would involve, so great was the belief that the old and trusted formula of secrecy, mercenaries, and cash would work as they had in the past. By the time it became obvious that this was not enough, the only alternative power with the capacity and desire to intervene was South Africa. At a stroke, South African intervention undermined the western groups' credibility in African opinion, overwhelmed the doubts that many African states (Nigeria in particular) had about the MPLA and its friends, and made large-scale Soviet and Cuban assistance to Neto the lesser evil.

The Soviets had their own special reasons for being sensitive to the role of Zaire in the Angolan crises. Zaire had been the scene of Soviet humiliation during the early 1960s. It had been precisely because of unhappy Soviet experiences in places like the former Belgian Congo that the Soviet Union embarked on a major buildup in long-distance support capacity. The Soviets, who had only been able to provide Patrice Lumumba in the Belgian Congo with sixteen transport planes and a few trucks in 1960, were able, in 1975, to provide Agostinho Neto with $200 million in military assistance by sea and air, to establish an air bridge with some forty-six flights of Soviet medium and heavy air transports, and to airlift in Soviet IL-62s a sizable part of the 11,000 Cuban combat troops sent into Angola during this period.[12]

In 1975, direct Soviet aid to the MPLA began in the form of arms deliveries by sea and air via Brazzaville. In March, Russian cargo planes began delivering military equipment, which was later transshipped to Cabinda or Luanda; in April, some hundred tons of arms were delivered in chartered Bristol Britannias, from Dar es Salaam to MPLA-controlled airfields in central Angola. In April, Paulo Jorge of the MPLA visited Cuba in search of specialists to assist with the sophisticated equipment now arriving from the Soviet Union and Eastern Europe, which the MPLA's own forces were not yet trained to handle.[13]

Cuban military men knowledgeable enough to use sophisticated equipment were beginning to take part in combat operations by the late spring of 1975. In July, the MPLA approached the Soviets for a Soviet troop presence in addition to military training experts. The Soviets balked at the suggestion as being too provocative and advised the MPLA to seek such assistance from Cuba. In early August, an MPLA mission visited Havana to urge Castro to supply them with troops. In mid August Castro authorized the logistical planning necessary to mount the sea- and airlift of troops, equipment, and supplies across the Atlantic to Angola. The operation was a complex one, involving the simultaneous arrival in Angola of troops from Cuba and armaments from the USSR.

On July 18, the United States decided to step up support to the anti-MPLA forces. The United States interagency policy group that advised the president on covert action, known as the "40 Committee," and to which the CIA was responsible, authorized $14 million in covert assistance to be paid in two installments to the FNLA and UNITA (a sum increased to $25 million in August and $32 million in November). A week before, on July 14, the MPLA expelled its rival from Luanda. By taking the offensive, it had by October seized control of twelve of the sixteen district capitals of Angola. South Africa's support for the FNLA seems to have begun in July and its support for UNITA in September. In mid August two Zairian paratrooper companies joined the action in support of the FNLA. Three Cuban merchant ships left Cuba for Angola in early September after urgent appeals from the MPLA, which now feared a large-scale South African invasion augmented by US assistance, via Zaire, to the FNLA and UNITA. The Soviets had abandoned the idea of a political coalition in March; they were now portraying the FNLA and UNITA in their propaganda as "splinterists" and describing the war in Angola not as a "civil war" but as a "war of intervention."

Unfortunately for Angola, the war was both a civil war and a war in which outside intervention occurred on a massive scale. The Chinese, looking on from their vantage point in Zaire, decided to cut their losses. On October 27, 1975, they withdrew all their military instructors from the FNLA.

By November, the Portuguese army in Angola was a helpless bystander. The last official Portuguese representative, Commander Leonel Cardoso, and his staff scuttled quietly away from Luanda the day before independence. In fact, at the moment independence was declared in Luanda, the MPLA held little more than the capital and a strip of central Angola inland toward Shaba and Cabinda.[14] South African advisers and South African antitank weapons had helped to stop an MPLA advance on Nova Lisboa (Huambo) in early October. Nova Lisboa was the center of UNITA strength and the site of a declaration of an independent state (the "Social Democratic Republic of Angola") by UNITA and the FNLA on November 11. By October, the South Africans had helped turn the tide in the south against the MPLA. A South-African-led combat group with Chipenda's troops, code-named Zulu, with armored cars and mortars, had traveled 400 miles from the Namibian border in two weeks, overwhelming the MPLA and Cubans in Benguela and Lobito, thus seizing control of the terminal of the Benguela railroad. In central Angola, a second South African combat unit, code-named Foxbat, with a squadron of armored cars, had moved 500 miles north toward Luanda and inflicted a severe defeat on the Cubans at Bridge 14 (north of Santo Combo), killing over 200 of them as well as 200 MPLA troops. North of Luanda, the FNLA and Zairian troops had again reached Caxito, within a short drive of the capital.[15]

A big Cuban buildup started on November 7, when 650 combat troops were flown to Angola via Barbados and Guinea-Bissau. On November 27, a Cuban artillery regiment and a battalion of motorized and field troops landed on the Angolan coast after a sea crossing of twenty days. The Soviets had, meanwhile, deployed a naval force in Angolan waters which provided protection to the ships unloading and transshipping arms from Pointe-Noire (Congo) to Angola. Soviet military transports were airlifting reinforcements and arms from late October. The Soviet and Cuban intervention was decisive. It saved the MPLA and their regime, and it profoundly altered the balance of power in Southern Africa.

Henry Kissinger, like the South Africans, was shaken by the scale of the Soviet and Cuban response. The CIA's Angolan task force had been so confident of success by the Zairian and South African regulars that on November 11 the members had celebrated Angolan independence with wine and cheese in their crepe-paper-decorated offices. The arrival of Soviet and Cuban ships and planes at Pointe-Noire and Brazzaville was observed by US intelligence surveillance, but the unloading of troops had taken place at night, and strictly imposed discipline during the sea voyage concealed the presence of troops.[16] Not until November did the CIA realize that 4,000 Cuban combat troops were deployed in Angola, a figure which had grown to 15,000 by January 1976. By February 1976, the combined Soviet–Cuban sea- and airlift had transported 38,000 tons of weapons and supplies to Angola.[17] Although South African foreign policy had consistently played up the communist threat to Africa, it had clearly not given serious attention to the consequences of a strong conventional communist military presence in the form of some 20,000 Cuban troops. Although South Africa lost only forty-three dead in Angola of its over 2,000 troops deployed there, it had by the end of 1976 concluded that, for military and political reasons, it was not in a position to take on a superpower. As a result of press leaks in the fall, the United States was effectively removed from the Angolan competition on December 19, 1975, when overwhelming majorities in both houses of Congress banned covert aid to the FNLA and UNITA. The OAU, in response to the fact that South African intervention had become public knowledge in November, swung from its former neutrality to support of the MPLA as the legitimate government of Angola. South African intervention was especially decisive in the case of Nigeria, the MPLA going so far as to bring a captured South African soldier to Lagos to prove that South African regulars were in fact involved in the Angolan fighting.

CHAPTER 8

The revolution tamed

The classical case of wooing the mother in order to marry
the daughter, and the daughter is Angola.
                    Admiral Rosa Coutinho (November 1975)

Let us put aside for one moment the ideologies which inspire
us and humbly note the fact that whereas nearly all the
people were with our revolution, today we have to recognize
that this is not the case. The march of the Revolution has
gained a pace which the people have not the capacity to
absorb.
            General Costa Gomes to the Armed Forces Movement
                                    Assembly (July 1975)

General Vasco Gonçalves wants us to believe that the
dilemma before us in Portugal is "revolution or counter-
revolution" . . . we refuse this false and simplistic dilemma
[which] deforms Portuguese reality.
                            Mário Soares (August 1975)

I

The scale of outside intervention in Angola remained largely
hidden from public view until December 12, 1975 when a story
by David Binder on the *New York Times* front page revealed the
full extent of US clandestine involvement. Most public attention
over the summer and autumn of 1975 remained focused on
Portugal. The land seizures in the south, and some highly pub-
licized but isolated seizures elsewhere in the country thoroughly
alarmed small landowners and scared them into mutual political
action and collaboration in August 1975. Often encouraged by
local priests, mobs burned and sacked at least forty-nine of
the Communist Party's offices in central and northern Portugal,

virtually expelling the Communist Party from these regions. More ominously, armed civilians blocked the road and rail links between Lisbon and northern Portugal at Rio Maior, making it clear more than once that it was in their power to cut Lisbon off from the whole north and center of the country if they chose to do so. Cunhal, surprised by this unanticipated uprising of small proprietors, was to note a year later that there had been "without doubt deficiencies and errors" in the party's activities over these months, preeminently in "understanding the importance of these classes." He spoke by then from bitter experience.[1]

It was a great irony of the Portuguese experience of these months that those who supposedly based their political analysis on a reading of social and economic conditions totally misread the social dynamic of Portugal. As a consequence, the psychological errors committed by the communists only hastened the polarization of the country along fundamental social and economic lines. The communists also totally misread the international reaction to their actions or the manner in which their equivocations could be used against them. The attack on the newspaper *República*, which the communists may not have initiated, but which they supported, became an international *cause célèbre*, and the attempt to monopolize the mass media proved to be entirely counter-productive for the communists. The attack and takeover of the Catholic church's radio station in Lisbon, where again the communists followed as much as initiated the seizure, also had major negative repercussions, especially among the highly religious peasantry of the north. And as if to confirm the image of Stalinist high-handedness, Cunhal chose precisely this moment to give an interview to Oriana Falacci, the well-known Italian journalist, which soon became notorious throughout Europe. "If you think the Socialist Party with its 40 percent and the Popular Democrats with its 27 percent constitutes the majority," he said, "you're the victim of a misunderstanding. . . . I'm telling you the elections have nothing or very little to do with the dynamics of a revolution. . . . I promise you there will be no parliament in Portugal."[2]

The preemptive agreements forced upon the political parties prior to the 1975 election had demoted any future parliament to a role co-equal with the MFA Assembly. The two assemblies were to be jointly responsible for the indirect election of the president of the republic. With these constraints, and in the face of constant harassment from the far left and the communists, the majority of the members of the constituent assembly (the deputies of the Socialist Party, of the PPD, and the CDS) spent most of their energies in this period defending what civil liberties they could within the overall conditions established by the MFA.

But, above all, the PCP had overestimated the tenacity of its friends and underestimated that of its enemies. In the civilian sphere, the socialists showed a much greater capacity to mobilize, and even to take to the streets, than the communists had anticipated, and Mário Soares proved much tougher than even his closest friends expected. On July 11 the socialists withdrew from the government, followed by the PPD ministers on July 17. On July 13, over 10,000 Catholics demonstrated in Aveiro against the takeover of Rádio Renascença, and on the same day at Rio Maior, 200 angry farmers and Catholics destroyed the headquarters of the Communist Party. It was by now apparent that a formidable popular coalition was forming against the fragmented left.

The communists' alliance with the military radicals was already severely strained. The communists, as Cunhal recognized later, "badly evaluated the situation in the armed forces and were overoptimistic as to the outcome of the internal conflicts within the military."[3] The group associated with the prime minister, Colonel Vasco Gonçalves, became increasingly isolated as the summer wore on, and the military's initiative passed to an MFA faction associated with Major Melo Antunes. Alarmed by the growing estrangement between the country as a whole and Lisbon, Melo Antunes' group increasingly objected to the vanguard role usurped by the Gonçalvists, and believed that a broader base of social support than that provided by the PCP was essential if the MFA was not to be placed in opposition to the majority of the population. Meanwhile, the influence of the extreme left was growing within the command structure of COPCON and in several of the key regiments in the Lisbon area, especially the light artillery and the military police. But the power of these units was undermined by the indiscipline that populism brought with it. COPCON was no more than a coordinating agency, and the growth of political passions in the barracks tended to undermine its effectiveness, so that the troops under its nominal command disaggregated into their component parts. The most radical units tended to become the most chaotic, and a communist attempt to subvert the more disciplined units, especially the commandos, failed miserably when the tough and popular commando colonel won over his troops in the consequent showdown. In fact it was a fourth group in the army, little noticed at the time, which was most active behind the scenes as the summer drew to a close. Known at times as the "operationals," this fourth group was composed of officers who reflected the professional interests of the officer corps, a current of which had been a powerful element in the original captains' movement. A leading figure in this group was Colonel Ramalho Eanes, the future president of Portugal.[4]

There were several factors beyond the PCP's control that help explain the communists' behavior in this critical period. From a rump clandestine organization with most of its leadership living abroad, the party had expanded, by the summer of 1975, to over 100,000 members. Few of these newcomers had received the ideological indoctrination or long experience within party organizations which would have made them a reliable and disciplined force. Many of the rank and file were to the left of the party leadership, and tensions emerged between "new" and "old" communists. The new communists were also, according to Cunhal's own retrospective criticism, highly sectarian, intolerant, and indiscreet. The rapidly moving political situation in Portugal thus caught the PCP in a state of mutation, no longer the sleek clandestine organization it had been, but not yet a mass party, and with a leadership steeped in secrecy and suspicion, distrustful of spontaneity and surprisingly out of touch with the cultural changes which had swept Europe after the 1960s.[5]

A second factor was the important role played by the large and noisy factions of the far left which continued to make their presence felt during these months. Events – as with the nationalization of the banks, the land seizures, and the takeovers of *República* and the Lisbon Catholic radio station – often moved faster under grassroots pressure than the central committee of the PCP might have wished. Cunhal was right in believing that the staying power of the far-left factions was limited and their ideological formation and commitments fragile; yet the PCP was always obliged during this period to treat the criticism of the far left seriously and to counter its impact among industrial workers, students, the military, and rural laborers.

Towards the end of August and during the first week of September, the PCP suffered two serious setbacks. In the civilian sphere, a powerful coalition had formed around Mário Soares and the socialists. While Soares initiated the move to oppose Gonçalves and led his party out of the fourth provisional government in July, his action was soon followed by the PPD. Soares' move was a critical one because it immediately brought solid democratic credibility to the opposition or the "resistance" as the anticommunist movement became known. No one could claim Soares was a "fascist," given his strong anti-Salazarist past and the charge, when levied against him, was hard to sustain. By August, the socialists were providing cover for large and at times violent popular demonstrations against the rump of communists and fellow-travelers appointed by Vasco Gonçalves to the fifth provisional government. No less important in the military sphere, an equally formidable coalition had formed around Melo Antunes and his so-called "Group of Nine." The "Nine" were officers who had all been important members of the MFA from the beginning and included the military commanders in the center and south of Portugal. Thus, unlike the old line generals or even the followers of Spínola, this coalition, like Soares, enjoyed the credibility of having made the original democratic opening possible in the first place. They too could not so easily be dismissed as "fascists." The units in the north, commanded by an officer close to Gonçalves, were refusing to obey him and had placed themselves at the disposition of the central military region.

General Vasco Gonçalves was forced out of office on August 29. The three days before, the "Group of Nine" had closed down the Fifth Division of the General Staff closing off thereby the Gonçalvist's propaganda arm. At a dramatic assembly of the Armed Forces movement at Tancos on September 5, Melo Antunes contested Vasco Gonçalves' attempt to become chief of the general staff and his political line, defeating him decisively. It was to be the last assembly of the MFA. A sixth provisional government was established which brought back the socialists, the popular democrats, and many of the original members of the MFA who, led by Melo Antunes and Captain Vasco Lourenço, had conducted the struggle with Gonçalves over the summer.

But the new situation was a critical one. The crisis had split the MFA wide open. The armed forces themselves had fragmented to such an extent that almost every unit found it necessary to define itself politically.[6]

The specter of civil strife became real. With the removal of Vasco Gonçalves from government power and the gradual purge of communist militants and sympathizers, which began throughout the armed forces, the PCP found itself squarely in opposition to a provisional government for the first time since the coup. Faced with this situation, the communists chose to ally themselves with the radical left. This threat to the new government presented the moderate left with only two alternatives: that of moving against the radical left quickly and seeking to disarm it or run the risk of being overthrown by an armed insurrection in Lisbon. The radical left, for its part, viewed the sixth government as an immediate threat to its own position, and believed that the longer it waited, the more vulnerable it would become. Thus, the radical left had every incentive to act sooner rather than later, especially as the provisional government began at once to establish a loyal elite military intervention force (AMI), threatening thereby to circumvent the remnants of the COPCON command structure under Otelo Saraiva de Carvalho.

The demands which "internationalist" solidarity placed on the Portuguese communists may also explain the behavior of the PCP in this period. As early as August 1975 Cunhal was privately urging caution on the PCP central committee. Yet, in October, he publicly led the PCP into a front with the previously despised far-left factionalists, an action which further alienated many Portuguese and helped consolidate a very broad-based coalition of forces against the communists. The PCP, however, had never hidden its belief that the Soviet Union was, to use Cunhal's word, the "sun" of the communist movement. And it is at least worth noting that, between August and November 1975, the PCP's behavior provided a very convenient smokescreen which did much to cover the beginning of large-scale Soviet and Cuban intervention in Angola as well as the rapid extension of its power among the peasants seizing land in the Alentejo.[7]

The west moved rapidly to shore up the sixth government. The United States and the EC quickly granted Portugal $272 million in emergency aid in early October 1975, following the ousting of Gonçalves. Both Washington and Brussels made it clear that this aid was seen as political support for the moderate socialists who had gained the initiative within the MFA and the government. The United States also pledged on October 14 to double its refugee airlift from Angola. Much clandestine assistance was also deployed on both sides of the Portuguese political divide. Associated Press reported on September 25 that the CIA had sent between $2 million and $10 million per month to the Portuguese socialists since June. The West German social democrats also contributed several million dollars to the Soares party much of it to buy printing presses, pay and train party activists and maintain offices throughout the country. Support from the Soviet Union to the PCP was placed at $45 million since the April coup, although British prime minister Harold Wilson claimed on September 5, 1975 that Moscow had spent $100 million on the PCP. Henry Kissinger had become increasingly vocal in warnings to the Soviet Union over the summer of 1975; and President Ford noted pointedly that despite the Helsinki Accorde signed in July, détente was "not a licence to fish in troubled water".

The most significant, if unexpected, element from the point of view of the communists was the fact that the western powers, and in particular the United States, did not follow the usual Cold War blueprint in the anticommunist struggle. Instead, they reverted in many respects to the strategy employed in the immediate post-World War II period in Italy and France. Here, with the memory of fascism very much on their minds, US leaders threw their overt and clandestine support behind the political parties of the center, be they social democrat or christian democrat. Since, by 1975, there was no serious christian democratic alternative in Portugal, the most obvious parties of the center were the popular democrats and the socialists. Of the two leaders of these parties, Mário Soares possessed the most developed foreign connections, in particular to the ruling German social democrats and the British Labor Party; Sá Carneiro was, in this period, sick in Spain and he had not impressed Washington as a potent leader. The PPD attempts to join the Socialist International had been blocked by Soares.

The west did not support the far right, now arrayed in a clandestine grouping ostensibly behind General Spínola in the

MDLP (the Democratic Movement for the Liberation of Portugal) or the more radical ELP (Army for Portuguese Liberation. These movements committed some terrorist bombings in Portugal in 1975 and had cells organized in Salamanca, Madrid, and Brazil as well as among the Portuguese immigrant communities within the United States and Venezuela. The position in favor of a right-wing military action was most publicly argued by Robert Moss, the editor of the *Economist*'s "Confidential Report", a subscription-only "insiders'" world report that often contained leaks from western intelligence agencies. In "A Ticket to Lisbon: The Civil War" in *Harper's Magazine* (December 1975), he argued that Mário Soares and his party were "bent on the socialization of the means of production, distribution, and exchange." He saw "long odds against a peaceful solution in Portugal," and reported on "many hours" spent in Spain and northern Portugal with the leaders of the underground army that had been preparing for an eventual civil war in Portugal. The Portuguese liberation army (ELP) was aligned with the Salazarist right, according to Moss, and had as its operational chief Barbieri Cardoso, a former deputy chief of PIDE/DGS. The directorate of the MDLP was composed of close supporters of Spínola. With the MDLP, Moss was struck by their commitment to Angola as well as Portugal. The three operational chiefs were Commander Alpoim Galvão, Colonel Dias de Lima, the former head of Spínola's military household, and Colonel Santos e Castro, who headed a mercenary force in Angola fighting with Holden Roberto of the FNLA. Alpoim Galvão had led the Portuguese invasion of Guinea Conakry in 1970. The MDLP claimed to have an armed 1,000-man strike force on hand in Spain whose presence was acquiesced to by the Spanish authorities. Moss complained that this "seems to have been largely ignored by the Agency [CIA] and its sister services in western Europe."[8]

Tenuous relations between the MDLP and right-wing political figures and intelligence officers in both the United States and Brazil certainly existed; but government policy in both countries repudiated them in the end. Here, the role of the American ambassador in Lisbon, Frank Carlucci, and his deputy, Herbert Okun, were critical in steering clear of the far right and in combatting the gloomy and knee-jerk reaction of the powerful secretary of state, Henry Kissinger, who was, at this time, also continuing to serve as national security adviser to President Gerald Ford. Unusual for an American ambassador, Carlucci was able to circumvent Kissinger and get his views directly to the president via the influence of his old Princeton college friend and wrestling mate, Donald Rumsfeld, the White House chief of staff. Thus, the embassy urged Washington to support the middle course and argued that the constituent assembly elections had clearly demonstrated the resonance that such a position enjoyed among the Portuguese people. The alternative which the communists and Moscow may well have anticipated was that the United States and its allies would support a violent armed action against them, which would have surely allowed them to justify their activities under the broad cover of nationalism, as had so often been the case in various third-world countries during the 1950s and 1960s. But, this was denied them; the United States steered clear of Spínola in exile and the Brazilian government did likewise.[9]

No less dangerous was the provocation of Spain. On September 27, in reaction to the execution of five anti-Franco militants by the Spanish authorities, mobs attacked and burnt the Spanish embassy and consulate general in Lisbon and the consulate in Oporto. The Portuguese armed forces and police provided no protection. General Costa Gomes was visiting Poland at the time. In conversation with the Catalan historian Josep Sánchez Cervelló, some years later, he blamed COPCON for the failure of the Portuguese military authorities to act in time. Fortunately no one was hurt, and the government in Madrid behaved with unexpected moderation and caution. Any Spanish military intervention in the Portuguese situation would have been disastrous for both countries, damaging to Spain's post-Franco transition to democracy (Franco died on November 20, 1975) and highly inflammatory in the extremely unstable circumstances in which Portugal found itself at that moment, providing perhaps the only force capable of reuniting the left and the right against the common and traditional enemy of Portuguese independence. In early October, in fact, even the new prime minister, Admiral Pinheiro de Azevedo, was convinced that Spanish troops and tanks were massing on the frontier. They were not, despite the rumors to the contrary encouraged by the Portuguese army's intelligence services. Some retaliatory measures were taken by

Spain, but the assault on the embassy and consulates was seen as an attempt to destabilize the sixth provisional government, and the west did all it could to prevent that from happening.

The center and the democratic right also acted with great skill and restraint during these months, far beyond what the communists might have expected, considering past experience. As far as one can tell, the anticommunist military in Portugal was scrupulous in keeping a distance between themselves and those nostalgic for a return to the old regime. Moreover, on several occasions when large-scale violence might have discredited and split the anticommunist alliance now forming between socialists, noncommunist leftists, moderates in the military, and civilian and church leaders in central and northern Portugal, caution and restraint prevailed.

The most dangerous moment had occurred on November 13, when a large number of construction workers (perhaps 100,000 strong) besieged the constituent assembly and members of the government, including the prime minister, in the parliament building in Lisbon. Ben Pimlott, the English political scientist and author, who was trapped inside the building with the deputies, was told by a journalist that "the Assembly with the Prime Minister's residence attached would be a symbolic Winter Palace as a place to storm." Protracted negotiations between the prime minister and the committee representing the construction workers led to a peaceful resolution of the stand-off, but at the cost of the government's capitulation to the workers' demands. It was obvious to all that the government lacked any authority, not least over the military. Within a week, the government declared itself to be "on strike", and a political solution to the crisis of authority became every day increasingly unlikely. The commandos in fact had wanted to go in and clear the crowd from the square in front of the parliament building. But they were held back by President Costa Gomes, who, despite his own very equivocal behavior during this period, was not prepared to see Portugal plunged into civil war, which any bloodshed at this critical moment might have provoked. The caution and the defensive strategy of the noncommunist military paid off when officerless radical soldiers in the paratroop corps led the "leftist" uprising that provided the excuse for the anticommunist alliance under the command of Colonel Eanes to crush them decisively on November 25, 1975.[10]

Finally, it must be noted that the confused situation in the country allowed for effective action by *agents provocateurs*. Foreign intelligence operatives from the NATO countries were very active in Portugal between June and November 1975. The sudden emergence (and just as sudden disappearance) of a "revolutionary" movement (SUV) within the ranks during this period, for instance, is remarkably similar in its tone and impact to the sergeants' "movement" in Brazil in 1964, which helped precipitate the coup of that year by conservative generals and politicians. In Portugal, as might have been anticipated, this development had a similar sobering effect on the Portuguese officer corps – even the leftists within it. The communist flirtation with the rank and file during the time they were associated with the Revolutionary Front, and growing chaos and indiscipline among soldiers, sailors, and airmen, also helped to cement the officer corps back together again.

In any event, it was the PCP's isolation in the country, together with the isolation of the Gonçalvists within the military, which made possible the formation of a temporary alliance of anticommunist forces after August 1975. During the November 25, 1975 showdown, this alliance delivered the decisive *coup de grâce* to the dream of socialist revolution so avidly espoused a few months before by Alvaro Cunhal and his allies.

II

Throughout the whole period of political turmoil, social upheaval, and military factionalism, the Constituent Assembly was at work. The assembly, reflecting as it did in composition the electoral returns of April 1975, existed for much of its lifetime within a political climate in which history seemed to have passed it by. Key developments, such as decolonization, agrarian reform, and the nationalizations of banks and industries, for instance, all occurred outside the purview of the Constituent Assembly and preempted and circumscribed its powers. Certain broad conditionalities, however, remained from the first phase of democratic aspiration and euphoria immediately following the coup d'état. This period, from April until September 1974, which had seen the emergence of new political parties, also found that a general consensus existed among them as to the type of institutional structure the Portuguese wished to see develop. At this stage, the main new political parties (PS, PPD, CDS) all sought a semipresidential system. In doing so, they were driven by a strong desire to avoid the dual legacy of Portuguese political history of the twentieth century: the experience of a weak and unstable parliamentary system that had arisen from the 1911 constitution, and the memory of an undemocratic, authoritarian, and overly centralized system that had been set up in the 1933 constitution.

This early consensus was shaken by the turn of events in Portugal after September 1974, when an increasing radicalization of the young officers who had made the coup, the aggressive role assumed by the Portuguese Communist Party, and the popular mobilizations in the towns and southern countryside, changed the parameters of the constitutional debate. The result of these developments was to insert a strong tutelary role for the military into the institutional structure and to radicalize the terms of the constitutional discourse. Although remaining semipresidentialist in form, when the text of the 1976 constitution was eventually approved, it contained aspects of a "guided democracy," with a strong, rhetorical Marxist overlay. The 1976 constitution retained the Council of the Revolution, established in the most radical period of the transition; the armed forces remained independent of government control; and restrictive clauses affected the economic life of the country. Moreover, the constitution-writing process itself was constrained by two major pacts between the civilian political parties and the armed forces. These agreements, dated April 13, 1975 and February 26, 1976, marked critical moments in contemporary Portuguese political history. The first established major powers for the Armed Forces Movement; the latter modified these powers but also retained many of the limitations on the ability of future governments to take economic or political measures to modify or undo the socialist aspirations embodied in the constitution. These constraints were very much a product of the historical moment, the fluidity and uncertainty of power, the roles played by various factions in the armed forces, and the generalized desire to avoid a deterioration of a tense situation into violence or even civil war. Nevertheless, the constitutional constraints on political and, above all, economic life were to lead to an excessively legalistic debate over the constitution during the first two decades of the new regime. Throughout the late 1970s, the Marxist aspects of the constitution remained highly contentious issues, capable of provoking demonstrations on the streets and conflicts between military factions and few felt able to challenge them. In this, Portugal's slow process of transition to a fully democratic system of government was very different, for example, from the Spanish constitutional experience, where all parties (with the exception of the Basque separatists) accepted the new Spanish constitution of 1978 and the intra-party negotiations which had led to its formulation were deliberately kept secret, with a collective agreement between the participants, including the communists, to avoid any divisive public debate until the essential agreements were reached.[11]

The Portuguese constitution also reflected the pact made on February 26, 1976, which in turn represented the shift in political forces following the November 25, 1975 defeat of the radicals. The MFA and the political parties drastically revised their earlier agreements and the most significant change was that the election of the president of the republic was to be by universal suffrage and secret ballot. The MFA Assembly disappeared completely from the institutional structure as a result of the February agreement. Yet, the original context within which the constitution-making process of 1975–6 occurred meant that the constitution of 1976 still remained, as the left liked to claim at the time, a "very advanced" document. The constitution explicitly committed Portugal to a "transition to socialism" and a collectivization of the means of production. The nationalization and land expropriations of 1975 were declared to be "irreversible." The MFA retained an important role through the Council of the Revolution which was transformed into an advisory organ of the presidency. In addition, the Council of the Revolution acquired the very significant power to judge the constitutionality of acts by the Assembly of the Republic and constitutional revision was made very difficult – any revisions being precluded before 1981, and then changes being made possible only with a two-thirds vote of the Assembly.

Adding to these confusions, the constitution also contained a built-in diffusion of power incorporating powerful centers of influence with conflicting goals. The Council of the Revolution, a nonelected appointive body, was intended to guarantee the progressive intent of the MFA's action in overthrowing the old regime in 1974. The government, on the other hand, was to be based on the balance of power between the political parties represented in the Assembly, which was elected under a system of proportional representation. The position of the president of the republic, on the other hand, was legitimized by a direct popular vote. The president, moreover, did not necessarily depend on party support, or at least on one party's support. The presidential vote was to be determined by a majority, over two rounds should a majority not be achieved at the first attempt.

As was agreed by the pact of February 1976 the first constitutional president was not a civilian politician. The continuing ascendancy of the armed forces and the military victory of the moderates in November was ratified by the choice of Colonel (by now General) Ramalho Eanes as the first constitutional president, and his candidacy was supported by a broad coalition of political parties, excluding only the communists. In the 1976 presidential election General Eanes, moreover, gained a clear majority, which none of the parties alone could muster, and hence enjoyed considerable autonomy from them. Thus, General Eanes took office in June 1976, standing at the apex of the two major forces – military and civilian – which had achieved victory in the armed confrontation of November 25, 1975 and General Eanes accumulated the powerful positions of elected president of the republic, commander-in-chief of the armed forces, chief of the general staff of the armed forces, and head of the Council of the Revolution.

III

The constitutional regime inaugurated in 1976 also inherited two distinct historical legacies which strongly affected the attitudes of those who had to work within its rules. One legacy came from the reaction against half a century of right-wing dictatorship, but no less important was the legacy which came from the traumatic encounter with the authoritarian left. The politicians, especially the socialists, entered the constitutional regime with as clear a view of the threat to them represented by the communists as they did of the threat from the far right. Thus, as far as the political system was concerned, two processes were at work: a desire to escape the authoritarian tradition of the right, but also the need to overcome the challenge of the authoritarian left. The strength of the Socialist Party leader Mário Soares' popular appeal very much derived from his ability to capitalize on his opposition to both Salazar before the revolution and communism after the revolution. Soares, despite the fact that his domestic political position was weaker than Eanes' in 1976, enjoyed one formidable advantage over the new president. Unlike Eanes, he was a cosmopolitan, as much at ease in Paris as in Lisbon. Even if he had not begun as Kissinger's favorite, he had become indispensable to the American vision of a democratic Portugal. He exemplified the western and European alternatives to the dual legacies of the recent past and was the pivotal Portuguese connection between the civilian democratic forces in Portugal and the political and governmental forces in Western Europe and the United States, some overt, some covert, which had assisted the anticommunist struggle over the previous months.

Yet, this same heritage, while Soares' personal strength, was also a source of weakness for his party. Socialist predominance in the dramatic political struggle of the mid 1970s had rested on an enforced and uneasy compromise between two powerful, antagonistic, and regionally defined social and political movements. The socialists took the lead in the anticommunist counter-offensive in the summer of 1975, but the commitment of many of their supporters to the party's principles was tenuous at best. The socialists, in fact, over the "hot" summer of 1975, were much less scrupulous than the military moderates had been about accepting rightist support and foreign money. Once the balance of power had changed after the November 1975 counter-coup, it was almost inevitable that, in time, many who had supported the socialists in the anticommunist struggle of 1975 would find their way back to more congenial and traditional surroundings. And given the ambiguous outcome of the struggles of 1975, the socialist governments, in particular, found it very difficult to implement measures that threatened the unspoken demarcation upon which a tenuous social peace had been reestablished in late 1975.

Because of the failure in 1976 of any one party to obtain a clear majority, the formation of parliamentary alliances in the new regime was an extremely complicated affair. One possible majority – a coalition on the left between communists and socialists – was completely out of the question. An alliance with the PCP, quite apart from its intrinsic domestic impossibility after the bitter disputes of the revolutionary period, was strenuously opposed by Washington and the West Germans, whose economic support for the floundering economy was increasingly essential. Yet a coalition between the socialists and the right was not easy either. The church and the conservatives had supported the socialists as a bulwark against communism during the crisis months of 1975. Yet both church and conservatives, especially in the north of the country, had been reinvigorated in the process. Moreover, the socialists remained secular republicans, many of them with close links to freemasonry, that old bugaboo of the right and the church, and they supported reform on many social issues such as divorce and abortion which the church and conservatives opposed.

The election for the first democratic parliament, the Assembly of the Republic, on April 25, 1976, confirmed the voting patterns that had emerged in the first free elections a year before, and this further complicated the building of political consensus. The context within which the elections were held had, of course, now totally changed. In April 1975, the radical military leadership closely allied to the PCP was in the ascendancy. In April 1976, the radical left had been deposed and the colonels who had defeated them on November 25 held the reins of power. The army, which in 1975 talked of itself as a "revolutionary vanguard" and a "movement of national liberation," by 1976 praised "hierarchy" and "discipline." Yet, despite this dramatic reversal of circumstances, the Portuguese electorate voted much as they had a year before. The Socialist Party (with 35 percent of the vote) again gained a plurality in 1976 and was thus confirmed as the key element in any political equation. Certainly, no general governmental coalition could function long without them. The parties of the center and the right, the popular democrats (with 24 percent of the vote) and the Democratic and Social Center (with 16 percent), did not gain sufficient support to form a majority of the right. The PCP, (with 12 to 15 percent), would not join a majority coalition with the strongly anticommunist Popular Democrats and Democratic and Social Center against the socialists, although a tactical alliance on individual issues was not impossible.

One possible alternative to a minority socialist government, a coalition to the right with the popular democrats, which would have provided a viable majority in the Assembly, presented major domestic complications. The Popular Democrats were long-time supporters of a liberal capitalist solution to Portugal's economic problems and to join them would risk immediate confrontation with the still potent labor unions and military and the communist-dominated rural areas of the south. Mário Soares and Francisco Sá Carneiro, leader of the PPD (soon to be renamed the Social Democratic Party, PSD), strongly disliked and distrusted each other, not least because Soares enjoyed strong foreign support which Sá Carneiro did not. In the face of these constraints, the socialists decided to go it alone, and the first constitutional government formed under Mário Soares' leadership was a minority government based on the socialist bloc in the Assembly.

The leadership of the new democracy in this critical early period was thus in the hands of two men of very different character and experience. President Eanes, a taciturn military man with no international experience, faced the immediate task of reestablishing military discipline and bringing about an orderly retrenchment and modernization of the armed forces as a whole. Prime Minister Soares, the gregarious lawyer, former exile and cosmopolitan, and the socialist minority government he led, faced a chaotic situation throughout the country, in which the authority of the state had largely broken down or been preempted by powerful regionally based popular movements. Together, the first constitutional president and prime minister, had to make parliamentary democracy work in a country where this had never happened.

The most sensitive area for the new government was how to deal with the rural crisis. Conditions in the countryside remained agitated in the wake of the seizures of large estates by landless workers, although the communists rapidly asserted their control over large sectors of the Alentejo through their rural unions. The system of orderly transport and supply to the cities had largely broken down or been preempted by special deals between rural collectives and industrial workers in the city. The provision of fertilizers, technical assistance, the improvement of crop yields, and funds for the replacement of lost breeding stock were all desperately needed. The provision of basic grain supplies became precarious at times, especially in the south, and Portugal remained a chronic importer of essential foodstuffs. The Alentejo was Portugal's breadbasket but the socialist government did not want to provide unconditional support to these areas which remained under the effective control of the communist collectives. The small landowners in the center and north of the country, meanwhile, had to be assured that the new government was strong enough to prevent more seizures of land. These small and medium proprietors had formed the backbone of the anticommunist riots in the summer of 1975.

The industrial sector was also in crisis. Based on oil, petrochemicals, and motor-vehicle assembly plants (with US, West European, and Japanese ownership), the economic viability of Portugal's industries was buffeted by the inflation in oil prices after 1973 and the changed social conditions in Portugal after 1974. The industrial expansion of the 1960s had been predicated on cheap energy. After 1974 Portugal's balance of payments deficits reached huge proportions, drawn by increased oil prices and exploding consumer demand arising from a steep rise in disposable income. By 1976, the Portuguese government was faced with the necessity of emergency recourse to foreign, especially United States, assistance. In return for IMF support, the socialists had to implement stringent austerity measures and Portuguese economic policy came increasingly under strict international supervision. The Portuguese socialists found themselves in the invidious position of being the political favorites of the very international political and economic interests that insisted on policies which threatened to undermine the socialists' political base. The socialists paid a heavy price in popular support for the economic measures they were compelled to patronize. Yet, ironically, at the same time that the socialists were obliged to pursue policies that could only weaken their popular support, they remained sufficiently of the left to be very wary of totally abandoning the nationalizations and social policies which a clear embrace of a market-oriented economic agenda would have implied.

The socialist minority government sought parliamentary support for its legislation from both the left and right. But, in 1978, outside economic pressures became so onerous that the socialists' attempt to go it alone collapsed when the socialist's IMF-inspired austerity package failed to obtain sufficient support in the assembly. Mário Soares managed to cobble together a second constitutional government, based on a shaky parliamentary coalition with the CDS led by Freitas do Amaral, but this too soon fell apart over the question of land reform. Since the CDS's key supporters were located in some of the most conservative and Catholic segments of the population of the north, they tended to view the socialists' measures as too modest and were hesitant to help. President Eanes, facing this parliamentary impasse and claiming that it was impossible to form a new government based on the political parties alone, dismissed Soares and attempted to install a "presidential" government led by a technocrat. But the Assembly was no more amenable to presidential directive than it had been to the socialist minority government, and after two failures in this effort to establish presidential governing, General Eanes was forced to install a caretaker government under Portugal's first woman prime minister, Maria de Lourdes Pintasilgo, and to call a general election for December 2, 1979.

In order to fight this election, the leader of the Social Democratic Party, Francisco Sá Carneiro, formed a coalition with the CDS and the small Popular Monarchist Party (PPM), which he called the "Democratic Alliance" (AD). The AD was also joined by several former socialist ministers, the self-styled "reformers," who had quarrelled with Mário Soares. The 1979 election results gave a small parliamentary majority to this newly formed coalition alliance.

The socialists, who had received 37.9 percent of the votes in 1975 and 35.0 percent in 1976, could now muster only 24.6 percent and were the major losers in 1979. In the municipal elections, held on December 16 of the same year, the socialist defeat was even greater. The party lost control of Portugal's two principal cities, Lisbon and Oporto. The communists, meanwhile, staged a surprising comeback and took 19 percent of the votes – improving their position not only in their traditional bastions but also receiving 10 percent of the vote even in such places as Braga, one of the centers of the anticommunist movement in 1975. This recovery of the communists came as a shock to many who thought they were a spent force. The communists had used the period of socialist preeminence to purge the opportunists who had flocked to the banner in 1974 and 1975 and, consciously evoking the Italian communist precedent, where communists had been successful in administration at the municipal level, the PCP had hoped to turn Evora, the major city of the Alentejo, into a "Portuguese Bologna." The party's objectives had shifted, in effect, from a flirtation with an attempt to seize hegemony in the nation to the attempt to consolidate their hegemony over the left. The communists' union organization also expanded its influence. In 1979 the party claimed 164,000 militants.

The communists, of course, were benefiting from the fact that they were in opposition in the years 1976–9, a period during which the socialist governments had been obliged to take stringent economic measures, which caused a dramatic deterioration of workers' purchasing power. This deterioration, moreover, followed the substantial improvement the workers had enjoyed over the 1974–6 period. Thus, while a space had been opened up to the benefit of the communists by the socialist government's austerity measures, the social democrats to their right and the social democratic leader Francisco Sá Carneiro, also saw an opportunity to preempt the center and right of the political spectrum with a frontal attack on the whole constitutional settlement of 1976 and its Marxist overtones, especially those clauses concerning the nationalizations and land expropriations which the socialists found it hard to abandon. Hence, by the time the October 1980 general election approached, the Democratic Alliance had skillfully staked out a clear position that opposed the cooperative and collective farms that had replaced the *latifúndio* in the south, condemned the nationalizations, and challenged the legitimacy of the 1976 constitution itself, calling into question for the first time all the so-called "conquests of the revolution." In a mirror image of this preemptive political offensive from the Democratic Alliance, the communists now claimed these "conquests" as their own, which of course in part they were: at the time these expropriations had occurred they had been a consequence of a broad social movement from below, which the communists, far from supporting, had at times sought to contain and preempt.

Some part of the blame for the socialists' failure to consolidate their hold on the center of the political spectrum during the first and second constitutional governments rests on their own shoulders. Mário Soares proved to be a poor administrator and the socialists in government did not display great competence. The party was divided into internal clans and permeated with personal jealousies. The socialists also took full advantage of their positions to place their cronies in choice jobs in public administration or in the nationalized industries. But Soares also faced a formidable economic dilemma in the late 1970s and early 1980s, not unlike that which affected the political system, which the socialists were ill-placed to confront. Portugal in many ways straddled the divide between a capitalist transformation that was only partly completed, and a socialist revolution that had no more than begun, suffering the disadvantages of both and the benefits of neither. Land and enterprises remained expropriated and nationalized under the constitutional regime established in 1976. Many of those who had lost their patrimony remained uncompensated, bitter, and unsatisfied. The two principal areas from which the old oligarchy had been expelled – the modern industrialized enterprises and the grain-producing plateau of the south – were, ironically, precisely the areas on which Portugal most depended for the increased productivity in both industry and agriculture needed to bring Portugal's payments deficits into balance and to prepare Portugal for European competition. Yet, the nationalizations had severely limited Portugal's ability to bargain effectively in the international arena, and by taking so vast a sector of Portuguese industrial enterprise into the hands of the state, and by simultaneously allowing foreign enterprise to remain inviolate, the inadvertent and paradoxical result of the revolution had been a denationalization of the economy as a whole. Outsiders, in any case, preferred to place their investments in private and foreign-affiliated businesses. The state, because of the political deadlock among the parties and the paralysis of the parliament, was in no position, in any case, to argue against the predispositions of the international financial community, while the bloated state sector itself, and its political holdings, now formed a formidable lobby against any change in the status quo. One consequence of this impasse was that in order to secure economic reform, Portuguese politicians turned increasingly to an outside stimulus – the European Community.

CHAPTER 9

Picking up the pieces

I could have been the Fidel Castro of Europe.
                    Otelo Saraiva de Carvalho (August 1975)

Europe is with us.   Socialist Party manifesto

Something like this happened after April when the ants woke
up, when poor people were allowed to smile and Portugal
learned to say *tu*. It was the foretaste. But the heavy hand
of bourgeois good sense tamed the revolution [and] put it
in a straight jacket.   Urbano Tavares Rodrigues

I

Francisco Sá Carneiro, the social democratic leader and the new
prime minister, had placed constitutional reforms at the top of
the political agenda in the 1980 election campaign, but the fact
that a two-thirds vote in the Assembly of the Republic was
needed to achieve constitutional change required the Democratic
Alliance to seek the support of the Socialist Party to achieve
these reforms. This, in turn, immediately created a major internal
debate among the socialists over the extent to which they should
collaborate in this revision process. A "letter of intent" agreed
to between the socialists and President Eanes before the second
presidential election in December 1980 (in which Eanes was
reelected), however, became central to the choice between a
presidential or a parliamentary route for the revision process,
since both Eanes and Soares opposed the calling of a referendum
on the constitutional question as had been proposed by the prime
minister. But this potential for conflict was avoided when, towards

the end of the campaign, the prickly social democrat leader, Sá Carneiro, was killed in a plane crash on the eve of the election, and he was succeeded as prime minister by an individual more willing to compromise – the affable co-founder of the PSD, Dr. Francisco Pinto Balsemão.[1]

Mário Soares, since he had to retain a working consensus within the Socialist Party, refused to move on the economic clauses of the constitution and, in the end, the socialists were able to agree only on the political aspects of the revision agenda – especially those that limited the president's powers, abolished the Council of the Revolution, and established a mechanism for civilian control over the military. The deep personal antagonism which had developed between the erstwhile allies – socialist leader Mário Soares and President Ramalho Eanes – undoubtedly facilitated the building of an interparty coalition on a series of constitutional changes to limit Eanes' presidential powers. The 1982 revision of the constitution left intact, meanwhile, the provisions that were intended to block any backtracking on the "road to socialism"; in particular, the constitution still prohibited the privatization of public and nationalized enterprises.

Presidential elections, because they are decided by a straightforward majority, reflected a more ideological division than the parliamentary elections, though the linkage between ideological preferences and individuals fluctuated widely between Eanes' first and second elections. In 1976 General Eanes represented a center-right majority (he was opposed by candidates from the communists and the populist left), whereas in his second election bid he was essentially the candidate of the center left and was opposed by a unitary candidate on the center right. The voting patterns in each case were almost the exact reverse of the other.[2] In the 1986 presidential campaign Freitas do Amaral was able to considerably increase the center-right vote and had no opponent to his right flank. Mário Soares, on the other hand, faced a very difficult first round where he was challenged for the votes of the left by three other candidates. His narrow victory was both a triumph of his skill as a campaigner and thanks to the votes of the communists, who did not place a candidate of their own into the fray and, with some reservations, in the second round recommended to their faithful that Soares was the lesser of two evils.

Throughout this period, which on the surface looked highly unstable with short-lived governments following one another with barely time to introduce their programs and nominate their ministers, there was a surprising continuity within the new political elite. As far as the individuals in office were concerned, there was surprisingly little turnover. This is especially true of the PSD. The party participated in every government after 1980, even if the PSD often acted as if it was in opposition. The PSD had also participated in five of the six provisional governments between 1974 and 1970. Maria José Stock, more than anyone, has given some analytical substance to the question of the social composition of these new political elites.[3] She found the PSD and PS were essentially parties of the urban and rural middle classes. In the urban areas their electorate was composed essentially of people in the service sectors, especially within the lower-middle and middle classes. The PSD was strong among the smaller landowners in the north and center of Portugal, and among small landowners in the south. Here, the Socialist Party was stronger among agricultural wage earners. The PS, however, was weak in the labor unions and in the organizations which represented farmers, businessmen, and entrepreneurs. The social democrats were more successful among service sector unions; but both parties only obtained an effective representation in the union sector after the foundation of the anti-Communist central union, the UGT, in 1978.

The Communist Party at the grassroots level enjoyed a quasi-religious attachment among its members who came from a social group linked principally to the rural sector. Modernization and rationalization in the economy, however, was a threat to these bases. Cunhal, the leader of the PCP, was the last great survivor in a leadership role of a European party from the Stalinist era and the PCP remained, because of its long clandestine existence, its key role in the revolutionary period, and the nature of its leadership, closely tied to developments in the Soviet Union and particularly within the Soviet Communist Party. Hence the arrival of *perestroika* and *glasnost* under General Secretary Mikhail Gorbachev, followed by the collapse of the Soviet Union itself in 1991, had a profoundly disturbing impact.

The CDS was essentially a christian democratic party but, unlike its Italian counterpart, it suffered from the policy of the

Catholic church which, after Vatican II, had avoided direct political endorsement of political parties. During the revolutionary period, the party was also a lightning rod for left-wing hysteria and suffered much physical harassment. In the 1986 presidential election, its founder and leader, Diogo Freitas do Amaral, far outpolled Soares during the first round, where the leftist vote was divided between four candidates, and in the final count he came very close to matching Mário Soares' vote. Freitas do Amaral was a key figure in several governments and drew up the very important national defense law while deputy prime minister and minister of defense in the Democratic Alliance government led by Francisco Pinto Balsemão.[4] He had resigned from the leadership to prepare his presidential bid and the party was led in his absence by one of the few personalities of the old regime to make a career in the new – Adriano Moreira – but his past – even a comparatively liberal past in terms of the Salazar ministerial elite – was unquestionably a burden in public perception. Yet, just as the communists were able to embarrass the socialists if they strayed too far in the direction of capitalism, so the CDS was a sometimes embarrassing repository of ideological purity, always willing to attack the PSD for being insufficiently conservative or responsive to the private sector or traditional Catholic values, especially on social issues such as abortion and divorce, or on their slowness to confront constitutional matters such as the revision of their Marxist terminology or in privatizing the public sector.

II

In the early constitutional phase, political decision making still occurred outside the electoral or parliamentary sphere. These extra-parliamentary changes had a direct impact on the context within which political power could be exercised, and the most important area of this extra-parliamentary reform was the process by which the military were depoliticized.

The 1982 constitutional revision, designed to diminish the power of the president and to abolish the Council of the Revolution, involved a new law of national defense which fortified the government's authority over the armed forces. General Ramalho Eanes' role in the tortuous negotiations on civil-military relations and the revolution was critical, and indeed it is interesting how historically significant Eanes' intervention (both in a positive and in a negative sense) was at several of the most critical junctures in the process of democratic consolidation: first as commander of the military forces which won the confrontation in November 1975; second, in his position of chief of the general staff, as the protagonist in the successful rationalization, diminution, and depoliticization of the armed forces; third, as the antagonist in the struggle with the political leadership who so alienated both socialists and the social democrats that, although these political parties could agree on little else, they could combine in parliament to achieve a two-thirds majority in 1982 and override Eanes' veto of the National Defense Law. The abolition of the Council of the Revolution was achieved by Constitutional Amendment which the president could not veto.

The process of modernization of the Portuguese military and its subordination to effective civilian control, however, was a painfully slow one. The effective integration of the Portuguese armed forces into the democratic regime was bound to be a complex process, given the armed forces' role in the demise of the old regime and its experience in the turbulent months that followed. The army, in particular, which had been at the center of the revolutionary turmoil that followed the coup of 1974, was shattered by the experience. The end of the colonial wars and the passing of the traumatic encounter with revolution, made a major readjustment and redefinition of the role of the Portuguese military unavoidable. The process was simultaneously one of modernization and of political disengagement. Modernization involved three elements: reconstruction, diminution, and a change of role.

Because of the degree of the armed forces' disintegration between April 1974 and November 1975, which involved a series of purges and internal coups, and which led to the collapse of discipline and coordination and the misappropriation of arms and munitions, a major task of the armed forces was to effect a process of reconstruction. The area of internal security, moreover, had been largely abandoned by the government in the aftermath of the suppression of the dictatorship's secret police in 1974 and heavy communist infiltration of the army's intelligence division in 1975.

Until the National Defense Law of 1982 established the institutional mechanism for civilian control through the ministry of defense, and until in 1984, an Internal Security and Intelligence Service Law sought to regularize (or reestablish) organs for intelligence gathering, this process of reform was conducted largely in *de facto* autonomy by the government. These institutional reforms remained largely cosmetic, however, and civilian control only began to be exercised effectively in the early 1990s.

When the MFA overthrew the old regime in 1974, the Portuguese armed forces numbered over 200,000 men. By the early 1990s, the number had fallen to under 40,000. Thus, a key part of the reform process after 1976 involved a very considerable cutback in numbers and concentration of forces. Many of the conscripts who fulfilled the manpower demands of the colonial wars were rapidly shed. This, however, was not matched by a diminution in the officer corps, so that an inverted pyramid was created with more high-ranking than low-ranking officers. This created internal constraints on the promotion prospects of the officers, both commissioned and noncommissioned, causing discontent with status, pay, and prestige. The issue of conscription remained contentious, opposed by young people who saw it as a waste of time, but defended by the large military bureaucracy and infrastructure that existed to organize it. Personnel expenses, in comparison with other NATO countries, remained excessive in terms of percentages of military expenditures. The disproportionate expenditures on personnel (in effect, some 86 percent of total military expenditures in the late 1980s, if both military and civilian employees are considered) left no more than 9 percent for *materiel*. This is an extraordinary burden for a military faced with the urgent need for a near total renovation of its equipment.[5]

Until 1974, the Portuguese armed forces had been trained and equipped for counter-insurgency warfare. The battlefield experience was of Africa, and the commitment to NATO's European contingencies was tenuous at best. The scale of NATO involvement was limited by political constraints, as legislation in the United States and political pressures in the European countries prevented modern equipment and training from being provided to the Portuguese on any scale to be effective, although such assistance and training did continue on a small scale, sometimes clandestinely. The modernization of the Portuguese armed forces to NATO standards was thus no small matter, since at base it was a root-and-branch reform that was needed.

Eventually, in 1985, a document was prepared by the government, entitled the "Military Strategic Concept," which attempted to formally define the defense posture for the Portuguese armed forces. It contained a major contradiction between the espoused posture – emphasizing the airforce and naval interdiction function in the so-called "Portuguese triangle," which is composed of the maritime area between the Portuguese mainland, the Azores, and Madeira – and the realities of Portugal's military presence (or rather nonpresence) in this vast area. The Portuguese army, moreover, not the airforce or the navy, remained the dominant service in terms of the allocation of resources and personnel. These operational transformations, involving a process of modernization of tasks and military configuration, were, in many respects, still subordinate to the changing political context. For the military, this involved, in essence, depoliticization, the slow establishment of civilian control, and the imposition of government authority.

The depoliticization of the military after the dramatic events of the mid 1970s presented a formidable problem to civilian and military leaders alike. Hierarchy and discipline needed to be reestablished within the military itself. After 1982 the formal political and constitutional role played by politically active officers through the Council of the Revolution was abolished. With Mário Soares' election to the presidency of the republic in 1986 and his subsequent reelection in 1991, the political neutrality of the armed forces was, to all intents and purposes, achieved. By the mid 1980s, moreover, most of the remaining "political" officers of the 1970s were in retirement (even though they were comparatively young). Meanwhile, the parts of the military most enamored with the far left self-destructed. The amateur involvement in the terrorist underground of the leader and hero of the original coup, Colonel Otelo Saraiva de Carvalho, led to his arrest and conviction. He spent several years in jail and was largely abandoned by his former supporters. Significantly, no military candidates competed in either the 1986 or the 1991 presidential elections.

Until 1982 the military and civil authorities moved in autonomous areas. The key link between them was the president of the republic. President Eanes, however, was almost continually at loggerheads with the civilian government; indeed, he vetoed the measures establishing the ministry of defense in 1982. The program was nevertheless promulgated by the government of the Democratic Alliance with the support in parliament of the Socialist Party, then in opposition. With this *de facto* coalition of parliamentary support, the government was able to obtain the two-thirds majority needed to override the presidential veto. Under the new statutes, after 1982 the prime minister and the minister of defense had the key role in approving promotions to general officer rank although they would still be submitted to the National Defense Council over which the President presided. Despite these institutional changes, however, governmental instability until 1986 gave the armed forces a continuing influence and limited the effectiveness of civilian control.

There was an underlying cause of many of these problems in consolidating the democratic gains of 1976, and it was not confined to the military sphere. The state only slowly recuperated authority after the turmoil of the mid 1970s. In fact the particularity of the collapse of the old regime in Portugal explains part of the problem. In Portugal it was the authority of the state that collapsed rather than the bureaucracy itself. In other words, centralized and integrating governmental power collapsed but not the mechanism of administration. The Portuguese bureaucracy, already grotesque, archaic, and obstructionist, lost whatever supervision it had. Successive governments, which had little time to legislate, were nevertheless anxious to reward political friends and supporters by colonizing the bureaucracy with new layers of functionaries and political appointees. As a consequence, the size of the civil service expanded exponentially (by 89.1 percent between 1968 and 1979), while its quality declined and its corruptibility increased.

For a time, the military, via the Council of the Revolution, competed in this game. But after 1982 the military largely attended to its own affairs and its own considerable financial needs. By the mid 1980s these priorities involved the definition of tasks for the armed forces and the allocation of resources between the various service branches.

Given the comparatively small percentage of national expenditures devoted to the armed services (the percentage of public expenditures was, by the 1980s, lower than it was in the 1950s, prior to the African wars) and the negligible percentage of these expenditures available for *materiel*, as well as the lack of any strong political or public consensus in favor of increased military budgets, the role of foreign aid in the military domain became very important. Since the major source of military assistance had been the United States, this preoccupation tended to focus on the American use of the Azores base and the compensation the Portuguese expected to flow from their Atlantic alliance. This fact strongly influenced the military pressures on Portuguese negotiators of bilateral defense agreements. The military was particularly sensitive to "separatist" tendencies in the Azores, where on several occasions conflicts between the central government and the autonomous government in the Azores occurred – such as one over the precedence of the national and Azorean flags in 1986.

The internationalization of the crisis in Portugal during the period 1974–6 also tended to raise Portuguese expectations regarding foreign assistance, which exceeded the responses from outsiders once the immediate threat of a communist takeover had passed. It was inevitable, perhaps, that disappointment and frustration with the level of foreign assistance in the 1980s, especially military assistance, would increase among those military officers and civilian politicians most engaged in defending western liberal democratic values in the 1974–6 period. The feeling was exacerbated because the Portuguese military had not enjoyed the type of assistance that other NATO nations had received in the late 1950s and 1960s because of differences over Salazar's African policies. In addition, the Azores, as the location of the US base, had felt that its own needs were slighted – a feeling that could not be expressed under the authoritarian regime, but which, after the autonomy granted by the constitution of 1976, could be forcefully articulated even in the course of bilateral negotiations with the United States. The Azorean autonomous government was also much more skillful in mobilizing support among the Portuguese immigrants in the United States – many of them of Azorean origin – than was the central government, which was almost always heavy-handed and bumbling in its dealings with the United States, under governments of all political persuasions.

Anxiety over the definition of missions for the Portuguese

armed forces, the domestic political competition for resources, and the need for international collaboration to obtain these resources, therefore, remained acute throughout the first decades of the new regime. These uncertainties served to exaggerate fears among the Portuguese military of the superior resources and capabilities of Spain (especially in the question of the Atlantic area, where Portugal aspires to a role that it does not have the naval capabilities to carry out effectively and where Spain has now deployed a carrier task force) and also to increase dissatisfaction with the levels of foreign, especially US, assistance.

III

Portuguese foreign policy after 1974 had shifted from the strongly anti-Soviet and anticommunist position espoused by the old regime to a "third-world," quasi-neutralist position, reflecting a desire for nonalignment between the superpowers. Yet, as the balance of power shifted back to the political center after 1976, Portugal moved increasingly toward a European future, involving integration into the European Community in 1986 and into the Western European Union (WEU) in 1988. The Portuguese Socialist Party and especially Mário Soares, strongly urged a European future for Portugal and made accession to the EC the highest priority among foreign policy objectives. This aspiration on the part of the Portuguese was encouraged by the strong role played by outsiders in the struggle for Portuguese democracy, especially, although not exclusively, by the Germans. In fact, the engagement with Europe is the preeminent event of these years.

Portugal's relationship with the United States after democratization was smoother on the whole than that with Spain, and Portugal, because of the struggle of the mid 1970s, was more comfortable with the anti-Soviet rationale behind western defense strategy during the Cold War. In polls taken in the mid 1980s Portuguese opinion in favor of NATO was as high as 64 percent, compared with a mere 17 percent in Spain.[6] In fact, during the Carter administration, many democratic Portuguese, who had only recently faced down a communist-inspired takeover bid, thought the US administration insufficiently hard-line in its policy toward the Soviet Union. Yet tensions did emerge in the 1980s and did so more as the result of the management of relations since democratization than the result of past US associations with the Salazar regime.

The period 1973–4 was, however, an important watershed which saw a major shift of emphasis by Portugal. Until then, it had been Portugal that was attempting, via the Azores, to engage the United States, and by extension NATO, in so-called "out of area" concerns – principally in southern Africa. After 1973–4 the shoe was on the other foot since now it was the United States that became interested in the Azores for "out of area" uses – especially the Middle East and the Persian Gulf.

US–Portuguese relations were certainly not helped by the long absence of a US ambassador from Lisbon (October 1986 until January 1988), caused by the opposition of Senator Jesse Helms to President Reagan's nominee in the Foreign Relations Committee (the nominee eventually withdrew). This vacancy coincided with the critical first year of the Cavaco Silva government, a government representing a more nationalistic element in Portugal than the previous socialist regimes and generally representing political forces that did not enjoy strong personal links with or experience in American affairs.

Spain's entry into NATO in 1982 also created new anxieties in Portugal, even though Spain's relationship to NATO is conditional as far as command structures are concerned. The Portuguese categorically reject serving in any capacity under a unified Iberian command based in Madrid. Curiously, there is a tendency in some Portuguese military circles to believe that the US favors Spain or at least an "Iberianist" view of the peninsula as a geostrategic unit. They also believe that Spain is more effective in its efforts to influence US policy, although this assumption is very surprising since it is dramatically opposed to the actual experience of those Americans involved in the Spanish relationship during the 1980s, among whom much personal antagonism developed, in particular among those involved in the Torrejón base negotiations. If Washington pays more attention to Madrid than to Lisbon, this is more a function of Spain's size and role in Europe than of any hostility to Portugal in the US bureaucracy.

IV

Over the course of the 1980s, however, Brussels far surpassed Washington as a source of financial aid and assistance. As far as foreign policy is concerned, the European Union does not yet impose the conditionalities mandated on its members in economic questions. To be sure, individual EU countries seek to coordinate foreign policies through the EPC (European Political Cooperation), but they still often take individual positions that reflect differing national perceptions or interests, and, for Portugal in particular, its trans-Atlantic and South Atlantic interests remain considerable. However, it is probably fair to say that Portugal's political role is considerably enhanced by EU membership.

Other areas of primary importance to Portugal are: the bilateral relationship with Spain; the African dimension; the relationship with Brazil; the Asian dimension, especially Macau and Timor; and the Arab world, especially Morocco. The African dimension of Portuguese foreign policy continues to receive a high priority in Lisbon. Portugal has established relationships with all the former colonies in Africa and has played a constructive role in regional peacemaking. In Angola, for instance, the government of Cavaco Silva initially took a more even-handed approach than the US administration, which continued to supply clandestine support to Jonas Savimbi in the ongoing civil war in that former Portuguese territory, but was then able to use the changed international environment (especially improved east-west relations) to broker a peace accord in Angola in May 1991. The war in Angola soon revived; but for Portugal, the important point was that the former colonial power had returned, not as a participant, and then bystander, as it had been for almost thirty years in the making of war, but as part of an international effort to bring peace.

Conclusion

The collapse of Portuguese rule in southern Africa in 1975 ended the last of Europe's overseas empires. Five and a half centuries after the conquest of Ceuta, for the first time the Portuguese standard was no longer hoisted above a fortress in Africa. The events of the mid 1970s in Portugal also played a significant and precocious part in the great ideological conflict of the twentieth century. The triumph for anticommunist democrats in the Portuguese domestic conflicts between 1974 and 1976, on the one hand, together with the initial victory of the communist-backed forces in Angola in the same period on the other, set in motion many of the forces which would help bring about the end of the Cold War in Europe, by reinvigorating democracy at the grassroots and by escalating the costs of proxy conflicts in the third world. By the 1990s, some political scientists, most notably Samuel Huntington, looking back at the 1970s, came to regard Portugal's democratization as the beginning of the "third wave" of democratization, which would see the fall of the communist regimes in eastern Europe and eventually in the Soviet Union itself, a period comparable to that of the 1820s and the 1940s in world history.[1]

The chain of events set in motion by the April 1974 coup thus had widespread and long-lasting international ramifications. In the United States the crisis reached a high salience in the foreign policy concerns of the presidency of Gerald Ford. The civil war in Angola, sparked by the helter skelter withdrawal of the Portuguese and by outside intervention, helped undermine *détente*, threatened the credibility of the Carter administration when the Cubans with Soviet support extended their activities to Ethiopia and the Ogaden, and later on provided justification for the huge military buildups which contributed to the burdens of military expenditure that, in the end, broke the back of the Soviet Union.[2]

But, for a long while this mortal danger to the Soviet system was disguised by the apparent success of Soviet-supported nationalist movements in the third world. Few saw or admitted that these successes were pyrrhic and owed at least as much to local circumstances, and, in the case of Angola, to American miscalculations, as they did to the intrinsic power of the movements themselves, or the efficacy of their ideological solutions to African third-world dilemmas, so that easy success for the Soviet-backed forces in Africa bred a dangerous overconfidence elsewhere, where circumstances were different and grassroots popular opposition to the Soviet expansion was more formidable – places like Afghanistan, the perennial graveyard of those with imperial pretensions.

In the mid 1970s the Portuguese upheaval had more immediate consequences. The behavior of the Portuguese communists discredited the Eurocommunist movement when, during the summer of 1975, they made the last serious communist attempt to take power in western Europe. For many European and North American radicals, Portugal provided for a time a reasonably close and safe way to experience a revolution in progress and first hand. Not unlike Nicaragua during the 1980s, Portugal was invaded by would-be revolutionary groupies and not a few ambitious journalists on the make. Out of this influx emerged some very good books, but the purveyors of quick solutions to old problems were rarely there to pick up the pieces once the euphoric moment had passed and new vicarious thrills presented themselves.

In southern Africa, meanwhile, the loss of the white-ruled buffer provided by the Portuguese colonies sealed the fate of white Rhodesia and, in time, that of white South Africa itself. On the periphery of the empire, however, the collapse of central authority produced less fortuitous results than it did in Europe. Portugal's former colonies in southern Africa were to experience bitter first decades of independence, with civil war and civil violence on a scale far surpassing that of the colonial conflicts that preceded them. The virulence of the African conflicts, especially that in Angola, was very much a consequence of the Portuguese events of 1974–1976, and of the intrusion of Cold War proxy struggles into that region. These conflicts also displayed and, in some ways, foreshadowed the ferocity of the ethnic conflicts that later marked the periphery of the old Soviet empire when it collapsed in the late 1980s and early 1990s.

In Spain, on the other hand, with its own tragic history of civil war very much in mind, all parties to the political transition following Franco's death in late 1975 behaved with great caution and good sense, striving to avoid repetition of the Portuguese collapse. The democratization of the Iberian peninsula presented the European Community (EC) with new opportunities; above all it removed the old excuse for excluding Spain and Portugal from the new Europe.[3] When Portugal joined the EC in 1986 it broke a five-hundred-year-old pattern in its international posture, one that had been overwhelmingly oceanic and Atlantic-facing, thereby marking a historic watershed.

The international context was always an important backdrop to the events in Portugal. But international factors alone do not explain the outcome of the social and political struggles in Portugal. These struggles, as this book has sought to demonstrate, must also be seen in their domestic context. In many respects the most remarkable feature of the emergence of democracy in Portugal was the triumph of the moderates. In the mid 1970s such an outcome was far from obvious. Alistair Horne, in his brilliant book on the bitter struggles of French decolonization in North Africa, *A Savage War of Peace*,[4] noted "the lesson of the sad, repeated failure of the moderates, or a third force to compete against opposing extremes." This lesson, Horne continued, "is one of constant relevance to the contemporary scene, whether it be in Northern Ireland, South Africa, or Latin America. As in 1793 or 1917 in modern revolutions," Horne concluded, "it is the Montagne that triumphs over the Gironde."

Portugal, of course, broke this pattern. It was not the Girondistes who were defeated by the Montagnards as during the French Revolution; or, more to the point in the case of Portugal in 1975, the Bolsheviks who defeated the Mensheviks. Despite the triumphalism espoused by the Portuguese Communist Party leader Alvaro Cunhal, despite the atavistic authoritarianism of the fallen regime, despite the "third worldism" espoused by the young military radicals who soon took power in Lisbon after the coup, despite the machinations of a far-right nostalgia for the past, despite Portugal's social and economic backwardness, and despite the chronic political instability which followed the promulgation of the constitution in 1976, and despite Henry Kissinger's gloomy progmostication, the Portuguese were able to create a representative and pluralistic system of government, fully comparable to the Western European mainstream. In the context of the Portuguese revolution, it was Kerensky who survived, not Lenin. It was the moderate socialist Mário Soares who eventually became president of the republic and the radical military populist Otelo Saraiva de Carvalho who went first to jail and then into obscurity. In this, Portugal was a precocious forerunner of the largely peaceful transitions from authoritarianism to democracy of the late 1980s in Latin America and in Eastern Europe.

Notes

1 PRISONERS OF HISTORY

1 C. R. Boxer, *The Portuguese Seaborne Empire, 1415–1825* (Oxford, 1963).
2 The word "Portugal" was derived from Portus Cale, the old Roman name for Oporto, now the country's second largest city.
3 K. M. Pannikar, *The Vasco da Gama Epoch* (London, 1959).
4 Lord Tyrawly, cited by A. R. Walford, *The British Factory* (Lisbon, 1940), p. 20.
5 Arthur William Costigan, *Sketches of Society and Manners in Portugal*, 2 vols. (London, 1787), II, p. 29.
6 Boxer, *The Portuguese Seaborne Empire*, p. 189.
7 Cited in J. Levinson, ed., *The Age of the Baroque in Portugal* (New Haven, 1994), p. 53.
8 Susan Schneider, *O marquês de Pombal e o vinho do Porto* (Oporto, 1980), p. 8.
9 Kenneth Maxwell, *Pombal, Paradox of the Enlightenment* (Cambridge, 1995).
10 Voltaire, *Candide*, cited in T. D. Kendrick, *The Lisbon Earthquake* (London, 1956) which provides the best overview of the impact of the catastrophe on European thinkers of the period.
11 Cited by Schneider, *O marquês de Pombal*, p. 169.
12 António Ribeiro dos Santos, cited by Kenneth Maxwell, *Pombal, Paradox of the Enlightenment*, p. 2.
13 Douglas L. Wheeler, "The Portuguese Revolution of 1910," *Journal of Modern History* 44 (June 1972), pp. 172–94.
14 There are several good accounts of Salazar and his system. The best ones in English are: Hugh Kay, *Salazar and Modern Portugal: A Biography* (New York, 1970), which is written from a sympathetic perspective, and António de Figueiredo, *Portugal: Fifty Years of Dictatorship* (London, 1975), which is written from the point of view of the opposition. On corporatism in Portugal, see Philippe C. Schmitter, *Corporatism and Public Policy in Authoritarian Portugal* (London and Beverly Hills, 1975). The most comprehensive coverage in English is by Howard J. Wiarda, *Corporatism and Development: The*

Portuguese Experience (Amherst, 1977). Salazar's own view can be seen in António de Oliveira Salazar, *Doctrine and Action: Internal and Foreign Policy of the New Portugal 1928–1939* (London, 1939), and Oliveira Salazar, *Como se levanta um estado* (Lisbon, 1977). A good overview of the Salazar and Caetano period is provided by Manuel de Lucena in *A evolução do sistema corporativo português*, 2 vols. (Lisbon, 1976). For Salazar himself, see the multivolume biography by Franco Nogueira, *Salazar* (Lisbon, 1977–1990).

15 On PIDE see Nuno Vasco, *Vigiados e perseguidos: Documentos secretos da PIDE/DGS* (Lisbon, 1977); *Dossier PIDE: Os horrores e crimes de uma "polícia"* (Lisbon, 1974). Tom Gallagher, "Controlled Repression in Salazar's Portugal," *Journal of Contemporary History* 14, 3 (July 1979), p. 392. Douglas Wheeler, "In the Service of Order: The Portuguese Political Police and the British, German, and Spanish Intelligence, 1932–1945," *Journal of Contemporary History* 18 (1983). On opposition, see D. L. Raby, *Fascism and Resistance in Portugal* (Manchester, 1988).

16 René Backman, "Portugal: Les archives de tortionnaires," *Le Nouvel Observateur* (Paris, September 2, 1974); also see António Costa Pinto, *O salazarismo e o fascismo europeu* (Lisbon, 1992). Details of treatment of political prisoners, the use of torture and the names of the political prisoners during the Caetano period were published by the National Commission for Assistance to Political Prisoners, *Presos políticos: documentos, 1970–1971* (Oporto, 1972) and *Presos políticos: documentos, 1972–1974* (Oporto, 1974).

17 António de Oliveira Salazar, *Antologia, 1909–1966: Discursos, entrevistas, artigos, teses, notas, relatórios* (Coimbra, 1966).

18 George Ball, *The Past has another Pattern* (New York, 1982), p. 278.

19 Salazar, *Antologia*. A good overview of the Salazar years can be obtained in Tom Gallagher, *Portugal: A Twentieth Century Interpretation* (Manchester, 1983).

20 On Portuguese colonialism, see R. J. Hammond, *Portugal and Africa 1815–1910: A Study in Economic Imperialism* (Stanford, 1966); James Duffy, *Portugal in Africa* (Cambridge MA, 1962); and René Pélissier, *Résistance et révolte en Angola (1845–1961)*, 3 vols. (privately printed, 1976). Also David Abshire and Michael A. Samuels, eds., *Portuguese Africa: A Handbook* (New York, 1969).

21 The most prominent proponent of the theory of "luso-tropicalism" was the Brazilian sociologist Gilberto Freyre, who published his influential *O mundo que o português criou* ("The world the Portuguese created") in Rio de Janeiro in 1940.

22 See especially Amílcar Cabral, *Unité et lutte*, 2 vols. (Paris, 1975).

23 Josep Sánchez Cervelló, "La inviabilidad de una victoria portuguesa en la guerra colonial: el caso de Guinea-Bissau," *Hispania* 49, 173 (Madrid, 1989), pp. 1017–44. Also, *Resenha histórico–militar das cam-*

panhas de África, 1961–1974, I (Lisbon, 1988), p. 251. For complete statistics on casualties see pp. 255–66.

24 On numbers of white settlers in Angola on the eve of decolonization, see Gerald Bender and Stanley P. Yoder, "Whites on the Eve of Independence: The Politics of Numbers," *Africa Today* 21 (Fall 1974), pp. 23–37. Bender and Yoder give minimum figures; the Portuguese colonial authorities gave maximum figures. It should be noted that the Portuguese population increased by 10 percent between 1974 and 1980 as a result of the flight of settlers from the African territories during the process of decolonization. Estimates placed Portugal's population at 8,200,000 in 1974 and at over 9,000,000 by 1980. For an overview, see René Pélissier, "Conséquences démographiques des révoltes en Afrique portugaise (1961–1970): Essai d'interprétation," *Revue Française d'Histoire d'Outre-Mer* 61, 222 (1974), pp. 34–73.

25 On liberation movements in Africa, see Ronald H. Chilcote, *Emerging Nationalism in Portuguese Africa* (Stanford, 1972); John A. Marcum, *The Angolan Revolution*, 2 vols. (Cambridge, MA, 1968 and 1976); Basil Davidson, *The Liberation of Guinea: Aspects of an African Revolution* (Harmondsworth, 1969); Davidson, *In the Eye of the Storm* (Harmondsworth, 1972). There is some useful comparative perspective in Kenneth W. Grundy, *Confrontation and Accommodation in Southern Africa: The Limits of Independence* (Berkeley and Los Angeles, 1973), especially chapters 5 and 6, and in Richard Gibson, *African Liberation Movements* (Oxford, 1972).

26 See especially S. Sideri, *Trade and Power: Informal Colonialism in Anglo-Portuguese Relations* (Rotterdam, 1970). Also Mariam Halpern Pereira, *Assimetrias de crescimento e dependência externa* (Lisbon, 1974); William Minter, *Portuguese Africa and the West* (Harmondsworth, 1972); and Minter, *Imperial Network and External Dependency: The Case of Angola* (Beverly Hills, 1972).

27 For *Comparative Statistics on Portugal and OECD Countries* see Portugal *Annual Economic Survey* (Paris, 1974). Also Alvin C. Egbert and Hyung M. Kim, *A Developmental Model for the Agricultural Sector of Portugal* (World Bank, Washington, DC, 1975).

28 Silva Martins, J., *Estruturas agrárias em Portugal continental*, 2 vols. (Lisbon, 1973); Ian Rutledge, "Land Reform and the Portuguese Revolution," *Journal of Peasant Studies* 5, 1 (October 1977), pp. 79–98.

29 Background information on social and demographic factors can be found in Massimo Livi Bacci, *A Century of Portuguese Fertility* (Princeton, 1971). On agrarian structure see Alvaro Cunhal, *A situação agrária em Portugal* (Rio de Janeiro, 1970) and José Cutileiro, *A Portuguese Rural Society* (Oxford, 1971). For a good overview on migration trends, see Heinz-Michael Stahl, "Portuguese Migration and Regional Development," *11 Conferência Internacional sobre Economia*

Portuguesa (Lisbon, 1979). On the church, see S. Cequeira, "L'église catholique et la dictature corporatiste portugaise," *Revue Française de Science Politique* 23 (June 1973), pp. 473–513.

30 Francisco Pereira de Moura, *Por onde vai a economia portuguesa?* (Lisbon, 1974); Organization for Economic Cooperation and Development, *[OECD] Annual Economic Survey: Portugal* (Paris, 1974, 1976, 1977); The Economist Intelligence Unit, *Portugal: Quarterly Economic Review*, nos. 1–4 (London, 1974) and *Annual Supplement* (1974); Eugénio Rosa, *A economia portuguesa em números* (Lisbon, 1975) and *Problemas actuais da economia portuguesa: Os monopólios e o 25 de abril* (Lisbon, 1974). For a succinct overview of the Portuguese economy on the eve of the revolution see Economist Intelligence Unit, *Portugal: Quarterly Economic Review* 1 (1974).

31 Maria Belmira Martins, *Sociedades e grupos em Portugal* (Lisbon, 1973). For concentration of land ownership and financial institutions in Portugal prior to 1974, see Ramiro da Costa, *O desenvolvimento do capitalismo em Portugal* (Lisbon, 1975).

32 Franco Nogueira, *Diálogos interditos* (Lisbon, 1979).

33 For useful economic and geographical background on Angola and Mozambique, see William A. Hance, *The Geography of Modern Africa*, 2nd edn. (New York, 1975), pp. 484–509.

2 THE PRAETORIAN GUARDS

1 Philippe C. Schmitter, "Still the Century of Corporatism?" *Review of Politics* 36 (January 1974) pp. 85–131; Howard J. Wiarda, "The Portuguese Corporative System: Basic Structures and Functions," *Iberian Studies* 2 (Autumn 1973), pp. 73–80.

2 For accounts of General Spínola's accomplishments in Guinea, see António de Spínola, *Linha de acção* (Lisbon, 1970). Also see Al Venter, *Portugal's War in Guinea-Bissau* (Pasadena, 1973) and Lars Rudebeck, *Guinea-Bissau: A Study of Political Mobilization* (Uppsala, 1974). For accounts of the war from the side of the PAIGC, see Davidson, *The Liberation of Guinea*. Marcello Caetano's own account of the meeting with Spínola is in Marcello Caetano, *Depoimento* (Rio de Janeiro, 1975).

3 For the Spínola–Caetano exchange see Caetano, *Depoimento*, pp. 191–2 and António de Spínola, *País sem rumo: Contributo para a história de uma revolução* (Lisbon, 1978). Caetano's comments on this exchange may also be found in Joaquim Veríssimo Serrão, *Marcello Caetano: Confidências no exílio* (Lisbon, 1985), pp. 234–5.

4 António de Spínola, *Portugal e o futuro* (Lisbon, 1974); the opening quotation is from the first manifesto of the Armed Forces Movement published in Jacinto Baptista, *Caminhos para uma revolução* (Lisbon, 1975), appendix III. General Spínola's book, *Portugal e o futuro*, was

published by Arcadia (Lisbon), a subsidiary of the CUF group, in February 1974. For a review of the book, see Kenneth Maxwell, "Portugal: A Neat Revolution," *New York Review of Books*, June 13, 1974, pp. 16–21.

5 Spínola, *Portugal e o futuro*.

6 On censorship under the old regime see Alberto Arons e Carvalho, *A censura e as leis de imprensa* (Lisbon, 1973).

7 Spínola, *Portugal e o futuro*.

8 For a comprehensive collection of MFA internal documents, see Diniz de Almeida, *Origens e evolução do movimento dos capitães* (Lisbon, 1977). Comprehensive background discussion in Maria Carrilho *Forças Armadas e Mudança Política em Portugal no séc.* xx. (Lisbon 1985). Especially pp. 295–472.

9 See discussion by Douglas Porch, *The Portuguese Armed Forces and the Revolution* (London, 1977), pp. 45–53, citation from p. 47.

10 Comment made to author in Lisbon, April 1974.

11 After Salazar's overthrow, Caetano pointed out that both Alvaro Cunhal, the communist leader, and Mário Soares, the socialist leader, unlike himself or Salazar, came from wealthy bourgeois families. See Veríssimo Serrão, *Marcello Caetano*, p. 333.

12 Caetano, *Depoimento*; also see Col. Antonino Cruz and Vitoriano Rosa, *As mentiras de Marcello Caetano* (Lisbon, 1974).

13 See good discussion of Caetano in Wiarda, *Corporatism and Development*, pp. 254–68.

14 Caetano's own views on this period can be found in Veríssimo Serrão, *Marcello Caetano*, p. 214. In 1973 Balsemão founded *Expresso*, an independent weekly newspaper which came to wield exceptional influence during the transition period. See discussion by Mario Mesquita on role of press in *Portugal 20 Anos de Democracia* ed. António Reis, Lisbon 1994) pp. 360–405; and Kenneth Maxwell, *The Press and the Rebirth of Iberian Democracy* (Westport and London, 1983).

15 See *Nós Nunca Seremos A Geração da Traição: 1 Congresso dos combatentes do ultramarino 1–7 June 1974* (Lisbon, 1974).

16 Spínola, cited by Avelino Rodrigues, Cesário Borga, and Mário Cardoso in *O movimento dos capitães e o 25 de abril* (Lisbon, 1974), p. 283.

17 See Nuno Vasco, *Vigiados e perseguidos: Documentos secretos da PIDE-DGS* (Lisbon, 1977). The outside world was not completely unware of tensions within Portugal during this period: the "Three Marias" case and reports of massacres in Mozambique both received wide coverage in the international press in 1973 and early 1974.

3 COUP D'ÉTAT

1 "National Security Council Interdepartmental Group on Africa. Study in Response to National Security Memorandum 39: Secret AF/NSC-IG/69-8, August, 15, 1969, p. 56.

This memorandum was published as *The Kissinger Study of Southern Africa*, edited and introduced by Barry Cohen and Mohamed A. El-Khamas (Westport, CT, 1976).

2 This contingency planning was confirmed by a senior State Department official in December 1974. Letter from Linwood Holton, Assistant Secretary of State for Congressional Relations, to Honorable Charles Diggs, Chairman, Subcommittee for Africa, Foreign Affairs Committee, published in "Review of State Department Trip through Southern and Central Africa," *Hearing Before the Subcommittee on Africa*, Foreign Affairs Committee, US House of Representatives, 93rd Congress.

3 See José Freire Antunes, *O factor africano, 1890–1990* (Lisbon, 1990), p. 50.

4 For background of Azores agreements, see José Calvet de Magalhães *et al.*, *Portugal: paradoxo atlântico* (Lisbon, 1993) and R. E. Vintras, *The Portuguese Connection: The Secret History of the Azores Base* (London, 1974). Also overview by Alvaro Vasconcelos, "Portuguese Defense Policy," in John Chipman ed., *NATO's Southern Allies* (London, 1989), pp. 86–139.

5 See R. E. Vintras, *The Portuguese Connection*.

6 George Kennan to Oliveira Salazar, Lisbon October 25, 1943, *Dez anos de política externa (1936–1948): A nação portuguesa e a Segunda Guerra Mundial* (Lisbon, in progress) vol. XIII 1986, pp. 489–96 also, Freire Antunes, *O factor africano*, p. 38.

7 Freire Antunes, *O factor africano*, p. 43.

8 Cited by Freire Antunes, based on the personal diaries of Franco Nogueira in *O factor africano*, p. 36.

9 See John Marcum, *The Angolan Revolution*, I, pp. 135–147; Henrique Galvão, *Santa Maria: My Crusade for Portugal* (Cleveland, 1961).

10 See Richard Mahoney, *JFK: Ordeal in Africa* (New York, 1983), p. 207.

11 Franco Nogueira, *Um político confessa-se: Diário 1960–1968* (Oporto, 1986); also Viana de Lemos, *Duas Crises, 1961–1974* (Lisbon, 1977); José Freire Antunes, *Kennedy e Salazar: O leão e a raposa* (Lisbon, 1991); Richard Mahoney, *JFK: Ordeal in Africa*, especially chapters 7 and 8; and Whitney Schneidman, "American Foreign Policy and the Fall of the Portuguese Empire, 1961–1976," Ph.D. dissertation (University of Southern California, 1982), chapter 2.

12 *Resenha histórico–militar das companhas de Africa, 1961–1974* (Lisbon, 1988).

13 On the Kennedy period see Minter, *Portuguese Africa*. For covert support for nationalism see Mahoney, *JFK: Ordeal in Africa*.

14 Cited in the personal diaries of Franco Nogueira, *Um político confessa-se*, October 22, 1962 and September 5, 1962; also cited by Antunes, *O factor africano*, p. 64.

15 Cited by Whitney Schneidman, "American Foreign Policy."
16 Mahoney, *JFK*, p. 193.
17 For Nogueira's account see *Diálogos*, II, pp. 261–70. Nogueira believed that at this point the United States and Portugal came close to an accord on a plan for self-determination. See note, p. 290.
18 See Marcello Mathias to Oliveira Salazar, concerning Arthur Schlesinger, Jr.'s book on the Kennedy administration, Paris, February 20, 1966, pp. 544–6; and Salazar to Marcello Mathias, February 22, 1966, pp. 547–51. Salazar's report on the conversation with Ball can be seen in Oliveira Salazar to Marcello Mathias, June 1, 1963, pp. 467–9, *Correspondência Marcello Mathias/Salazar*, preface by Professor J. Veríssimo Serrão (Lisbon, 1984).
19 Also see Franco Nogueira, *Diálogos*, II, pp. 19–27.
20 Letter from Marvine Howe to Bill Moyers, October 15, 1965. Aides file, Lyndon Baines Johnson Library, Austin, TX. Cited by Whitney Schneidman, "American Foreign Policy and the Fall of the Portuguese Empire," pp. 177 and 230.
21 Nogueira, *Diálogos interditos*, II, p. 191.
22 Nogueira, *Diálogos interditos*, II, pp. 249–52.
23 See Barry Munslow, *Mozambique: The Revolution and its Origins* (New York, 1983), p. 111.
24 Walter Isaacson, *Kissinger: A Biography* (New York, 1992) pp. 511–524: José Freire Antunes *Nixon & Caetano: Promessas e abandono* (2nd Edition, Lisbon, 1992) pp. 264–304. The second edition of Freire Antunes book contains information on the "Red Eye" missile affair not contained in his first edition (1986) based on interviews with General Costa Gomes, see p. 304. In reaction to the first edition of Freire Antunes' book the discussions between Kissinger and Portuguese Foreign Minister Rui Patrício were described with unusual frankness by a participant, J. Calvet de Magalhães in *Estratégia* (Lisbon, 1987) no. 3, especially, pp. 40–43.
25 Vasco Lourenço quote from *MFA: rosto do povo* (Lisbon, 1975), pp. 16–17.
26 Political Committee draft program. Published with other documents in Jacinto Baptista, *Caminhos para uma revolução* (Lisbon, 1974), pp. 292–323.
27 The MFA program has been published in several places. See Orlando Neves, ed., *Textos históricos da revolução* (3 vols Lisbon, 1975) vol. I.
28 For Spínola's amendments see documents 1 and 2 in Diniz de Almeida, *Ascensão, apogeu e queda do MFA* (Lisbon, 1976), pp. 306–370.
29 See discussion by Insight Team of the *Sunday Times* (London), *Insight on Portugal* (London, 1975), pp. 71–97.

30 There is a good discussion of the songs of the revolution in Thomas J. Braga, "The Lyrics of a Revolution: Zeca Afonso's Cantigas de Maio," *Journal of the American Portuguese Society* 13 (1979), pp. 2–18.

31 On labor disputes after the coup see Maria de Lourdes Lima Santos, Marinus Pires e Lima, and Vítor Matias Ferreira, *O 25 de abril e as lutas sociais nas empresas* (Oporto, 1976) and José Pires, *Greves e o 25 da abril* (Lisbon, 1976).

32 On schools see B. Pimlott and J. Seaton, "How Revolution Came to the Schools of Portugal," *New Society*, December 9, 1976.

33 For Spínola's own account of this period see António de Spínola, *País sem rumo: Contributo para a história de uma revolução* (Lisbon, 1978). For other analyses of the first year of the revolution see Robin Blackburn, "The Test in Portugal," *New Left Review* 87/88 (September–December 1974); Paul Sweeney, "Class Struggles in Portugal," *Monthly Review* 26/27 (September–October 1975); Michael Harsgor, "Portugal in Revolution," in *The Washington Papers* (Beverly Hills, 1976).

34 Spínola's account in António de Spínola, *País sem rumo*, pp. 113–121.

4 CONFLICTS AND CONFUSIONS

1 A very comprehensive collection of documents, newspapers, reports and communiqués was compiled at the time as *Coleção documentos do nosso tempo*, 3 vols. (Lisbon, n.d. [1974]): I, *A revolução das flores do 25 de abril ao governo provisório*; II, *O governo de Palma Carlos*; III, *O governo de Vasco Gonçalves até ao acordo de Lusaka*.

2 The background on Cunhal is from the "official" biographical material provided by the editors in the introduction to his book, Alvaro Cunhal, *Pela revolução democrática e nacional* (Lisbon, 1975).

3 For background on opposition see Figueiredo, *Portugal*. For a background on the military plots, see Douglas Wheeler, "The Honor of the Army," in *Contemporary Portugal*, eds. Graham and Mackler; also see Hermínio Martins, "Opposition in Portugal," *Government and Opposition* 4, 2 (Spring 1969), p. 263; Peter Freyer and Patricia McGowan-Pinheiro, *Oldest Ally: A Portrait of Salazar's Portugal* (London, 1961), and Raby, *Facism and Resistance*.

4 Valério Ochetto, *Em pro da verdade: O como e o porquê de um crime político – a morte de Delgado* (Amadora, 1978).

5 For points of view expressed by the opposition in 1973, see *Congresso de oposição democrática, Aveiro, 4–8 abril, 1973, teses* (Lisbon, 1974). This was available in Lisbon bookstores in March 1974. For William Colby's comments on Portugal, see *Honorable Men* (New York, 1978). On the CIA in Portugal prior to the coup, see *The Pike Report* (Nottingham, 1977). These comments are also based on my own

access to PIDE files in January and February 1975. For a discussion of the PCP by a former PIDE inspector see Fernando Gouveia, *Memórias de um inspector da PIDE: A organização clandestina do PCP* (Lisbon, 1979).

6 For a useful compendium of articles and documents published at the time on the role of the church, see "The Church and Revolution," *International Documentation on the Contemporary Church*, 1 (New York 1975).

7 See comments by Caetano in Veríssimo Serrão, *Marcello Caetano*, pp. 334–5. An important source for the new political class was SEDES (Association for Economic and Social Development) founded in 1970.

8 See in particular, Cunhal's speech in Barreiro, June 8, 1974, in Alvaro Cunhal, *Discursos políticos: Documentos políticos do partido comunista português* (Lisbon, 1974), p. 56. For a valuable collection of essays on the PCP, see Carlos Gaspar and Vasco Rato, *Rumo à memória: Crônicas da crise comunista* (Lisbon, 1993), pp. 13–58. Also, J. A. Silva Marques, *Relatos da clandestinidade – O PCP visto por dentro* (Lisbon, 1976).

9 On Kissinger's reactions the best account is Tad Szulc, "Lisbon and Washington: Behind the Portuguese Revolution," *Foreign Policy* 21 (Winter 1975/76), pp. 3–62.

10 General George Brown in *The Times* (London) October 11, 1974. See also Drew Middleton, "Importance of US Munitions to Israel Assayed," in *New York Times*, September 2, 1974.

11 At the beginning of 1974 the army consisted of 51,000 in metropolitan Portugal and 142,395 in the overseas territories, of which 65,512 were in Angola, 51,403 in Mozambique, and 32,035 in Guinea. See *Resenha histórico-militar das companhas de Africa* 1, pp. 251–9.

12 For COPCON see Almeida, *Ascensão*, pp. 370–2.

13 See *Sabotagem económica: Dossier Banco Espírito Santo* (Lisbon, 1975).

14 Law no. 7174 of July 26, 1972, "Direito das colônias à independência" and "Comunicado Portugal – ONU 4/8/74" which formally ratified Portugal's acceptance of the right to self-determination and independence of all the territories under the administration. See texts in Fernando Ribeiro de Mello, ed., *Dossier: 2a República* (Lisbon 1976–7), pp. 250–4.

15 Vasco Lourenço quote from *MFA: rosto do povo* (Lisbon, 1975), pp. 16–17.

16 See discussion by Porch, *The Portuguese Armed Forces and the Revolution* (London, 1977), pp. 114–115.

17 Alvaro Cunhal to the seventh congress of the PCP in *Documentos políticos do partido comunista português*, 7th Congresso (extraordinário) do PCP em 20/10/1974 (Lisbon, 1974), p. 46.

18 *Ibid.*

19 For a useful inside view of the MFA of this time see Almeida, *Ascensão*.

20 For Brazilian policy I have relied on "Palestra proferida na escola superior de guerra por Italo Zappa," 31 May 1976 (unpublished paper deposited with the background materials for this book in the Special Collections division of Princeton University Library).

21 Chronology of March 11 in Fernando Ribeiro de Mello, ed., *Dossier: 2a República*, I, pp. 165–73. For a discussion of the number of political prisoners in this period see Nicholas Ashford. *The Times* (London, April 12, 1975).

22 Caetano, *Depoimento*.

23 Szulc, "Lisbon and Washington," *Foreign Policy*, pp. 3–62.

24 For Soares' contacts with Neto, see Mário Soares, *Quelle révolution?* (Paris, 1975).

25 The American decision to support Roberto at this time was also reflective of a more widespread view of the MPLA's factionalism. Basil Davidson, for instance, wrote in 1963 that "the MPLA has fractured, split and reduced itself to a nullity. With Roberto ... gathering strength and allies, the MPLA has ceased to count." Davidson, *In the Eye of the Storm* (Harmondsworth, 1972), p. 207.

26 On MPLA and Neto, see Marcum, *The Angolan Revolution* vol. I, pp. 37–40.

27 See Marcum, *The Angolan Revolution* vol. II, pp. 221–40.

28 At the time of the Lisbon coup, the CIA was attempting to exchange Captain Pedro Rodrigues Peralta, a Cuban captured by the Portuguese in Guinea in 1969, for Lawrence K. Lunt, an American businessman held in Havana. Peralta was elected to the central committee of the Cuban Communist Party in late 1975, and represented Cuba at the declaration of the People's Republic of Angola in Luanda on November 11, 1975. For Peralta see *Presos políticos: documentos, 1970–1971* (Lisbon, 1973), p. 136.

29 The most accessible summaries of the view of US academic experts on Portugal in this period are contained in Howard J. Wiarda, *Transcending Corporatism? The Portuguese Corporative System and the Revolution of 1974*, Institute of International Studies, essay series II (University of South Carolina, 1976). This draws on reports by Douglas Wheeler, Lawrence S. Graham, and Wiarda himself prepared for the Office of External Research, Department of State (16 October 1974). Also Philippe C. Schmitter. "Liberation by *Golpe*: Retrospective Thoughts on the Demise of Authoritarian Rule in Portugal." *Armed Forces and Society* 2 (November 1975) pp. 5–33.

5 AFRICA DILEMMAS

1 From background confidential print made available to the author by the then editor of the *Observer*, Neal Ascherson.

2 Spínola, *País sem rumo*. Also Kenneth Maxwell, "The Thorns of the Portuguese Revolution," *Foreign Affairs* (January 1976), pp. 250–70, and Kenneth Maxwell, "The Legacy of Decolonization" in Richard J. Bloomfield (ed.) *Regional Conflict and U.S. Policy: Angola and Mozambique* (Boston, 1988) pp. 7–39.

3 Jean Daniel, "L'armée portugaise face à l'anticommunisme," *Le Nouvel Observateur*, August 11, 1975, pp. 16–18.

4 The articles from the MFA *Boletim* may be found in *MFA: Motor da revolução portuguesa* (Lisbon, 1975).

5 The most comprehensive account remains John Marcum, *The Angolan Revolution*, Vol. II, pp. 243–63.

6 Rosa Coutinho, "Interview with Revolutionary Council member Admiral," in *Diário de Notícias* November 10, 1975, pp. 7–8; reported by *FBIS-WEU Daily Report* 75–224, vol. 7, no. 224, p. 78.

7 Spínola, *País sem rumo*, pp. 142, 151, 159.

8 Rosa Coutinho, *FBIS-WEU: Daily Report* 75–224, November 10, 1975.

9 Comment made to author, Lisbon, January 1975.

10 Jane Kramer, "A Reporter at Large (Portugal)," *The New Yorker* December 15, 1975, pp. 92–131.

6 REVOLUTION

1 Chronology and communiqués in Fernando Ribeiro de Mello, ed., *Dossier: 2a República*, I, pp. 165–73.

2 "Costa Gomes: da posse ao conselho da revolução 30 março 75," in *Dossier: 2a República*, I, pp. 174–5.

3 For a comprehensive collection of MFA texts of the period, most from the *Boletim 25 de abril*, see *MFA: Motor da revolução portuguesa* (July 1975), coordinated by Serafim Ferreira.

4 Cited in *MFA: Motor da revolução*.

5 For a text of decrees see *A revolução em ruptura: Textos históricos da revolução*, (3 vols. Lisbon 1975), vol. II organized by Orlando Neves.

6 For election returns and analyses, see Jorge Gaspar and Nuno Vitorino, *As eleições de 25 de abril: Geografia e imagem dos partidos* (Lisbon, 1976). Also see analyses by John Hammond in Lawrence S. Graham and Harry M. Mackler, eds., *Contemporary Portugal: Culture, Economy and Politics in Comparative Perspective* (Austin, 1979) and Ben Pimlott and Jean Seaton "Ferment of an Old Power," *New Society* July 24, 1975, p. 202.

7 For analyses of elections see Maria Emília Arroz et al., *As eleições legislativas: Algumas perspectivas regionais* (Lisbon, 1976).

8 Ambassador Carlucci's comment from "Military and Economic Assistance to Portugal," *Hearing before the Subcommittee on Foreign*

Assistance of the Committee of Foreign Relations, US Senate 95th Congress, 1st session on S. 844, etc., February 25, 1977 (Washington DC, 1977); Carlucci had a distinguished career after his posting in Lisbon. He became deputy director of the CIA on his return to Washington, then secretary of defense and national security adviser.

9 Cunhal's comments from Alvaro Cunhal, *A revolução portuguesa, o passado e o futuro* (Lisbon, 1976).

10 For an interesting summary and critical look at the writing on the "land reform" in Portugal see Rutledge, "Land Reform and the Portuguese Revolution." Also see Claude Collin, "Enquête sur les coopératives agricoles au Portugal," *Les temps modernes* 364 (1976).

11 On Angola in this period see Ernest Harsch and Tony Thomas, *Angola: The Hidden History of Washington's War* (New York, 1976); Jim Dingeman, "Angola: Portugal in Africa," *Strategy and Tactics* 56 (May/June 1976); Colin Legum, "The Role of the Big Powers," and Tony Hodges, "How the MPLA Won," in *After Angola: The War Over Southern Africa* (New York, London, 1976).

12 See interview with João van Dunem by Fernando J. Andresen in *Camões Center Quarterly* vol. 5, nos. 1/2 (Winter 1993/94), p. 28.

13 See interview with João van Dunem in *Camões Center Quarterly* vol. 5, nos. 1/2 (Winter 1994/95), p. 26.

14 See Kenneth Maxwell "Portugal and Africa: The Last Empire". In Prosser Gifford and William Roger Louis, eds. *The Transfer of Power in Africa: Decolonization 1940–1960* (New Haven, 1982) pp. 337–85; and Aquino de Bregança and Basil Davidson "Independence and Decolonization: Mozambique 1974–1975" in Gifford and Louis, eds., *Decolonization and African Independence* Newhaven, 1988) pp. 427–43.

15 Among them the Export–Import Bank, the First National City Bank, the Chase Manhattan Bank, and Continental Illinois.

16 Excellent accounts of the tense negotiations over Zaire's debt and economic problems can be found in Nancy Bellieveau, *Institutional Investor* (March 1977), pp. 23–28, and Crawford Young, "Zaire: The Unending Crisis," *Foreign Affairs* (Fall 1978), pp. 169–85.

17 On private lines of communication and their impact on Zairian–US-Angolan relations, see Bruce Oudes' reports in *Africa Contemporary Record*, ed. Colin Legum (New York: Africana Publishing Company), especially vol. VII (1974–1975), pp. A87–A101, and vol. VIII (1975–1976), pp. A118–A126 (1975–1976).

18 See "US Policy on Angola," *Hearing Before the Committee on International Relations*, House of Representatives, 94th Congress, 2nd Session, January 26, 1976 (Washington DC: 1975), p. 13. Also see, "Security Supporting Assistance for Zaire," *Hearing Before the Subcommittee on African Affairs and the Subcommittee on Foreign Assistance of the Committee on Foreign Relations*, US Senate, 94th Congress, 1st Session, October 24, 1975 (Washington, DC: 1975), p. 32. Also Kenneth Maxwell,

"A New Scramble for Africa," in *The Conduct of Soviet Foreign Policy*, ed. Erik Hoffman and Frederick Fleron, Jr. (Hawthorne, 1980), pp. 515–34.

19 Mulcahy's comment in "US Policy on Angola," *Hearing Before the Committee on International Relations*, p. 13. Also see "Security Supporting Assistance for Zaire," *Hearing Before the Subcommittee on African Affairs and the Subcommittee on Foreign Assistance of the Committee on Foreign Relations*, p. 32.

20 For Spínola's own account of this episode, see Spínola, *País sem rumo*. See also, Stephen R. Weissman's testimony before the Committee on International Relations, January 26, 1976 (see n. 18), and his book, *American Foreign Policy in the Congo 1960–1969* (Ithaca, 1974), as well as John Stockwell, *In Search of Enemies: A CIA Story* (New York, 1978). There has been much speculation about what was discussed between Spínola and Nixon at their June 19, 1974 Azores meeting. The two men met alone with only an interpreter present, and officials on both sides were left in the dark as to the topics covered. Spínola has now given his version of the conversation in *País sem rumo*, pp. 158–168.

21 See especially Weissman, *American Foreign Policy in the Congo*.

22 Stockwell, *In Search of Enemies*.

7 COUNTER-REVOLUTION

1 For a good account of the complicated *República* and Rádio Renascença cases see Phil Mailer, *Portugal: The Impossible Revolution?* (New York, 1977).

2 Jacques Fremontier, *Portugal: Les points sur les i* (Paris, 1976).

3 For an excellent account of the different reactions of the French and Italian communist parties to events in Portugal see Alex Macleod, *La révolution inopportune: les parties communistes française et italienne face à la révolution portugaise (1973–1975)* (Montréal, 1984).

4 Jane Kramer, "A Reporter at Large (Portugal)," *The New Yorker* December 15, 1975, pp. 92–131.

5 Cunhal, *Pela revolução democrática e nacional* (Lisbon, 1975).

6 Alvaro Cunhal, *Radicalismo pequeno burguês da façada socialista* ([Lisbon?] 1971), p. 82; see also Cunhal, *A revolução portuguesa, o passado e o futuro* (Lisbon, 1976).

7 Jane Kramer, "A Reporter at Large."

8 For the struggle within one family-owned textile enterprise in the north, see *O caso dos 17 da textil Manuel Gonçalves: um documento para a história da luta dos trabalhadores* (Oporto, 1976).

9 For the economy see the volumes of the two International Conferences on the Portugaise economy (1977, 1979) held in Lisbon,

sponsored by the Gulbenkian Foundation and the German Marshall Fund in the US.

10 See especially John L. Hammond, *Building Popular Power: Workers and Neighborhood Movements in the Portuguese Revolution* (New York 1988) pp. 77–87, 98–105, 147–77.

11 Helmut Sonnenfeldt, "American-Soviet Relations: Informal Remarks," *Parameters: Journal of the US Army War College* 6, 1 (an article adapted from an address before the 22nd Annual National Security Seminar at the US Army War College, June 3, 1976), pp. 15–16. On Soviet policy, "The Soviet Union and the Third World: A Watershed of Great Power Rivalry," *Report to the Committee on International Relations*, House of Representatives, by the Senior Specialists Division, Congressional Research Service, Library of Congress, May 8, 1977 (Washington, DC: 1977). Kissinger had encouraged a series of highly secret contacts with the Castro regime aimed at a detente between the U.S. and Cuba as late as August of 1975. This in part explains the surprise in Washington at Castro's Angolan intervention. See "Dialogue with Castro: A Hidden History" by Peter Kornbinh and James G. Blight, *New York Review of Books* (October 6, 1994), pp. 45–49.

12 Gerald J. Bender, "Angola, the Cubans, and American Anxieties," *Foreign Policy* 31 (Summer 1978), pp. 3–33; John A. Marcum, "The Lessons of Angola," *Foreign Affairs* 54, 3 (April 1976), pp. 407–25; Kenneth Adelman and Gerald J. Bender, "Conflict in Southern Africa: A Debate," *International Security* 3, 2 (Fall 1978), pp. 67–122; Gerald J. Bender, "Kissinger and Angola: Anatomy of Failure," *American Policy in Southern Africa* (Washington DC, 1978), pp. 65–143; and Marcum, *The Angolan Revolution*, II (which deals with this period); Robert Moss, "Castro's Secret War Exposed," *The Sunday Telegraph* (London), January 30, 1977, February 6, 1977, February 30, 1977; Gabriel García Márquez, "Operation Carlota: Cuba's Role in Angolan Victory," *Cuba Update* 1, Center for Cuban Studies (April 1977). This is an abbreviated account based on the original in Spanish published in Mexico. A good overview is Arthur Jay Klinghoffer, *The Angolan War: A Study in Soviet Policy in the Third World* (Boulder, 1980). Also see Stephen R. Weissman, "CIA Covert Action in Zaire and Angola: Patterns and Consequences," *Political Science Quarterly*, 94, 2 (Summer 1979). For background on Cuba's role in Africa, see Nelson P. Valdes, "Revolutionary Solidarity in Angola," *Cuba and the World*, ed. Cole Blasier and Carmelo Mesa-Lago (Pittsburgh, 1979), pp. 87–117; William M. LeoGrande, "Cuba–Soviet Relations and Cuban Policy in Africa," *Cuban Studies* (January, 1980), pp. 1–48.

13 See the excellent accounts by Hodges and Legum, eds., in *After Angola: The War over Southern Africa* (New York, 1978); Charles K.

Ebinger, "External Intervention in Internal War: The Politics and Diplomacy of the Angolan Civil War," *Orbis* (Fall 1976), pp. 669–99; as well as the first-hand report by Stockwell, *In Search of Enemies: A CIA Story* (New York, 1978) and Nathaniel Davis, "The Angola Decision of 1975: A Personal Memoir," *Foreign Affairs* (Fall 1978), pp. 109–24. On South Africa's intervention, see Robert S. Jaster, "South Africa's Narrowing Security Options," *Adelphi Papers* 159 (London, 1980). For early Cuban contacts with the MPLA, see Fernando Andressen Guimarães' interview with two MPLA dissidents in *Camões Center Quarterly* vol. 5, nos. 1/2 (Spring 1994).

14 For some interesting and well-informed comments on this aspect, see "The Battle for Angola," by Robert Moss, editor of the *Economist*'s confidential *Foreign Report*, November 12, 1975, pp. 1–6. Moss was in southern Angola with the South Africans and was one of the observers best placed to know their thinking on this question. Also see comments by Cord Meyer, *Facing Reality: From World Federalism to the CIA* (New York, 1981). Cord Meyer was the CIA station chief in London over this period.

15 Colin Legum "Foreign Intervention in Angola" in *African Contemporary Record 1975–76* (New York, 1976) pp. A3–38.

16 Marcum *The Angolan Revolution* Vol. 2, pp. 272–81.

17 These figures are pieced together from Mark M. Lowenthal, "Foreign Assistance in the Angolan Civil War," in appendix 3 to "Mercenaries in Africa," *Hearing Before the Special Subcommittee on International Relations*, House of Representatives, 94th Congress, 2nd session, August 9, 1976 (Washington, DC), and from *World Military Expenditures 1967–1976* (Washington, DC) and *Strategic Survey 1977* (London 1976 and 1977), p. 27.

8 THE REVOLUTION TAMED

1 Alvaro Cunhal, *Pela revolução democrática e nacional* (Lisbon, 1975), especially pp. 7–10.

2 Alvaro Cunhal, *L'Europeo*, June 15, 1975 (Milan).

3 See Cunhal, *A revolução portuguesa, o passado e o futuro* (Lisbon, 1976), p. 383.

4 For the struggle in the military see Avelino Rodrigues, Cesário Borga, and Mário Cardoso, *Abril nos quarteis de novembro* (Lisbon 1979). Also, José Gomes Mota, *A resistência* (Lisbon, 1976).

5 See Kenneth Maxwell, "Portuguese Communism" in George Schwab, ed. *Eurocommunism* (Westport, 1981) pp. 269–99: *A Report on West European Communist Parties Prepared by the Foreign Affairs and National Defense Division of the Congressional Research Service* (Washington D.C. 1977); Carlos Gaspar and Vasco Rato *Rumo à Memória Crónicas da Crise Comunista* (Lisbon, 1992).

6 For the summer disputes in the military, see Ramiro Correia, Pedro Soldado, and João Marujo, *MFA e a luta de classes: subsídios para a compreensão do processo histórico português* (Lisbon, n.d.). This collection contains important extracts from speeches in MFA assemblies, etc. For a collection of articles from the MFA *Bulletin* see *MFA: Motor da revolução portuguesa* (Lisbon, 1975). For the speeches of the prime minister see Vasco Gonçalves, *Discursos, conferências, entrevistas*, introduction by J. J. Teixeira Ribeiro (Oporto, 1976). See also *Citações de Vasco Gonçalves: Livro verde da revolução* (Amadora, 1975). Also Sánchez Cervelló, *A Revolução Portuguesa* p. 243–5.

7 The PCP's view of the summer is contained in Alvaro Cunhal, "A crises político-militar: discursos políticos" in *Documentos políticos do PCP* 15 (Lisbon, 1975) which published comments made by Cunhal but these were suppressed in the party's bulletins put out at the time. The PCP had abandoned Vasco Gonçalves on August 10, 1975. Also see Jean-Pierre Faye, *Portugal: The Revolution in the Labyrinth* (Nottingham, 1976). For Soviet attitudes in this period, see the analysis by Carlos Gaspar, "O lugar de Zarodov: A engenharia política leninista e a revolução portuguesa," in Gaspar and Rato, eds., *Ruma à memória* (Lisbon, 1992), pp. 59–92.

8 Robert Moss, "A Ticket to Lisbon: The Civil War in Portugal," *Harper's Magazine* (1975), pp. 89–93.

9 Carlos Dugas, *MDLP-ELP – que são? A verdade sobre os dois movimentos clandestinos* (Alfragide, 1976).

10 See Correia, Soldado, and Marujo, *MFA e luta de classes*. For Pimlott's eyewitness account of the siege of the constituent assembly and government see Ben Pimlott, *Frustrate their Knavish Tricks: Writings on Biography, History and Politics* (London, 1994), pp. 262–68. Also for this period see José Freire Antunes, *O segredo do 25 de novembro, O verão quente de 1975 e os planos desconhecidos do grupo militar* (Lisbon 1980). The "moderates" and their western backers were not fully confident of victory on 25 November. Plans had been made to establish a government in the north of the country in the event that Lisbon was lost to the far left; this was the "commune of Lisbon" scenario. Groups in the Azores were also poised to declare independence from Lisbon in this eventuality. Even after the victory of 25 November in Lisbon, Kissinger remained committed to increased covert action in Angola, including the introduction of American advisers. This was an inflamatory position to take in the year South Vietnam had fallen. Predictably the news leaked, and led directly to the congressional ban of US assistance to the anti-MPLA forces. While in Indonesia in mid December, President Ford and Kissinger turned a blind eye to Indonesia's brutal invasion of East Timor where tens of thousands died. On his return to Washington, furious that the news of American complicity might leak, he complained:

"And we can't construe a communist government in the middle of Indonesia as self-defense?" It was another example of Kissinger's indifference to the human consequences of his actions which will continue to mar his historical reputation as a statesman. For a detailed account the Angolan and Timor episodes see Isaacson, *Kissinger* pp. 673–85; the quotation about Timor is from p. 681.

11 Kenneth Maxwell and Scott C. Monge, eds., *Portugal: The Constitution and Consolidation of Democracy, 1976–1989* (New York, 1991); Andrea Bonime-Blanc, *Spain's Transition to Democracy: The Politics of Constitution Making* (Boulder, 1987).

9 PICKING UP THE PIECES

1 Dr. Balsemão has provided his own view of the period in "The Constitution and Politics: Options for the Future" in K. Maxwell, ed., *Portugal in the 1980s: The Dilemmas of Democratic Consolidation* (Westport, New York, and London, 1986), pp. 197–232.

2 Luís Salgado de Matos, "Significado e consequências da eleição do presidente por sufrágio universal – o caso português," *Análise Social* 19, 2 (1983), pp. 235–59.

3 Maria José Stock, "O centrismo político em Portugal: gênese do Bloco Central e análise dos partidos da coligação," *Análise Social* 21, 1 (1985), pp. 45–81 and "A base social de apoio e o recruta- mento dos líderes do PSD," in *Revista de ciência política* (1985), pp. 103–21.

4 See Diogo Freitas do Amaral, *A lei de defesa nacional e das forças armadas: Textos, discursos e trabalhos preparatórios* (Coimbra, 1983).

5 Alvaro de Vasconcelos, "Portuguese Defense Policy: Internal Politics and Defense Commitments," in John Chipman, ed., *NATO's Southern Allies* (London, 1988), pp. 86–136. See also Kenneth Maxwell (ed.) *Portuguese Defense and Foreign Policy since Democratization* (New York, 1991).

6 Vasconcelos, "Portuguese Defense Policy," pp. 130–1. Also the comprehensive discussion by Lawrence S. Graham, *The Portuguese Military and the State* (Boulder, 1993).

CONCLUSION

1 Samuel P. Huntington, *The Third Wave: Democratization in the Late Twentieth Century* (Norman, 1991).

2 For the impact of Angola on Kissinger's subsequent policy in Africa see Walter Isaacson *Kissinger: A biography* (New York, 1992) pp. 607–29; pp. 673–92; also Coral Bell *The Diplomacy of Détente: The Kissinger Era* (New York, 1977) pp. 156–83.

3 For an account of Spain's transition, Kenneth Maxwell and Steven Speigel, *The New Spain: from isolation to influence* (New York, 1994).

4 Alistair Horne, *A Savage War of Peace* (London, 1977).

Bibliographical essay

There are four major sets of questions which have interested scholars in recent years and provide a context for the period covered by this book. The first concerns the old regime; the second, the question of Portuguese colonialism in Africa; the third, the revolution; and the fourth, the consolidation of the democratic system. This essay touches only on the major questions and contributions since each of these areas is vast.

There are now the beginnings of bibliographical and documentary aids to scholars interested in this period. The most important depository of documentation on the post-April 25 period is at the Centro de Documentação 25 de Abril, founded by Professor Boaventura de Sousa Santos at the University of Coimbra. This center has already published a bilingual and annotated bibliography by Ronald H. Chilcote, *The Portuguese Revolution of 25 April 1974* (Coimbra, 1987). Most of the documentation I have used for this book has been deposited with the Special Collections division at Princeton University where a comprehensive guide will also be available in the future, and the materials of which will be available to scholars. The Conference Group of Modern Portugal has also published a good bibliographical guide by William Lomax, *Revolution in Portugal, 1974–1976: A Bibliography* (Durham, 1978). For an excellent comparative bibliography see D. Nikiforos Diamandouros, Pilar Rivilla, Joaquim Lopez Novo, Huri Tursam, and Philippe Schmitter, *A Bibliographic Essay on Southern Europe and its Recent Transition to Political Democracy* (Florence, 1986).

The early works on corporatism by, among others, Howard Wiarda (*Corporatism and Development: The Portuguese Experience* (Amherst, 1977)) and Manuel de Lucena (*A evolução do sistema corporativo português*, 2 vols. (Lisbon, 1976)), were heavily theoreti cal, and the immediate post-coup analyses were polemical and denunciatory. The series of "black books on fascism," for example, were much less helpful to historians than they should have been and the commission on the dismantling of the secret police (PIDE and later DGS) became highly politicized. These archives are now at the National Archive in Lisbon and were opened to scholars in 1994, on the twentieth anniversary of the coup, though access is still circumscribed. Salazar's and Caetano's personal papers have only just begun to be exploited and are available to scholars on a very sporadic basis. However, there is an accumulating body of memoirs and published correspondence now available.

Several stalwarts of the old regime have published memoirs or histories of the period, most notably Salazar's former foreign minister, Franco Nogueira, who, after returning to Portugal from exile, spent his later years on a massive biography of Salazar (*Salazar*, 6 vols. (Lisbon, 1977–1985)). Nogueira also published his diary, or at least a sanitized version of it, as *Um político confessa-se: Diário, 1960–1968* (Oporto, 1986). His *Diálogos interditos: A política externa portuguesa e a guerra de Africa*, 2 vols. (Lisbon, 1979) is also extremely important for his comments on leading figures in Salazar's administration as well as Nixon and Kennedy. Other important memoirs are those of Marcello Mathias, also a Salazar intimate, foreign minister and long-time ambassador to Paris (Marcello Mathias, *Correspondência com Salazar, 1947–1968* (Lisbon, 1984)). José Freire Antunes has contributed several volumes of letters from the Caetano personal archive, including *Salazar e Caetano: Cartas Secretas 1932–1968* (Lisbon 1994) and *Cartas particulares a Marcello Caetano* (Lisbon, 1985) 2 vols. Marcello Caetano wrote his own memoirs in *Minhas memórias das Salazar* (Lisbon, 1977).

Among the most polemical and revealing verbatim conversations with Marcello Caetano is by the historian Joaquim Verríssimo Serrão, *Marcello Caetano: Confidências no exílio* (Lisbon and São Paulo, 1985). The book was enormously controversial, precisely because of its direct comment about people and events, so unlike the usual elliptical and indirect world of most Portuguese memories and commentary. The book contains Caetano's own annotations of General Spínola's book, *País sem rumo* (Lisbon, 1978). Veríssimo Serrão was rector of the University of Lisbon (now known as the Classical University of Lisbon) at the time of the coup, and he was purged from his position and chair. He was an old friend of Caetano, who had also been rector of the university and had resigned as a result of the government's reaction to student disturbances in 1961. Both men, in this period, were bitter about their treatment and the book, as a consequence, is more revealing than it might have been if it were written at any other point in time. Veríssimo Serrão later became president of the Portuguese Academy of History; Caetano died in Rio de Janeiro in 1980.

In addition, more detailed empirical studies of various aspects of the Salazar and Caetano regime have now been published. António Costa Pinto, for example, has tackled the comparative European dimension of Portuguese authoritarianism, summarizing the debates in "O Salazarismo e o fascismo europeu," in *Salazar e o Salazarismo*, ed. J. Brandão de Brito (Lisbon, 1989), pp. 155–89 and in his *salazarismo e o fascismo europeu: Problemas de interpretação nas ciências sociais* (Lisbon, 1992). There are several well-documented books on various aspects of the international relations of the old regime, especially in the 1940s, by António Telo, *Portugal na Segunda Guerra* (Lisbon, 1987); Fernando Rosas, *Portugal entre a paz e a guerra* (Lisbon, 1990); César Oliveira, *O salazarismo e a guerra civil de Espanha* (Lisbon, 1988), among others. For other aspects of the regime, Manuel Braga da Cruz has written on the political organization of the one party state in *O partido e o Estado no salazarismo* (Lisbon, 1988). Also, Silas Cequeira on the Catholic church in "L'église catholique et la dictature corporatiste portugaise," *Revue Française de Sciences Politiques* 23 (1973); D. L. Raby, *Fascism and Resistance in Portugal: Communists, Liberals, and Military Dissidents in the Opposition to Salazar, 1941–1974* (Manchester, 1988) and Hermínio Martins, "Opposition in Portugal," *Government and Opposition* 4, 2 (Spring 1969) on the opposition; Maria Filomena Mónica, *Educação e sociedade no Portugal de Salazar: A escola primária salazarista, 1926–1939* (Lisbon, 1978) on education; and José Maria Brandão de Brito, *A industrialização portuguesa na pós-guerra 1948–1965: O condicionamento industrial* (Lisbon, 1989) on industrial policy. A useful collection of chapters covering many aspects of the old regime from integralism to architecture resulted from a March 1980 conference, published as *O fascismo em Portugal* (Lisbon, 1982).

The second important series of issues concerns the nature of late Portuguese colonialism. Here there is a substantial body of work in several languages since it was the colonial wars and the defiance of the international community over decolonization that attracted a great deal of attention from foreigners as well as a propaganda effort by the Salazar and Caetano regimes. Some of the best work by American scholars grew out of an attempt to counter the idea of "Luso-tropicalism," a term which had been developed and popularized by the Brazilian sociologist Gilberto Freire in his influential *O mundo que o português criou* [The World the Portuguese Created] (Rio de Janeiro, 1940). Freire argued that the Portuguese tolerance and assimilation of tropical values distinguished them as pioneers of modern tropical civilizations. The focal point of the ideology of Luso-tropicalism was the notion of the unique non-racism of the Portuguese colonizer. For a discussion and demolition of his theory, see Gerald Bender, *Angola Under the Portuguese: The Myth and the Reality* (Berkeley and Los Angeles, 1978). See also Charles Boxer, *Race Relations in the Portuguese Colonial Empire 1415–1825* (Oxford, 1963). In this book Boxer challenged the theory with irrefutable evidence and was thoroughly vilified by the Salazar regime for having done so. There was, nevertheless, a difference in Portuguese colonial practice from that of the British, and there is a need for a thorough and unbiased account of the whole question of Portuguese colonialist mentality and myth which will strike a balance between a wholly materialist explanation espoused by scholars such as Bender or the wholly mythic interpretation espoused by the more fervent supporters of Salazar. Two recent excellent contributions to the overall debate on Portuguese colonialism are Gervase Clarence-Smith, *The Third Portuguese Empire, 1825–1975* (Manchester, 1985) and Malyn Newitt, *Portugal in Africa: The Last Hundred Years* (London, 1981). Also M. Anne Pitcher, *Politics in the Portuguese Empire: The State, Industry and Cotton 1926–1974* (Oxford, 1993).

This culturalist debate was linked, of course, to the debate about the nature of Portuguese Iberic consciousness developed by Wiarda (see below). Both, to some degree, rejected the more materialist interpretation of the underpinnings of the regime and of Portuguese colonialism. The Portuguese governmental elite, Salazar especially, categorically denied the economic argument

and were adamantly opposed to the opening-up of the Portuguese
territories in Africa to American capital until very late in the
conflict. José Freire Antunes has dealt with this in a general way
in his *O factor africano, 1890–1990* (Lisbon, 1990). Dependency
theory played an important role in the writing of William Minter
and others during the 1960s and 1970s. For Guinea-Bissau, see
Patrick Chabal, *Amílcar Cabral: Revolutionary Leadership and People's
War* (Cambridge, 1983) and the general overview by Joshua B.
Forrest, *Guinea-Bissau: Power, Conflict and Renewal in a West African
Nation* (Boulder, 1992). Among Basil Davidson's many works on
the Portuguese territories and the liberation movements are *In
the Eye of the Storm* (Harmondsworth, 1972) and *The Liberation of
Guinea: Aspects of an African Revolution* (Harmondsworth, 1969).
For Angola see Don Barnett and Roy Harvey, *The Revolution in
Angola: MPLA Life Histories and Documents* (New York, 1972).

The third general area concerned the nature of the revolution –
was it a revolution, and if so how revolutionary were the post-
April 25, 1974 developments? The question was asked most
directly by Ben Pimlott in an engaging article, "Socialism in
Portugal: Was it a Revolution?" *Government and Opposition* 12, 3
(Summer 1977), pp. 332–50 and his "Were the Soldiers Revolutionary? The Armed Forces Movement and the Portuguese
Revolution," *Iberian Studies* 7, 1 (Spring 1978). There is much
disagreement over this question, as there was at the time, and
the answer lies in a complex series of international, domestic,
and theoretical concerns, all of which have been addressed in
hundreds of publications, both contemporaneously and subsequently. The collection of essays contained in the volume edited
by Lawrence S. Graham and Douglas L. Wheeler, *In Search of
Modern Portugal: The Revolution and its Consequences* (Madison, 1983),
addressed various sides of these questions in often discordant
ways, as the thoughtful introductory essay by Joyce Riegelhaupt
pointed out at the time. The Graham and Wheeler volume, like
its predecessor edited by Graham and Harry Makler, *Contemporary
Portugal: Culture, Economy and Politics in Comparative Perspective*
(Austin, 1979), emerged from conferences organized by the International Conference Group on Modern Portugal. The degree to
which the revolutionary period has been sublimated is very well
presented in the comments in Richard Herr's introductory essay
to *The New Portugal: Democracy and Europe* (Berkeley, 1992).

Among the more accessible collections of published documents of the revolutionary period are several compilations published at the time, most notably *Textos históricos da revolução*, 3 vols., organized by Orlando Neves (Lisbon, 1975–6) and the *Revolução das flores*, 3 vols. (1975–6). In addition, there are important documents contained in Fernando Ribeiro de Mello, ed., *Dossier: 2a República* 2 vols. (Lisbon, 1976–7), as well as in the numerous publications by various members of the Armed Forces Movement (MFA) noted below and in the bibliography. These are all essential starting points.

As with the Salazar and Caetano period, there are now many memoirs and polemics by former leading figures in the revolutionary period. Many of these works need to be treated with caution and placed in their historical context. There are several important works on the origins of the MFA, as well as accounts by the leading participants in the movement. The best overview can be found in: Avelino Rodrigues, Cesário Borga, and Mário Cardoso, *O movimento dos capitães e o 25 de abril: 229 dias para derrubar o fascismo* (Lisbon, 1974); *Insight on Portugal* (by the Insight Team of the *Sunday Times* (London, 1975)); Otelo Saraiva de Carvalho, *Alvorada em abril* (Lisbon, 1977); Diniz de Almeida, *Origens e evolução do movimento dos capitães* (Lisbon, 1977); George Grayson, "Portugal and the Armed Forces," *Orbis* 19 (Summer 1975), pp. 335–78. There are important studies of the armed forces by Maria Carrilho, *Forças armadas e mudança política em Portugal no século XX* (Lisbon, 1985) and Josep Sánchez Cervelló, *A revolução Portuguesa e a sua influência na transição espanhola (1961–1976)* (Lisbon, 1993). See also Mário Moreira Alves, *Les soldats socialistes du Portugal* (Paris, 1975) and Douglas Porch, *The Portuguese Armed Forces and the Revolution* (London, 1977). Alves and Porch take differing views as to the importance of the African experience, Alves giving it a primary role in stimulating the MFA's radicalism, Porch arguing against the importance of Africa as a radicalizing influence. Porch, however, exaggerates his case, and the disagreement in this author's view is more to do with chronology than substance. The African component was vital to explain the process of politicization, not its ultimate outcome, about which Porch, by stressing the strength of the corporate identity of the officer corps, is undoubtedly right. Both authors draw heavily on my articles written at the time for the *New York Review of*

Books 21, 10 (June 17, 1974), pp. 16–21; 22, 6 (April 17, 1975), pp. 29–39; 22, 9 (May 29, 1975), pp. 20–30. Several distinguished books provide a detailed account of the popular movement in this phase, both in its rural and urban dimension. For the agrarian reform see Nancy Gina Bermeo, *The Revolution within the Revolution: Workers' Control in Rural Portugal* (Princeton, 1986) and António Barreto, *Anatomia de uma revolução: A reforma agrária em Portugal 1974–1976* (Lisbon n.d.); and on the urban movement John L. Hammond, *Building Popular Power: Workers and Neighborhood Movements in the Portuguese Revolution* (New York, 1988) and Charles Downs, *Revolution at the Grass Roots: Community Organization in the Portuguese Revolution* (Albany 1986). Also important is the lively and skeptical analysis by Phil Mailer, *Portugal: The Impossible Revolution* (London, 1977) which captures the spirit of the times better than the more academic studies.

The final series of questions concerns the success and vicissitudes of the new regime. How successfully consolidated is Portuguese democracy, how stable, what are its characteristics and strengths? On these issues too, there is now a large body of literature.

As to the stability of the new democratic regime, several distinct interpretations have emerged, though the authors of the various interpretations rarely, if ever, engage each other in direct debate. Thomas C. Bruneau (*Politics and Nationhood: Post-Revolutionary Portugal* (New York, 1984); and Thomas C. Bruneau and Alex Macleod (*Politics in Contemporary Portugal: Parties and the Consolidation of Democracy* (Boulder, 1980) best exemplify the consensus view. Bruneau was, from the beginning, generally optimistic about the prospects for democracy in Portugal and its continuance. Howard J. Wiarda, who wrote a major book on the Portuguese corporatist regime (*Corporatism and Development: The Portuguese Experience* (Amherst, 1977)), published shortly after the regime's collapse (though mainly written before 25 April), best exemplifies the more skeptical position. In *The Transition to Democracy in Spain and Portugal* (Washington, DC, 1989), Wiarda explained the imperfect (in his view) institutionalization of the new democracy in terms of behavioral continuities from the old regime which he claims have been underestimated by wishful-thinking observers. What Wiarda calls "Iberic consciousness" had not, he believed, "internalized" a democratic ethos.

Yet this point of departure seems to me to miss an important element. As this book has attempted to demonstrate, Portuguese democracy did not flow from the planning or pact-making of elites – something much more characteristic of the democratic transitions in Latin America and Spain and the subject of an excellent recent book edited by John Higley and Richard Gunther, *Elites and Democratic Consolidation in Latin America and Southern Europe* (Cambridge, 1992). Portuguese democracy, by way of contrast, emerged out of a turbulent breakdown of authority, out of a vivid clash between alternative visions of social and political organization and of the future. As I have emphasized in this book, Portugal is a democracy, that has been struggled for rather than negotiated; and in this fact lie the causes of some of its problems as well as its basic strength. Indeed, precisely because elections were so restrictive, unrepresentative, and so manipulated during the long years of the Salazar regime, the electoral act in Portugal today remains almost unique in contemporary democracies as an act of civic piety and is likely to remain so as long as the memories of the old regime persist among segments of the electorate. And, since democratization, no election has been attacked as having been manipulated, stolen, or fixed. This alone is a major achievement.

Dr. Wiarda also evokes the continuities of anti- or non-democratic practices. Yet he is not speaking here of social and economic obstacles or class antagonism, or how social segments of the population react or might react to changing economic circumstances – the type of analysis, for example, which has been carried out by Professor Boaventura de Sousa Santos and his colleagues at the University of Coimbra (*O estado e a sociedade em Portugal, 1974–1988* (Oporto, 1990)). These Portuguese scholars have sought to explain the resilience of Portuguese social structures in the face of economic and political trauma. They also point to the potential risks involved in the rationalization of these structures. This will presumably be one of the inevitable consequences of the rapid modernization of Portugal under the pressure emanating from European integration, pressure which may diminish the complexity of the social structure in Portugal and its imperfect or partial modernity, and hence perhaps eliminate the built-in compensatory mechanisms that provide individuals and families with relief in times of economic trouble. But this prognostication appears to have underestimated the rapid growth that would follow EC accession and the flow of foreign investment and EC funds.

Walter C. Opello, in "The Continuing Impact of the Old Regime on Portuguese Political Culture" (in Lawrence Graham and Douglas Wheeler, eds., *In Search of Modern Portugal: The Revolution and its Consequences* (Madison, 1983) pp. 199–222) has also been skeptical about Portugal's democratization base in his research on changes in local administration. Nevertheless his is a more nuanced and less cataclysmic view than that of Wiarda. Opello emphasizes the continuing over-centralization of the bureaucracy and the lack of fiscal autonomy at the local level. Continuity of personnel is a separate question, both within the administrative and the economic elites, and this remains a much understudied topic, despite the work by Harry Makler on industrialists before and after the April coup, and Lawrence Graham on bureaucrats and the military. The ongoing studies by Manuel de Lucena and his colleagues at the Instituto de Ciências Sociais at the University of Lisbon will provide very important data on these issues. See, in particular, Manuel de Lucena, "A desmantelamento da organização corporativa ao duvidoso fim do corporativismo," *Análise Social* 13, 3 (1977), pp. 541–92. A good review of the debate on political culture is contained in the review essay by Franz-Wilhelm Heimer, "A cultura política em Portugal," *Revista de Ciência Política* 4 (Lisbon, 1986), pp. 7–21. A fine analysis of institutional change in the rural area is Manuel de Lucena's *Revolução e instituições: A extinção dos grémios da Lavoura alentejanos*, III. This is one of eight volumes edited by António Barreto on agrarian reform, funded by the German Friedrich Naumann Foundation, (Lisbon, n.d.). For an overview of the "compensating mechanism" thesis see Boaventura de Sousa Santos "Social Crises and the State," in Kenneth Maxwell, *Portugal in the 1980s* (Greenwood, Westport, New York, London, 1986), pp. 167–95. Also Walter Opello, "Administração local e cultura política num concelho rural," *Análise Social* 15, 2 (1979), pp. 655–72 where he points to continuing administrative centralization and lack of financial autonomy.

We still have very few studies of what the parties represent in terms of interests or regions or business or organized labor. We know very little, at least in the social scientific literature, about how the various interest groups make themselves felt in Portuguese politics, although anecdotal evidence certainly suggests that they are very important. The parties have clearly sought to cement their political power by colonization of the bureaucracy and state enterprises with their loyalists. It is also evident that individual leaders have used political influence to reward and punish friends and opponents: something which has some consequences for scholarship as well, since key positions in the gift of the prime minister can be rewards for political and polemical fealty. It is perhaps an exaggeration to argue, as the sociologist Manuel Villaverde Cabral has, that all political analysis is "politically motivated," but there is certainly a germ of truth in this hyperbole (M. Villaverde Cabral, "Portugal since the Revolution," *Luso-Brazilian Review 24*, 1 (1987), pp. 79–86). The press is very much a captive of this all-pervasive political intrusion. The press is also a prime target for privatization, given the heavy state role in its ownership. Here again, the integration of Portugal into the EU has had a major impact, with the infusion of outside money into new media outlets and the competition for new means of access to electronic media. See comprehensive analysis by Mário Mesquita "Os meios de Communicação Social" in António Rais (ed) *Portugal 20 Anos de Democracia* (Lisbon 1994) pp. 360–96.

Data on the role of interest groups is sparse. Civil society was disarticulated by the coup and consequent social turmoil. The process of rearticulation has been slow but it is clearly different from what existed before. To take one very important example: the revolution effectively decapitated an economic system headed by small groups of family-oriented cartels. Through the nationalization of these huge enterprises the state became a direct participant in their management and financing. New associations or lobbies emerged against this background and the smaller businessmen and entrepreneurs as well as farmers and landowners also found the need to create new representative associations. José Manuel Durão Barroso pointed out that the "political articulation of these interests preceded the actual social organization of these groups." He was referring to organizations like the Portuguese Confederation of Industrialists (CIP), the Portuguese Farmers' Association (CAP), the noncommunist unions (UGT), and so on, all of which first emerged as political actors (José

M. Durão Barroso, "Capacidade de adaptação e incapacidade de decisão: o estado português e a articulação política dos intereses sociais desde 1974," *Análise Social* 20 (1984–5), pp. 453–4).

A number of Portuguese scholars are working within a Europewide comparative framework on some of these issues. Clearly, for any rounded analysis of the functioning of the Portuguese political system and for a realistic view of its penetration of society, we need to know much more about these interest groups, their activities, and their mode of operation, especially on a level of business-to-government and business-to-political-party levels (Emile J. Kirchner "The Relationship between Interest Groups in Greece, Portugal, and Spain and their European Counterparts," *Revista de Ciência Política* 1, 3 (Lisbon, 1986), pp. 61–9).

Much was made until 1987 of the built-in, constitutionally derived conflict between president and prime minister. There is a large body of work now on these topics; among the most influential is Marcello Rebello de Sousa, *Os partidos políticos no direito constitucional português* (Braga, 1983); Marcello Rebello de Sousa, *Sistema do governo português antes e depois da revisão constitucional*, 3rd edition (Lisbon, 1984); Vital Moreira, *Constituição e revisão constitucional* (Lisbon, 1980); and Joaquim Aguilar, *A ilusão do poder: Análise do sistema partidário português 1978–1982* (Lisbon, 1983). Most informed commentators in the mid 1980s believed that the major resolution of this conflict would come in the presidential elections of 1986; and via the evolution of a new presidentialist party. Joaquim Aguilar's article, "A fluidez oculta num sistema partidário ultra estável," in *Revista de Ciência Política* (1985), pp. 7–34, reflected this point of view most succinctly. Yet it was out of the parliamentary sector that the redefinition of power relationships and party balances occurred, precisely where the system seemed to have reached an impasse. The election of Professor Aníbal Cavaco Silva as leader of the PSD in May 1985; and the misjudgment of the presidentialist option (as reflected in the rise and decline of the Eanist party, the PRD) served to break the pattern established in 1975 and provide a mechanism for the shift of votes to the PSD from the PS as well as from the Communist Party and CDS which would have been very difficult otherwise. The election of 1985, which saw the new PRD take some 18 percent of the vote, was not unlike the by-election phenomenon in other parliamentary democracies where major protest votes often take place which do not always sustain themselves in the general election.

The PSD however, the victor in 1987 and again in 1991, and the first party to obtain a majority in Portugal, remains ironically very much characterized by the intrusion of traditional networks of clientelism, which some political scientists had pointed to as an impediment to such change, and where the most thoroughly traditional characteristics of Portuguese society had been internalized by a political party.

Another way of approaching this question is to see in the parties and *clientelas* the strength of a political system rooted in social reality in a manner which political scientists have tended to assume has been superseded in advanced modern societies. Not least among the comparative points which can be suggested from an analysis of Portuguese politics since 1976, therefore, is the need to reassess this rather negative view of parties in the modern polity. As Bruneau and Macleod argued in their *Politics in Contemporary Portugal: Parties and the Consolidation of Democracy* (Boulder, 1986), since 1976 Portuguese political parties have made themselves central to the political process. It is a phenomenon which deserves much more attention than it has so far received.

The role of outside advisers is also difficult to document. The West Germans, however, became critical actors within the Portuguese political system. The figures provided by Maria José Stock suggest that the parties rely almost exclusively on state subsidies and foreign support, the latter quantitatively providing the larger inputs. The election of Mário Soares to the presidency of the republic in 1986, and the elimination from the Socialist Party of many of Soares' closest collaborators after 1987, tended to break the close links provided by Soares between the party and the outside financial supporters (especially German sources such as the Ebert Foundation). In consequence the PS under Soares' immediate successor, Vítor Constáncio, faced severe financial constraints. This is an aspect of the evolution of the parties in Portugal which deserves more attention. The PS is, of course, not unique since the German foundations associated with the Christian Democrats (Adenauer) and the Free Democrats (Naumann) have also provided support. Overall, these interventions have been positive and well-intentioned. In addition the Germans funded "think tanks" such as the Institute for Development Studies, headed by very able foreigners, which have been a key source of excellent studies and blueprints for reforms, with direct consequences on governmental programs. For a look at some of these connections see Thomas Bruneau, "As dimensões internacionais da revolução portuguesa: apoios e constragimentos no estabelecimento da democracia," *Análise Social* 18, (1982), pp. 885–96. The role of the European Union, since Portugal's accession to the EC in 1986, as a source of funds and ideas has been quite central and will be in the future.

There has also been a tendency to use external factors or externally imposed conditionalities, to justify harsh economic or social measures the political system was unable to negotiate. The two harsh IMF-imposed austerity programs (1978, 1982) are a case in point. The voting public, however, has not failed to punish the parties which took such a route – the Socialist Party in particular. The integration with the EC was likewise often justified as providing the external jolt needed to bring about structural change within Portugal.

With the election of Mário Soares as president of the republic in 1986, the political eclipse of General Eanes, as a result of the disastrous experience of the PRD, and the emergence of Anibal Cavaco Silva as unchallenged head of a majority government after 1987, it seemed for a time that the constitutional issue had been subsumed and that the blockages of the past and conflicts between prime minister and president had indeed been personal and not institutional. Yet the honeymoon, or the period of cohabitation between Soares and Cavaco Silva, became quickly strained as the government began to confront the need to make structural changes which involved questions that directly challenged the social and economic clauses of the 1976 constitution – especially over labor legislation, over the privatization of state companies, and even over land and military reform. Thus, by 1988, the constitutional issue came back to center stage, and the old frictions reemerged between the Palácio de São Bento, the prime minister's residence, and the Palácio de Belém, the president's official home.

For Portuguese policy toward Africa, especially Portugal's former colonies, see José Manuel Durão Barroso, "Prospects for Peace and Development in Africa: A Portuguese View," *Camões Center Quarterly* Vol 1, Nos 3 & 4 (September & December

1989), pp. 1–3; António de Figueiredo, "Portugal and Africa," in Kenneth Maxwell, ed., *Portugal in the 1980s* (Westport 1986), pp. 89–108; and Carlos Gaspar, "Portugal's Policies toward Angola and Mozambique since Independence," in Richard J. Bloomfield, ed., *Regional Conflict and US Policy: Angola and Mozambique* (Reference Publications for World Peace Foundation, Boston 1986), pp. 40–74. I have discussed the decolonization process in "Portugal and Africa: The Last Empire," in Prosser Gifford and William Roger Louis, eds., *The Transfer of Power in Africa* (New Haven, 1982), pp. 337–85. In critical reaction to this chapter arguing that I overestimated the international dimensions, Aquino de Bragança and Basil Davidson provide a concise account of FRELIMO's views in "Independence and Decolonization: Mozambique 1974–1975" in Gifford and Louis, eds., *Decolonization and African Independence* (New Haven, 1988) pp. 427–43. For an unusually detailed analysis of the various "lobbies" at work within Portugal to influence Angolan policy, see the anonymous article, "Portugal e as conversações entre o MPLA e a UNITA," *Política Internacional* Lisbon, 1, 3 (Winter 1991), pp. 147–57. Portugal had hoped for a longer-term role in Africa as an intermediary for the EU, once the conflicts within Mozambique and Angola were resolved, but other EU countries are unlikely to defer easily to Portuguese interests here if they perceive a vacuum to be filled or economic possibilities to be exploited. Spain, in particular, has shown an increasing interest in southern Africa and provided peace-keeping forces to the UN for Namibia and Angola. France has always had ambitions in the Portuguese-speaking African countries, and both Britain and Germany have been in competition with the Portuguese. Thus in Africa the future is unlikely to be built on sentiment and wishful thinking, a large dose of which still pervades Portuguese thinking about Africa.

Portugal's position on the Middle East has, on the whole, been closer to that of the United States and less favorable to the Arabs than Spain's. In recent years, however, with an eye to the value of the Azores for the projection of US military power in the Middle East and in light of the 1973 experience, the Portuguese toyed with the idea of shifting their position of unqualified support for the United States (or at least giving the impression to Washington that they might) in order to strengthen their negotiating position with the United States over the Azores facilities. Simultaneously attempting to play "the other Middle East card," they have also been making an attempt to piggyback on the influence of the Israeli lobby in the US by stressing the value of the Azores to the security of Israel, something also demonstrated in 1973. It is probably no accident that, coincident with the opening of the Azores negotiations, Lisbon decided to send its first resident ambassador to Israel.

Like so much else, however, the ending of the Cold War in Europe in 1989 and the war in the Persian Gulf in 1991 changed many of these calculations, not only because the European NATO allies (including Spain) all permitted the US to use facilities for deployment against Iraq during the Gulf War, but the role of Israel as an exclusive US ally in the Middle East was also modified by the success of the US-led, UN-sanctioned coalition in the Gulf War and the consequential opening of peace negotiations between the Palestinians and Israelis. Egypt, for instance (the recipient of massive Soviet arms transfers in 1973), became a key US partner in any Middle East settlement. A remarkable series of volumes by José Freire Antunes covering US-Portuguese relations under the general title *Os Americanos e Portugal* is in progress. To date he has published *Kennedy e Salazar* (Lisbon 1991) and *Nixon e Caetano* (2nd edition, Lisbon, 1992). A recent American overview is provided by Scott B. MacDonald, *European Destiny, Atlantic Transformations: Portuguese Foreign Policy under the Second Republic* (New Brunswick, 1993).

It is too soon, of course, to know how the dramatic changes now underway in international relationships will work out. The Azores were important as a platform for resupplying US forces in the event of a European war – this was the basic rationale for the NATO use of the base and a function of equal interest to Europe and the United States. Now, however, the Warsaw Pact is a thing of the past and the Soviet Union has itself collapsed. None of which is to say that the Azores base is not important, but it is clear that two of the major Portuguese arguments – the exclusive value of the base for Middle East deployments and as a bastion of Cold War resupply – are greatly diminished in the new international environment.

The implications of these changes for Portugal, in its relationship with the United States in particular, are well summarized by Bernardo Futscher Pereira. "As a general rule," he observes, "the greater the solidarity between the US and Western Europe, the less relevant is the Portuguese position to the US. In contrast, the greater the division between the US and Western Europe, the smaller the number of European allies willing to collaborate in political and military actions, the greater will be the US interest in bilateral relations." [Bernardo Futscher Pereira "As relacões entre Portugal e os EUA: ensaio de prospectiva" dir. José Medeiros Ferreira, Projecto Portugal Ano 2000 (Lisbon 1986)].

The conclusions Futscher Pereira draws from his overview of Portugal's foreign relations through the prism of a discussion of US–Portuguese bilateral relations is that Portuguese and United States interests were very largely convergent after 1978, despite the difficulties and irritations that can emerge in specific negotiations. Public opinion in Portugal is little engaged in the question and is, of all European publics, one of the most pro-American (or at least one of the least anti-American at the popular level). Any anti-Americanism that does exist is largely confined to older establishment figures and some elements within the armed forces who still resent US opposition to Portugal's colonial pretensions in the 1960s. The Portuguese elite, of course, resent the sporadic nature of the attention the United States pays to their country. This resentment is further aggravated on occasions when the United States appears to view Portugal as a "Third World country," in the words of former Portuguese foreign minister Jaime Gama, or, even worse, as a province of Spain. [Jaime Gama, "Foreign Policy" in Kenneth Maxwell and Michael H. Haltzel eds., *Portugal: Ancient Country, Young Democracy* (Washington D.C., 1990), pp. 73–81.] However, as Europe becomes more integrated, nonsecurity issues increasingly enter its the European–Atlantic equation and will undoubtedly influence Portuguese policy with respect to the United States. In fact, it is this development more than anything else that will tend to diminish the role of international security issues in the overall US–Portuguese relationship. Not all the international consequences arising from Portugal's democratization have been resolved, even by the mid 1990s. Angola has yet to achieve some measure of internal peace, and in East Timor the tragedy of Indonesian repression and Timorese resistance continues. For a critical review of writing of post-independence Portuguese-speaking Africa see Patrick Chabal, "The Post Colonial State" in *Portuguese Studies*, vol. 8, 1992, pp. 189–202, and for Timor see "Focus on Timor" in *Camões Center Quarterly* vol. 5, nos. 3 and 4, autumn and winter 1992–93.

Bibliography

PRIMARY SOURCES

Africa Contemporary Record: Annual Survey and Documents 1974–1975. London, 1975

Africa Contemporary Record: Annual Survey and Documents 1975–1976. London, 1976

Africa Contemporary Record: Annual Survey and Documents 1976–1977. London, 1977

Africa Contemporary Record: Annual Survey and Documents 1977–1978. London, 1978

Coleção documentos do nosso tempo, 3 vols. Lisbon, n.d.

Congresso de oposição democrática, Aveiro, 4–8 abril, 1973, teses. Lisbon, 1974

Estado Maior do Exército. *Resenha histórico-militar das campanhas de África, 1961–1974* (Lisbon, 1988).

International Documentation and Communication Center (IDOC). Dossiers 1, 2, and 13

Ministério da Administração Interna. Instituo Nacional de Estadística. *Eleição Para Assembleia Constituinte 1975. Resultados por freguesias, concelhos e distritos do continente e ilhas adjacentes* 2 vols. Lisbon, 1975

Ministério dos Negócios Estrangeiros, Lisbon. *Dez anos de política externa, 1936–1948.* Lisbon, in progress

National Security Council. "National Security Council Interdepartmental Group on Africa. Study in Response to National Security Memorandum 39. Secret AF/NSC-IG 69–8. August 1969

Pike Report. Nottingham, 1977. (Also "The Pike Papers: House Select Committee on Intelligence, CIA Report." *The Village Voice* February 16, 1976

Relatório da comissão de averiguação de violências sobre presos sujeitos às autoridades militares. Lisbon, 1976

Relatório do 25 de novembro: Texto integral, 2 vols. Lisbon, 1976

US Congress. House of Representatives. "Angola: Should the US Support UNITA?" *Hearing Before the Select Committee on Intelligence.* 99th Congress, second session. March 1986

"The Complex of United States–Portuguese Relations: Before and

After the Coup." *Hearing Before the Subcommittee on Africa, Foreign Affairs Committee.* 93rd Congress, second session. March 14; October 8, 9, and 22, 1974

"Foreign Assistance in the Angolan Civil War." Statement by Mark M. Lowenthal, appendix 3. *Hearing Before the Special Sub-committee on International Relations.* 94th Congress, second session. August 1976

"Implementation of the US Arms Embargo." *Hearing Before the Subcommittee on Africa, Committee on Foreign Affairs.* 93rd Congress, first session. 1973

"Issues in US Relations with Spain and Portugal." *Report to the Subcommittee on Europe and the Middle East, Foreign Affairs Committee.* 96th Congress, first session. February 1979

"Military Assistance to Portugal for Fiscal Year 1977." *Hearing and Mark-up Before the Subcommittee on Europe and the Middle East, Committee of International Relations.* 95th Congress, first session. 1977

"Review of State Department Trip through Southern and Central Africa." *Hearing Before the Subcommittee on Africa, Foreign Affairs Committee.* 93rd Congress. December 1974

"The Soviet Union and the Third World: A Watershed of Great Power Rivalry." *Report to the Committee on International Relations.* Washington DC, 1977

"US Policy on Angola." *Hearing Before the Committee on International Relations.* 94th Congress, second session. January 1976

"US Policy towards Portugal." *Hearing Before the Subcommittee on International Political and Military Affairs, Committee on International Relations.* 94th Congress. May 1975

US Congress. Senate. "Implications of Angola for the Future of US Foreign Policy." Statement by Henry A. Kissinger. *Hearing Before the Subcommittee on African Affairs, Foreign Relations Committee.* January 1976

"Military and Economic Assistance to Portugal." *Hearing Before the Subcommittee on Foreign Assistance, Committee on Foreign Relations.* 95th Congress, first session. February 1977

"Mozambique and US Policy." *Hearing Before the Subcommittee on African Affairs, Committee on Foreign Relations.* 100th Congress, first session. June 1987

"Revolution into Democracy: Portugal After the Coup." *Report to the Committee on Foreign Relations.* August 1976

"Security Supporting Assistance for Zaire." *Hearing Before the Subcommittee on Foreign Assistance, Committee on Foreign Relations.* 94th Congress, first session. October 1975

"US – Angolan Relations." *Hearing Before the Subcommittee on Africa, Committee on International Relations.* 95th Congress, second session. May 1978

"US Involvement in Civil War in Angola." *Hearing Before the Subcom-*

mittee on African Affairs, Committee on Foreign Relations. 94th Congress, second session. January/February 1976

"US Policy Towards Southern Africa." *Hearing Before the Subcommittee on African Affairs, Committee on Foreign Relations.* 94th Congress, first session. June/July 1976

US Department of State. Bureau of Public Affairs. *Henry Kissinger – Press Conference: Angola, Pike Report, Latin American Trip, Relations with the USSR.* February 1976

US Department of State. US Arms Control and Disarmament Agency. *World Military Expenditures and Arms Trade, 1963–1973.* Washington DC, 1975

BOOKS

Abreu, Paradela de. *Do 25 de abril ao 25 de novembro: Memória do tempo partido.* Lisbon, 1983

Abshire, David and Samuels, Michael A., eds. *Portuguese Africa: A Handbook.* Washington, DC, 1969

Agee, Philip. *Inside the Company: CIA Diary.* Harmondsworth, 1975

Aguiar, Luiz. *Livro negro da descolonização.* Braga, n.d.

Aguilar, Joaquim. *A ilusão do poder: análise do sistema partidário português 1978–1982.* Lisbon, 1983

Almeida, Carlos and Barreto, António. *Capitalismo e emigração em Portugal.* Lisbon, 1974

Almeida, Diniz de. *Ascensão, apogeu e queda do MFA.* Lisbon, 1976

Origins e evolução do movimento de capitães. Lisbon, 1977

Antunes, Oliveira. *A ITT contra o 25 de abril.* Lisbon, 1977

Araújo, Miguel de, ed. *Os bispos e a revolução de abril.* Lisbon, 1976

Arons e Carvalho, Alberto. *A censura e as leis de imprensa.* Lisbon, 1973

Arroz, Maria Emília et al. *As eleições legislativas: Algumas perspectivas regionais.* Lisbon, 1976

Audibert, Pierre and Brignon, Daniel. *Portugal: Les nouveaux centurions.* Paris, 1974

Bacci, Massimo Livi. *A Century of Portuguese Fertility.* Princeton, 1971

Ball, George. *The Past has Another Pattern.* New York, 1982

Banco Espírito Santo. *Comissão de delegados sindicais do Banco Espírito Santo e Comercial de Lisboa.* Lisbon, 1975

Baptista, Jacinto. *Caminhos para uma revolução: sobre o fascismo em Portugal e sua queda.* Lisbon, 1975

Barnett, Don and Harvey, Roy. *The Revolution in Angola: MPLA Life Histories and Documents.* New York, 1972

Barreno, Maria Isabel, Horta, Maria Teresa, and Velho da Costa, Maria. *New Portuguese Letters: The Three Marias.* London, 1975

Barreto, António. *Anatomia de uma revolução: A reforma Agrária en Portugal 1974–1976* (Lisbon, n.d.)

Barrilaro Ruas, Henrique, ed. *A revolução das flores do 25 de abril ao governo provisório*. Lisbon, n.d.
  ed. *A revolução das flores: O governo de Palma Carlos*. Lisbon, n.d.
  ed. *A revolução das flores: O governo de Vasco Gonçalves até ao acordo de Lusaka*. Lisbon, n.d.
Bender, Gerald. *Angola Under the Portuguese: The Myth and the Reality*. Berkeley and Los Angeles, 1978
Bermeo, Nancy Gina. *The Revolution Within the Revolution: Workers' Control in Rural Portugal*. Princeton, 1986
Bonime-Blanc, Andrea. *Spain's Transition to Democracy: The Politics of Constitution Making*. Boulder, 1987
Borga, Cesário, Cardoso, Mário and Rodrigues, Avelino. *O movimento de capitães e o 25 de abril: 229 dias para derrubar o fascismo*. Lisbon, 1974
Boxer, Charles. *The Portuguese Seaborne Empire, 1415–1825*. Oxford, 1963
  Portuguese Society in the Tropics: The Municipal Councils of Goa, Macao, Bahia and Luanda, 1510–1800. Madison, 1965
  Race Relations in the Portuguese Colonial Empire 1415–1825. Oxford, 1963
Braga da Cruz, Manuel. *As origins da democracia cristã e o salazarismo*. Lisbon, 1980
  O partido e o estado no salazarismo. Lisbon, 1988
Brandão de Brito, José Maria. *A industrialização portuguesa na pós-guerra 1948–1965: O condicionamento industrial*. Lisbon, 1989
Bridgeland, F. *Jonas Savimbi: A Key to Africa*. London, 1986
Bruce, Neil. *Portugal: The Last Empire*. New York, 1975
Bruneau, Thomas C. *Politics and Nationhood: Post-Revolutionary Portugal*. New York, 1984
  and Macleod, Alex. *Politics in Contemporary Portugal: Parties and the Consolidation of Democracy*. Boulder, 1980
Cabral, Amílcar. *Unité et lutte*, 2 vols. Paris, 1975
Caetano, Marcello. *Corporative Revolution: Permanent Revolution*. Lisbon, 1969
  Depoimento. Rio de Janeiro, 1975
  Minhas memórias de Salazar, Lisbon 1977
Caldeira, Reinaldo and do Céu Silva, Maria, eds. *Constituição política da república portuguesa, 1976: Projectos, votações, e posição dos partidos*. Lisbon, 1976
Cardoso, António Lopes. *Luta pela reforma agrária*. Lisbon, 1976
Carrilho, Maria. *Forças armadas e mudança política em Portugal no séc. XX: Para uma explicação sociológica do papel dos militares*. Lisbon, 1985
Cartaxo, António, and Ribeiro, Jorge. *BBC versus Portugal: A história de um despedimento político*. Lisbon, 1977
Chabal, P. *Amílcar Cabral: Revolutionary Leadership and People's War*. Cambridge, 1983
Chilcote, Ronald H. *Emerging Nationalism in Portuguese Africa*. Stanford, 1972

The Portuguese Revolution of 25 April 1974. Coimbra, 1987

Clarence-Smith, Gervase. *The Third Portuguese Empire, 1825–1975.* Manchester, 1985

Cohen, Barry and El-Khamas, Mohamed A. eds. *The Kissinger Study of Southern Africa.* Westport, CT, 1976

Colby, William. *Honorable Men.* New York, 1978

Corregedor da Fonseca, Vasco. *Eleições para a constituente em processo revolucionário.* Lisbon, 1975

Correia, Ramiro, Soldado, Pedro and Marujo, João. *MFA e a luta de classes: subsídios para a compreensão do processo histórico português.* Lisbon, n.d.

Costa Pinto, António. *Salazarismo e o fascismo europeu: Problemas de interpretação nas ciências sociais.* Lisbon, 1992

Costigan, Arthur William. *Sketches of Society and Manners in Portugal,* 2 vols. London, 1787

Cruz, Antonino and Rosa, Vitoriano. *As mentiras de Marcello Caetano.* Lisbon, 1974

Cunhal, Alvaro. *Discursos políticos: Documentos políticos do partido comunista português.* Lisbon, 1974

Pela revolução democrática e nacional. Lisbon, 1975

Radicalismo pequeno burguês da Façada Socialista. Lisbon, [?] 1971

A revolução portuguesa: o passado e o futuro. Lisbon, 1976

A situação agrária em Portugal. Rio de Janeiro, 1970

Cutileiro, José. *A Portuguese Rural Society.* Oxford, 1971

Da Costa, Ramiro. *O desenvolvimento do capitalismo em Portugal.* Lisbon, 1975

Davidson, Basil. *In the Eye of the Storm.* Harmondsworth, 1972

The Liberation of Guinea: Aspects of an African Revolution. Harmondsworth, 1969

Dominguez, J. *To Make a World Safe for Revolution: Cuba's Foreign Policy.* Cambridge, MA, 1989

Downs, Charles. *Revolution at the Grass Roots: Community Organizations in the Portuguese Revolution.* Albany, 1990

Duffy, James. *Portugal in Africa.* Cambridge, MA, 1962

Dugard, John. *The Southwest Africa/Namibia Dispute: Documents and Scholarly Writings on the Controversy Between South Africa and the United Nations.* Berkeley and Los Angeles, 1973

Dugas, Carlos. *MDLP-ELP – O que são: a verdade sobre os dois movimentos clandestinos.* Alfregide, 1976

Duran Clemente, Manuel. *Elementos para a compreensão do 25 de novembro.* Lisbon, 1976

Durão Barroso, J. *Le système politique portugais face à l'intégration.* Lisbon, 1983

Egbert, Alvin C. and Hyung M. Kim. *A Development Model for the Agricultural Sector of Portugal.* World Bank, Washington, DC, 1975

Eleições 75 (Primeiras eleições livres): O programa do MFA e dos partidos políticos. Lisbon, 1975

Faye, Jean-Pierre. *Portugal: The Revolution in the Labyrinth.* Nottingham, 1976

Fernandes, Capitão [Alvaro Henrique]. *Portugal: Nem tudo está perdido: do movimento dos capitães ao 25 de novembro.* Lisbon, 1976

Ferreira, Hugo Gil and Marshall, Michael W. *Portugal's Revolution: Ten Years On.* Cambridge, 1986

Ferreira, Serafim, ed. *MFA: Motor da revolução portuguesa.* Lisbon, 1975

Figueiredo, António de. *Portugal: Fifty Years of Dictatorship.* London, 1975

Forrest, Joshua B. *Guinea-Bissau: Power, Conflict and Renewal in a West African Nation.* Boulder, 1992

França, Luis da. *Comportamento religioso da população portuguesa.* Lisbon, 1980

Freire Antunes, José. *Salazar e Caetano: cartas secretas 1932–1968* (Lisbon, 1994)

Cartas particulares a Marcello Caetano (Lisbon, 1985), 2 vols. Lisbon, 1990

Kennedy e Salazar: O leão e a raposa. Lisbon, 1991

O factor africano, 1890–1990. Lisbon, 1990

Os Americanos e Portugal: Os anos de Richard Nixon, 1969–1974, Lisbon, 1986, 2nd Edition, 1992.

O segredo do 25 de novembro: A verão quente de 1975 e os planos desconhecidos do grupo militar. Lisbon, 1980

Freitas do Amaral, Diogo. *A lei de defesa nacional e das forças armadas: Textos, discursos e trabalhos preparatórios.* Coimbra, 1983

Frémontier, Jacques. *Portugal: Les points sur les i.* Paris, 1976

Freyre, Peter and McGowan-Pinheiro, Patricia. *Oldest Ally: A Portrait of Salazar's Portugal.* London, 1961

Freyre, Gilberto. *O mundo que o português criou.* Rio de Janeiro, 1940

Gallagher, Tom. *Portugal: A Twentieth Century Interpretation.* Manchester, 1983

Galvão, Henrique. *Santa Maria: My Crusade for Portugal.* Cleveland, 1961

Galvão de Melo, General. *MFA: Movimento revolucionário.* Lisbon, 1975

Gaspar, Carlos and Rato, Vasco. *Rumo à memória: Crónicas da crise communista.* Lisbon, 1992

Gaspar, Jorge and Nuno Vitorino. *As eleições de 25 de abril: Geografia e imagem dos partidos.* Lisbon, 1976

Gibson, Richard. *African Liberation Movements: Contemporary Struggles Against White Minority Rule.* Oxford, 1972

Gomes, Varela. *A contra-revolução de fachada socialista.* Lisbon, 1981

Gomes Bandeira, José and Humberto, Luis. *Os trabalhadores e o lock-out em Vieira de Leiria.* Oporto, 1974

Gonçalves, Vasco. *Discursos, conferências, entrevistas.* With introduction by J. J. Teixeira Ribeiro. Oporto, 1976

Livro verde da revolução. Amadora, 1975

Gonçalves, Vasco and Ferreira, Serafim, eds. *Citações de Vasco Gonçalves*. Lisbon, 1975

Gouveia, Fernando. *Memórias de um inspector da PIDE: A organização clandestina do PCP*. Lisbon, 1979

Graham, Lawrence S. and Makler, Harry M., eds. *Contemporary Portugal: Culture, Economy and Politics in Comparative Perspective*. Austin, 1979

Graham, Lawrence S. and Wheeler, Douglas L. eds. *In Search of Modern Portugal: The Revolution and its Consequences*. Madison, 1983

Grundy, Kenneth W. *Confrontation and Accommodation in Southern Africa: The Limits of Independence*. Berkeley and Los Angeles, 1973

Halpern Pereira, Mariam. *Assimetrias de crescimento e dependência externa*. Lisbon, 1974

Hamilton, Iain, ed. *Portugal and Spain: Transition Politics*. London, 1976

Hammond, John. *Building People's Power: Workers and Neighborhood Movements in the Portuguese Revolution*. New York, 1988

Hammond, R. J. *Portugal and Africa 1815–1910: A Study in Economic Imperialism*. Stanford, 1966

Hance, William A. *The Geography of Modern Africa*, 2nd edn. New York, 1975, pp. 484–509

Harsch, Ernest and Thomas, Tony. *Angola: The Hidden History of Washington's War*. New York, 1976

Heimer, F. *The Decolonization Conflict in Angola, 1974–1976: An Essay in Political Sociology*. Geneva, 1979

Henriksen, Thomas H. *Revolution and Counterrevolution: Mozambique's War of Independence, 1964–1974*. New Jersey, 1983

Herr, Richard, ed. *The New Portugal: Democracy and Europe*. Berkeley, 1992

Hersch, Seymour M. *The Price of Power*. New York, 1982

Higley, John and Gunther, Richard. *Elites and Democratic Consolidation in Latin America and Southern Europe*. Cambridge, 1992

Horne, Alistair. *A Savage War of Peace*. London, 1977

Huntington, Samuel P. *The Third Wave: Democratization in the Late Twentieth Century*. Norman, 1991

Insight Team (*Sunday Times*). *Insight on Portugal: The Year of the Captains*. London, 1975

Isaacson, Walter, *Kissinger. A Biography* (New York, 1992)

Jardim, Jorge. *Moçambique: Terra Queimada*. Lisbon, 1976

Kay, Hugh. *Salazar and Modern Portugal: A Biography*. New York, 1970

Keefe, Eugene K. et al. *Area Handbook for Portugal*. Washington DC, 1977

Kissinger, Henry. *The White House Years*. Boston, 1979
Diplomacy. New York 1994

Klinghoffer, Arthur Jay. *The Angolan War: A Study in Soviet Policy in the Third World*. Boulder, 1980

Lake, Anthony. *The "Tar Baby" Option: American Policy Towards Southern Rhodesia.* New York, 1976

Leitão, Maria Lúcia and Freitas, Vera. *Análise das disparidades salarais no pós 25 de abril.* Lisbon, 1982

Lemos, Viana de. *Duas Crises, 1961–1974.* Lisbon, 1977

Lima Santos, Maria de Lourdes et al. *O 25 de abril e as lutas sociais nas empresas.* Oporto, 1976

Lourenço, Vasco. *MFA: rosto do povo.* Lisbon, 1975

Lucena, Manuel de. *A evolução do sistema corporativo português,* 2 vols. Lisbon, 1976

Macedo, Jorge Braga and Serfaty, Simon (eds) *Portugal Since the Revolution* (Boulder, 1981)

Macleod, Alex. *La révolution inopportune: Les partis communistes français et italiens face à la révolution portugaise.* Montréal, 1984

Mahoney, Richard D. *JFK: Ordeal in Africa.* New York, 1983

Mailer, Philip. *Portugal: The Impossible Revolution?* New York, 1977

Makler, Harry Marks. *A elite industrial portuguesa.* Lisbon, 1969

Marchetti, Victor and Marks, John. *The CIA and the Cult of Intelligence.* New York, 1974

Marcum, John A. *The Angolan Revolution,* 2 vols. Cambridge, MA, 1968, 1976

Martins, Maria Belmira. *As multinacionais em Portugal.* Lisbon, 1976

Sociedades e grupos em Portugal. Lisbon, 1973

Maxwell, Kenneth. *Pombal, Paradox of the Enlightenment.* Cambridge, 1995

ed. *Portugal: Ten Years After the Revolution.* New York, 1984

ed. *Portugal in the 1980s: The Dilemmas of Democratic Consolidation.* Westport, CT, New York, and London, 1986

ed. *The Press and the Rebirth of Iberian Democracy.* Westport, CT, 1983

and Monge, Scott C., eds. *Portugal: The Constitution and Consolidation of Democracy, 1976–1989.* New York, 1991

eds and Michael H. Haltzel *Portugal, Ancient Country, Young Democracy* (Washington, D.C., 1990)

ed. *Portuguese Defense and Foreign Policy Since Democratization* (New York, 1991)

Medeiros Ferreira, José, *Ensaio Histórico sobre a Revolução do 25 de abril* (Lisbon, 1983)

Portugal em Transe (1974–1985) *História de Portugal,* vol. 8 (Dir. by José Mattoso, Lisbon, 1995.

Meyer, Cord. *Facing Reality: From World Federalism to the CIA.* New York, 1981

Minter, William. *Imperial Network and External Dependency: The Case of Angola.* Beverly Hills, 1972

Portuguese Africa and the West. Harmondsworth, 1972

ed. *Operation Timber: Pages from the Savimbi Dossier.* Trenton, NJ, 1988

Mirajaia, Eduardo, Vieira, Joaquim and Vieira, Manuel. *Ramiro Correira: Soldado de abril.* Lisbon, n.d.

Mondlane, Eduardo. *The Struggle for Mozambique*. Harmondsworth, 1969
Mónica, Maria Filomena. *Educação e sociedade no Portugal de Salazar: A escola primária salazarista, 1926–1939*. Lisbon, 1978
Moreira Alves, Mário. *Les soldats socialistes du Portugal*. Paris, 1975
Morris, Roger. *Uncertain Greatness: Henry Kissinger and American Foreign Policy*. New York, 1977
Mota, Gomes. *A resistência*. Lisbon, 1976
Munslow, Barry. *Mozambique: The Revolution and its Origins*. New York, 1983
Neves, Orlando, ed. *Textos históricos da revolução*, 3 vols. Lisbon, 1975–6
Newitt, Malyn. *Portugal in Africa: The Last Hundred Years*. London, 1981
Nixon, Richard. *The Memoirs of Richard Nixon*, New York, 1978
Nogueira, Franco. *Diálogos interditos: A política externa portuguesa e a guerra de Africa*, 2 vols. Lisbon, 1979
    Um político confessa-se: Diário 1960–1968. Oporto, 1986
    Salazar, 9 vols. Lisbon, 1977–1990
Ochetto, Valério. *O como e o porquê de um crime político – a morte de Delgado*. Amadora, 1978
Oliveira, César. *O salazarismo e a guerra civil de Espanha*. Lisbon, 1988
Osório, Sanches. *O equívoco do 25 de abril*. Lisbon, 1975
Pacheco, Fernando de Amorim. *Portugal Traido*. Madrid, 1975
Pélissier, René. *Résistance et révolte en Angola (1845–1961)*, 3 vols. Privately printed, 1976
Pereira, Pedro Teotónio. *Memórias*. Lisbon, 1972
Pereira de Moura, Francisco. *Por onde vai a economia portuguesa?* Lisbon, 1974
Pimlott, Ben, *Frustrate their Knavish Tricks: Writings on Biography, History and Politics* (London, 1994)
Pina Cabral, João de Pina. *Sons of Adam, Daughters of Eve*. Oxford, 1986
Pires, José. *Greves e o 25 da abril*. Lisbon, 1976
Porch, Douglas. *The Portuguese Armed Forces and the Revolution*. London, 1977
    Portugal: O 25 de abril na imprensa estrangeira. Lisbon, 1974
    Portugal: na imprensa estrangeira – um ano depois. Lisbon, 1975
Poulantzas, Nicos. *The Crisis of the Dictatorships: Portugal, Greece, Spain*. London, 1976
Praça, Afonso *et al. 25 de abril: Documentos*. Lisbon, 1974
Raby, D. L. *Fascism and Resistance in Portugal: Communists, Liberals, and Military Dissidents in the Opposition to Salazar, 1941–1974*. Manchester, 1988
Rama, M. Manuela de S. and Plantier, Carlos. *Melo Antunes: Tempo de ser firme*. Lisbon, 1976
Rebello de Sousa, Marcello. *Os partidos políticos no direito constitucional português*. Braga, 1983
    Sistema do governo português antes e depois da revisão constitucional, third edn. Lisbon, 1980

Reis, António (ed) *Portugal 20 Anos de Democracia* (Lisbon, 1994)
Ribeiro de Mello, Fernando, ed. *Dossier: 2a República*, 2 vols. Lisbon
   1976–7
Rocha, Nuno. *Memórias de uma revolução: Itinerário de um jornalista na luta
   por um jornal.* Lisbon, 1975
Rodrigues, Avelino, Borga, Cesário and Cardoso, Mário. *Abril nos quarteis
   de novembro.* Lisbon, 1976
Rosa, Eugénio. *A economia portuguesa em números.* Lisbon, 1975
   Portugal: Dois anos de revolução na economia. Lisbon, 1976
   Problemas actuais da economia portuguesa: Os monopólios e o 25 de abril.
   Lisbon, 1974
Rosas, Fernando. *O Estado Novo nos anos trinta: Elementos para o estudo da
   natureza económica e social do salazarismo, 1928–1938.* Lisbon, 1986
   Portugal entre a paz e a guerra. Lisbon, 1990
   O Estado novo (1926–1994) Historia de Portugal Vol. 7. (dir. by José
   Mattoso) Lisbon 1994
Rudebeck, Lars. *Guinea-Bissau: A Study of Political Mobilization.* Uppsala,
   1974
Sá Carneiro, Francisco. *As revisões da constituição política de 1933.* Oporto,
   1971
   Por uma social-democracia portuguesa. Lisbon, 1975
Salazar, António de Oliveira. *Antologia, 1909–1966.* Coimbra, 1966.
   Como se levanta um estado. Lisbon, 1977
   Discursos, 5 vols. Coimbra, 1961
   *Doctrine and Action: International and Foreign Policy of the New Portugal
   1928–1939.* London, 1939
   Government and Politics. Lisbon, 1956
   Mais um passo na definição e consolidação do regime. Lisbon, 1949
   *The Principles and Work of the Revolution in their Internal and International
   Aspects.* Lisbon, 1943
Salgado Matos, Luis de. *Investimentos em Portugal.* Lisbon, 1973
Saldanha, Sanches, J. A. *O MRPP – Instrumento da contra-revolução.* Lisbon,
   1975
Sánchez Cervelló, Josep. *A revolução Portuguesa e a sua influência na transiçáo
   espanhola (1961–1976)* Lisbon 1993
Saraiva de Carvalho, Otelo. *Alvorada em Abril.* Lisbon, 1977
   Cinco meses que mudam Portugal. Lisbon, 1975
Saraiva, José António. *Do estado novo á segunda república.* Lisbon, 1974
Schmitter, Philippe C. *Corporatism and Public Policy in Authoritarian Portu-
   gal.* London and Beverly Hills, CA, 1975
Schneider, Susan. *O marquês de Pombal e o vinho do Porto.* Oporto, 1980.
Sideri, S. *Trade and Power: Informal Colonialism in Anglo-Portuguese Relations.*
   Rotterdam, 1970
Silva, Marques, J. A. *Relatos da clandestinidade – O PCP visto por dentro.*
   Lisbon, 1976

Silva, Martins, J. *Estruturas agrárias em Portugal continental*, 2 vols. Lisbon, 1973

Sklar, Richard L. *Corporate Power in an African State: The Political Impact of Multinational Mining Companies in Zambia*. Berkeley and Los Angeles, 1975

Soares, Mário. *Democratização e descolonização: Dez meses no governo provisório*. Lisbon, 1975
  Portugal amordaçado: Depoimento sobre os anos do fascismo. Lisbon, 1974
  Quelle révolution. Paris, 1975

Sobel, Lester, ed. *The Portuguese Revolution, 1974–76*. New York, 1976

Soldado, Pedro, Marujo, João and Correia, Ramiro. *MFA: dinamização cultural, acção cívica*. Lisbon, 1977

Soldados Unidos Vencerão. *Os SUV em luta: Manifestos, entrevistas, comunicados*. Lisbon, 1975

Sousa Santos, Boaventura de. *O estado e a sociedade em Portugal, 1974–1988*. Oporto, 1990

Spínola, António de. *Linha de acção*. Lisbon, 1970
  País sem rumo: Contributo para a história de uma revolução. Lisbon, 1978
  Portugal e o futuro. Lisbon, 1974

Stockwell, John. *In Search of Enemies: A CIA Story*. New York, 1978

Telo, António. *Portugal na segunda guerra*. Lisbon, 1987

Teixeira de Sousa, A. and da Freitas, Eduardo. *Subsídios para uma análise da população activa operária em Portugal*. Lisbon, 1974

Valença, C. Fernando. *As forças armadas e as crises nacionais: A abrilada de 1961*. Lisbon, n.d.

Vasco, Nuno. *Dossier PIDE: Os horrores e crimes de uma "polícia."* Lisbon, 1974
  Vigiados e perseguidos: Documentos secretos da PIDE/DGS. Lisbon, 1977

Veríssimo Serrão, Joaquim. *Marcello Caetano: Confidências no exílio*. Lisbon and São Paulo, 1985

Veríssimo, Serrão, Joaquim ed. *Correspondência Marcello Mathias/Salazar*. Lisbon, 1984

Venter, Al. *Portugal's War in Guinea-Bissau*. Pasadena, 1973

Vintras, R. E. *The Portuguese Connection: The Secret History of the Azores Base*. London, 1974

Walford, A. R. *The British Factory*. Lisbon, 1940

Wallraff, Gunter (and Hella Schlumberger). *A descoberta de uma conspiraçao: a acçaõ Spínola*. Lisbon, 1976

Weissman, Stephen R. *American Foreign Policy in the Congo, 1960–1969*. Ithaca, 1974

Wiarda, Howard J. *Corporatism and Development: The Portuguese Experience*. Amherst, 1977
  Transcending Corporatism? The Portuguese Corporative System and the Revolution of 1974. Institute of International Studies, South Carolina, 1976

The *Transition to Democracy in Spain and Portugal*. Washington, DC, 1989

ARTICLES

Adelman, Kenneth L. "Report from Angola." *Foreign Affairs* 53, 3 (April 1975)

Adelman, Kenneth and Bender, Gerald. "Conflict in Southern Africa: A Debate." *International Security* 3, 2 (Fall 1978) pp. 67–122

Ashford, Nicholas. "Number of Prisoners Mounts in Portugal." *The Times* (London, April 12, 1975)

Backman, René. "Portugal: Les archives de tortionnaires." *Le Nouvel Observateur* (September 2, 1974)

Balsemão, Francisco Pinto. "The Constitution and Politics: Options for the Future." In Kenneth Maxwell, ed., *Portugal in the 1980s: Dilemmas of Democratic Consolidation*. New York, 1986, pp. 197–232

Bandeira, António Rangel. "The Portuguese Armed Forces Movement: Historical Antecedents, Professional Demands, and Class Conflict." *Politics and Society* 6, 1 (1976)

Baynham, S. J. "International Politics and the Angolan Civil War." *Army Quarterly and Defense Journal* 107 (January 1977), 25–32

Bellieveau, Nancy. *Institutional Investor* (March 1977), pp. 23–28

Bender, Gerald. "American Policy toward Angola: A History of Linkage." In Bender, G., Coleman, J. and Sklar, R., eds., *African Crisis Areas and US Foreign Policy*. Berkeley, 1985

"Angola, the Cubans, and American Anxieties." *Foreign Policy* 31 (Summer 1978), pp. 3–33

"Angola: History, Insurgency and Social Change." *Africa Today* 19, 1 (Winter 1972), pp. 30–6

"The Continuing Crisis in Angola." *Current History* 82 (March 1983)

"The Eagle and the Bear in Angola." *Annals of the American Academy of Political and Social Science* 489 (January 1987), 123–32

"Kissinger and Angola: Anatomy of Failure." In *American Policy in Southern Africa*. Washington DC, 1978

"The Limits of Counterinsurgency: An African Case." *Comparative Politics* 4 (April 1972), pp. 331–407

Bender, Gerald and Yoder, Stanley P. "Whites on the Eve of Independence: The Politics of Numbers." *Africa Today* 21 (Fall 1974), pp. 23–37

Blackburn, Robin. "Portugal: Who Will Rule?" *Ramparts* (November 1974)

"The Test in Portugal." *New Left Review* 87–88 (September–December 1974)

Bossut, Michael. "Torture du sommeil – torture psychologue." Press conference organized by the Belgian League for the Defense of the Rights of Man. Brussels, 1973

Braga, Thomas J. "The Lyrics of a Revolution: Zeca Afonso's Cantigas de Maio." *Journal of the American Portuguese Society* 13 (1979), pp. 2–18

Bruneau, Thomas C. "Church and State in Portugal: Crisis of Cross and Sword." *Journal of Church and State* 18, 3 (Autumn 1976), pp. 463–90

"Portugal: Problems and Prospects in the Creation of a New Regime." *Naval War College Review* 29, 1 (Summer 1976), pp. 65–82

"Portugal: The Search for a New Political Regime." *The World Today* (December 1975)

Cabral, M. Villaverde. "Portugal since the Revolution." *Luso-Brazilian Review* 24, 1 (1987) pp. 79–86

Cardoso, Pires José. "Changing a Nation's Way of Thinking." *Index* (Spring 1972)

Cequeira, S. "L'église catholique et la dictature corporatiste portugaise." *Revue Française de Sciences Politiques* 23 (June 1973), pp. 473–513

Chabal, P. "People's War, State Formation and Revolution in Africa: A Comparative Analysis of Mozambique, Guinea-Bissau and Angola." *Journal of Commonwealth and Comparative Politics* 21, 3 (1983)

Collin, Claude. "Enquête sur les coopératives agricoles au Portugal." *Les Temps Modernes* 364 (1976)

Comissão Nacional de Socorro aos Presos Políticos (CNSPP). "Armando de Castro, Francisco Pereira de Moura, and Luis Felipe Lindley Cintra." March/April 1972

"Circular." February 6, 1973

"Political Repression in Portugal Worsening." Press release, May 9, 1973

Council of Europe. "Introductory Report on Human Rights in Portugal." April 8, 1970

Cunhal, Alvaro. "A crises político-militar: discursos políticos." *Documentos políticos do PCP* 15 (May/November 1975)

Davis, Nathaniel. "The Angola Decision of 1975: A Personal Memoir." *Foreign Affairs* (Fall 1978), pp. 109–24

Dingeman, Jim. "Angola: Portugal in Africa." *Strategy and Tactics* 56 (May/June 1976)

Duner, Bertil. "Cuba: Dependent Interventionism." *Nordic Journal of International Politics* 22, 1 (1987), pp. 35–47

Durão Barroso, José Manuel. "Prospects for Peace and Development in Africa: A Portuguese View." *Camões Center Quarterly* vol. 1, nos. 3 & 4 (September & December 1989)

"A dimensão esquerda-direita e a competição partidária na Europa do sul." *Revista de Ciência Política* 1 (Lisbon, 1985), pp. 35–60

Durch, W. J. "The Cuban Military in Africa and the Middle East: From Algeria to Angola." *Studies in Comparative Communism* 11, 1/2 (1978)

Ebinger, Charles. "External Intervention in Internal War: The Politics and Diplomacy of the Angolan Civil War." *Orbis* (Fall 1976), pp. 669–99

Fallaci, Oriana. "Disintegrating Portugal . . .: An Interview with Mário Soares." *New York Review of Books* (November 13, 1975)

"I Care Nothing for Elections, ha, ha!: An Interview with Alvaro Cunhal." *New York Times Magazine* (July 13, 1975)

Gallagher, Tom. "Controlled Repression in Salazar's Portugal." *Journal of Contemporary History* 14, 3 (July 1979)

García Márquez, Gabriel. "Operation Carlota: Cuba's Role in Angolan Victory." *Cuba Update* 1 (April 1977)

Grayson, George. "Portugal and the Armed Forces." *Orbis* 19, 2 (Summer 1975), 335–78

Griffith, William E. "Soviet Power and Policies in the Third World: The Case of Africa." *Adelphi Papers* 152 (London, 1979)

Guimarães, Fernando J. Andresen. "Interview with MPLA Dissidents." *Camões Center Quarterly* vol. 5, nos. 1/2 (Spring 1994)

Halperin, M. "The Cuban Role in Southern Africa." In Seiler, J., ed., *Southern Africa since the Coup*. Boulder, 1981

Harsgor, Michael. "Portugal in Revolution." *The Washington Papers*. Center for Strategic and International Studies, Georgetown University. Beverly Hills, 1976

Heimer, Franz-Wilhelm. "A cultura política em Portugal." *Revista de Ciência Política* 4 (Lisbon, 1986)

Henriksen, Thomas H. "Angola and Mozambique: Intervention and Revolution." *Current History* 71 (November 1976), pp. 153–7

Hodges, Tony. "How the MPLA Won in Angola." In Legum, Colin and Hodges, Tony, eds., *After Angola: The War Over Southern Africa*. London, 1976

Hottinger, Arnold. "The Rise of Portugal's Communists." *Problems of Communism* (Washington DC, 1975)

Jaster, Robert S. "South Africa's Narrowing Security Options." *Adelphi Papers* 159 (London, 1980)

Kennan, George F. "Hazardous Courses in Southern Africa." *Foreign Affairs* 49, 2 (January 1971), pp. 218–36.

Klinghoffer, Arthur J. "US–Soviet Relations and Angola." *Harvard International Review* 8 (January/February 1986), pp. 15–19

Kolm, Serge-Christophe. "Chile–Portugal: vers une théorie des processus révolutionnaires modernes." *Annaes: Economie, Société, Civilisation* (November/December 1976)

"Portugal: Quelle révolution vers quelle société?" *Les Temps Modernes* (December 1975)

Kramer, Jane. "A Reporter at Large (Portugal)." *The New Yorker* (December 15, 1975), pp. 92–131

"Letter from Lisbon." *The New Yorker* (September 1974)

Legum, Colin. "The African Crisis." *America and the World 1978*. New York, 1979, pp. 633–5

"The Role of the Big Powers." In Legum, Colin and Hodges, Tony, eds., *After Angola: The War Over Southern Africa*. London, 1976

"A Study of International Intervention in Angola." In Legum, Colin and Hodges, Tony, eds., *After Angola: The War Over Southern Africa*, 2nd ed. New York, 1971

LeoGrande, William M. "Cuba–Soviet Relations and Cuban Policy in Africa." *Cuban Studies* (January 1980), pp. 1–48

MacShane, Denis. "The Battle for Radio Renascença." *New Statesman* (July 18, 1975)

Malefakis, Edward. "The Iberian Land Reforms Compared: Spain 1931–1936 and Portugal 1974–1978." *A Agricultura latifundiária na península ibérica* Oeiras, 1979

Marcum, John A. "The Lessons of Angola." *Foreign Affairs* 54, 3 (April 1976) pp. 407–25

"Portugal and Africa: The Politics of Indifference." In *Eastern African Studies*, (1972)

Martins, Hermínio. "Opposition in Portugal." *Government and Opposition* 4, 2 (Spring 1969)

"Portugal." In Woolf, S. J., ed., *European Fascism*. London, 1968

Maxwell, Kenneth. "The Emergence of Democracy in Portugal." In Herz, John, ed., *From Dictatorship to Democracy: How Eight Countries Have Coped with the Legacy of Authoritarianism and Totalitarianism*. Westport, CT, 1982, pp. 231–50

"A New Scramble for Africa." In Fleron, Frederick and Hoffman, Erik, eds., *The Conduct of Soviet Foreign Policy*. Hawthorne, 1980, pp. 515–34

"Portugal: A Neat Revolution." *New York Review of Books* (June 13, 1974), pp. 16–21

"Portugal and Africa: The Last Empire." In Gifford, Prosser and Louis, William Roger, eds., *The Transfer of Power in Africa: Decolonization 1940–1960*. New Haven, 1982, pp. 337–85

"Portuguese Communism." In Schwab, George, ed., *Eurocommunism*, Westport, CT, 1986, pp. 269–302

"Prospects for Democratic Transition in Portugal." In Whitehead, Lawrence, Schmitter, Philippe and O'Donnell, Guillermo, eds., *Transitions from Authoritarian Rule: Prospects for Democracy*. Baltimore, 1986, pp. 198–203

"The Thorns of the Portuguese Revolution." *Foreign Affairs* (January 1976), pp. 250–70

"The Legacy of Decolonization." In Richard J. Bloomfield (ed.) *Regional Conflict and U.S. Policy: Angola and Mozambique* (Boston, 1988, pp. 7–39)

Michael, Carl and Brooks, Julie, "ELP: Mercenaries Prepare to Invade Portugal." *Counterspy* 3, 1 (Spring 1976), pp. 40–5

Mitchell, Alex and Law, Roger. "The Pit: Aftermath of the Portuguese Coup – The Fall of Dr. Caetano's Secret Police." *The Sunday Times Magazine* (London) (July 14, 1974), pp. 8–20

Moss, Robert. "The Battle for Angola." *Economist Foreign Report* (November 12, 1975), 1–6

"Castro's Secret War Exposed." *The Sunday Telegraph* (London) (Jan. 30, 1977, Feb. 6, 1977, Feb. 30, 1977)

"A Ticket to Lisbon: The Civil War in Portugal." *Harper's* (December 1975)

Mujal-Leon, Eusebio M. "The PCP and the Portuguese Revolution." *Problems of Communism* (Washington D.C., 1977)

Oldberg, Ingmar. "The Portuguese Revolution of 1974–1975 and US. Foreign Policy: Cooperation and Conflict." *Nordic Journal of International Politics* 17, 3 (1982), pp. 179–89

Patriarca, Maria de Fátima. "Contrôle operária em Portugal: Documentos." *Análise Social* 47, 3 (1976) and 48, 4 (1976)

Pélissier, René. "Conséquences démographiques des révoltes en Afrique portugaise (1961–1970): Essai d'interprétation," *Revue Française d'Histoire d'Outre-Mer* 61, 222 (1974), pp. 34–73

Pimlott, Ben. "Parties and Voters in the Portuguese Revolution: the Elections of 1975 and 1976." *Parliamentary Affairs* 30, 1 (Winter 1977), pp. 35–58

"Universities Spark Revolution and Go on Fighting." *Times Higher Education Supplement* (August 15, 1975)

"Socialism in Portugal: Was it a Revolution?" *Government and Opposition* 12, 3 (London, Summer 1977), pp. 332–50

"Were the Soldiers Revolutionary? The Armed Forces Movement and the Portuguese Revolution." *Iberian Studies* 7, 1 (Spring 1978)

Pimlott, Ben and Seaton, Jean. "How Revolution Came to the Schools of Portugal." *New Society* (December 9, 1976)

— "Sacking the Censor: Portuguese Broadcasting since April 1974." *Index* (London, Summer 1976)

Rutledge, Ian. "Land Reform and the Portuguese Revolution." *Journal of Peasant Studies* 5, 1 (October 1977), pp. 79–98

Salazar, António de Oliveira. "Realities and Trends of Portugal's Policies." *International Affairs* 34 (April 1963), pp. 169–83

Salgado de Matos, Luís. "Significado e consêquencias da eleição do presidente por sufrágio universal – o caso português." *Análise Social* 19, 76 (1983), pp. 235–59

Sánchez Cervelló, Josep. "La inviabilidad de una victoria portuguesa en la guerra colonial: el caso de Guinea-Bissau." *Hispania* 49, 173 (Madrid, 1989), pp. 1017–44

Schmitter, Philippe C. "Impact and Meaning of Non-Competitive, Non-Free and Insignificant Elections in Authoritarian Portugal, 1933–1974." In Hermet, D., Rose, Richard and Rouquier, Alain, eds., *Elections Without a Choice*. London, 1978

"Liberation by *Golpe*: Retrospective Thoughts on the Demise of Authoritarian Rule in Portugal." *Armed Forces and Society* 2 (November 1975), pp. 5–33

"Le parti communiste portugais entre le "pouvoir social" et le "pouvoir politique." *Etudes Internationales* 6, 3 (September 1975), pp. 375–88

Seaton, Jean. "Ferment of an Old Power." *New Society* (July 24, 1975), p. 202

Smith, Diana. "An Interview with the Editor of Expresso, Lisbon." *Index* (London, 1975)

"Letter from Portugal." *Index* (London, 1976)

"Portuguese TV: No Room for Debate." *Index* (London, 1977)

Sonnenfeldt, Helmut. "American-Soviet Relations: Informal Remarks." *Parameters: Journal of the US Army War College* 6, 1 (1976), pp. 15–16

Stahl, Heinz-Michael. "Portuguese Migration and Regional Development." *11 Conferência Internacional sobre Economia Portuguesa* (Lisbon, September 1979)

Stern, Laurence and Griffin, Dan. "A Washington View: The Portuguese Connection." *Ramparts* 13, 8 (May/June 1975), pp. 41–4.

Stock, Maria José. "A base social de apoio e o recrutamento dos líderes do PSD." *Revista de Ciência Política* 1 (1985), pp. 103–21

"O centrismo político em Portugal: gênese do Bloco Central e análise dos partidos da coligação." *Análise Social* 85, 21 (1985), 45–81

Sweeney, Paul M. "Class Struggles in Portugal." *Monthly Review* 26–27 (September–October 1975)

Szulc, Tad. "Lisbon and Washington: Behind the Portuguese Revolution." *Foreign Policy* 21 (Winter 1975/76), pp. 3–62

Tavares, Jean. "Les paysans, l'église et la politique dans un village portugais." *Les Temps Modernes* (July 1976)

Texeira de Sousa, A. and Freitas, Eduardo. "Subsídios para uma análise da população activa operária em Portugal." *Cadernos* 12 (March 1974)

Ulsamer, Edgar. "New Look at USAF Strategic Air-Lift." *Airforce Magazine* (February 1975), 24–31

Urban, Joan Barth, "Contemporary Soviet Perspectives on Revolution in the West" *Orbis* (Winter 1975–76), pp. 1359–1402

Valdes, Nelson P. "Revolutionary Solidarity in Angola." In Blasier, Cole and Mesa Lago, Carmelo, eds., *Cuba and the World*. Pittsburgh, 1979, pp. 87–117.

Vasconcelos, Alvaro de. "Portuguese Defense Policy: Internal Politics and Defense Commitments." In Chipman, John, ed., *NATO's Southern Allies*. London, 1988, pp. 86–136

Walker, Darcy A. "Cuban Military Involvement in Angola." *Congressional Research Service*. Washington DC, 1976

Weissman, Stephen R. "CIA Covert Action in Zaire and Angola:

Patterns and Consequences." *Political Science Quarterly* 94, 2 (Summer 1979)

"The CIA and US Policy in Zaire and Angola, 1975." In Lemarchand, R., ed., *American Policy in Southern Africa: The Stakes and the Stance.* Washington DC, 1978

Wheeler, Douglas. "In the Service of Order: The Portuguese Political Police and the British, German, and Spanish Intelligence, 1932–1945." *Journal of Contemporary History* 18 (1983)

"The Portuguese Revolution of 1910." *Journal of Modern History* 44 (June 1972), pp. 172–94

"Thaw in Portugal." *Foreign Affairs* 48 (July 1970) pp. 769–181

Wiarda, Howard J. "Corporatism and Development in the Iberic-Latin World: Persistent Strains and New Variations." *Review of Politics* 36 (January 1974), pp. 3–33

"The Portuguese Revolution: Toward Explaining the Political Behavior of the Armed Forces Movement." *Iberian Studies* 4 (Autumn 1975), pp. 53–61

"Toward a Framework for the Study of Political Change in the Iberic-Latin Tradition: The Corporative Model." *World Politics* 25 (January 1973), pp. 206–235

Yergen, Daniel. "Lisbon and Brussels." *The New Republic* 16, 173 (October 18, 1975)

Young, Crawford. "Zaire: The Unending Crisis." *Foreign Affairs* (Fall 1978), pp. 169–85

UNPUBLISHED DISSERTATIONS

Guimarães, Fernando J. Andresen. "The origins of the Angolan Civil War: International Politics and Domestic Political Conflict 1961–1976". London School of Economics and Political Science, PhD. 1992

Schneidman, Witney. "American Foreign Policy and the Fall of the Portuguese Empire 1961–1976". University of Southern California, 1982

Index